The War against the Americans

The War against the Americans
Resistance and Collaboration in Cebu: 1899–1906

RESIL B. MOJARES

ATENEO DE MANILA UNIVERSITY PRESS

ATENEO DE MANILA UNIVERSITY PRESS
Bellarmine Hall, Katipunan Avenue
Loyola Heights, Quezon City
P.O. Box 154, 1099 Manila, Philippines
Tel.: (632) 426-59-84 / Fax: (632) 426-59-09
Email: unipress@admu.edu.ph
Website: www.ateneopress.com

Cover design by J. B. de la Peña

The National Library of the Philippines CIP Data

Recommended entry:

Mojares, Resil B.
    The War against the Americans :
resistance and collaboration in
Cebu, 1899–1906 / by Resil B. Mojares.
– Quezon City : ADMU Press, c1999
    1 v

    1. Cebu – History – 1899–1906.
I. Title.

DS688.C4 959.599523 1999 P991000043
ISBN 971–550–298–9 (pbk.)

Contents

Prologue

T O UNDERSTAND the Filipino-American War is to understand a large part of the groundwork of contemporary Philippine society. Yet, despite much scholarship in this area in the past two decades, this war remains marginal to popular consciousness. A war we ambiguously lost, it is not as much a remembered event as the war against the Japanese, one we ambiguously won. This is not just a matter of temporal distance, it is also a question of colonial memory.

We rediscovered this war in the 1960s, in part because the needs of a new nationalism required a critical redefinition of Filipino-American relations and in part because the trauma of the Vietnam War resurrected antecedents in America's "imperial adventure" in the Philippines. Since the 1960s much historiography has been done on the U.S. occupation of the Philippines. Recent studies call into question the myth of U.S. rule as one of "benevolent assimilation," Filipino-American "partnership for progress," and Filipino receptivity towards American institutions. They stress such themes as the collaborative role of the Filipino elite in the shaping of the new order, mutual manipulation by Filipinos and Americans, the problematic impact of American rule on Filipino politics, culture, and economics, and the many-sided character of Filipino resistance to U.S. occupation.[1] Several of these studies focus on local theaters of the conflict, on war and politics as carried out in specific regions and provinces of the country. By hewing close to what happened "on the ground," these studies have occasioned revisions of some of the generalizing statements in the older scholarship.

The present book is a contribution to this continuing rediscovery of an important aspect of our past. Its reconstruction of the war as it happened in the province of Cebu brings to light a great deal of new data. The book, however, is impelled less by the motive of presenting an original contribution to scholarship as making a particular history better known to a determinate body of readers. Hence, it is written in the style of a popular narrative addressed to a Filipino (and, particularly, Cebuano) readership.

The book attempts to give a full and rounded history of the war in Cebu province. It is animated by the sense that beneath the surface drama of a war lies more. A war is an epiphanic event in the life of a society: It renders painfully—at times, gloriously—visible what, in ordinary times, is often masked or disguised. A war turns society inside out: It bares the motions of deep-lying forces, articulates social formations, and exposes and sharpens inner contradictions. It brings the past forward in time (at a pace quicker than usual) and raises something of the shape of the future (in terms more compelling than in ordinary times). It necessarily implicates us, for—in the case of the Filipino-American War—*we* are now the shape of that future.

This book was not done under the formal auspices of an institution. Hence, work on it has been a drawn-out, off-and-on affair. Based on data mainly compiled in 1982, the writing did not begin until 1986 and then again in 1989. Except for very minor revisions, the present text is as it was completed in 1989.

A few explanatory notes are in order. In the text, I frequently use the term "insurgent." I must point out that I do not subscribe to the bias that sees the anti-American resistance as an "insurrection" rather than what it really was, a war between nations. My use of the term is occasioned by its standard use in both primary and secondary sources and the lack of a convenient alternative from the other terms used by the Cebuanos themselves during the war (*nacionalistas, revolucionarios, guerrillas*).

The research on which the book draws would not have been possible without the assistance of various agencies and individuals. I acknowledge my indebtedness to the Council for the International Exchange of Scholars (CIES) for a fellowship that allowed me to examine Visayan source materials in 14 libraries and archives in the United States over a nine-month period in 1982. The Cebuano Studies Center of the University of San Carlos provided time and resources which enabled me to do work that, in various ways, contributed to the making of this book.

I thank Juan Francisco (Philippine-American Educational Foundation), Jennifer O'Keefe and Linda Gunter (CIES), Fr. Theodore Murnane (University of San Carlos), Fe Susan Go, Michael Price (who generously provided photographs from his collection for this volume), and many individuals in the U.S. for their friendship and assistance in the course of my research work in 1982. In particular, I thank Michael Cullinane (University of Michigan and University of Wisconsin-Madison), who shared data and insights and has been, in all ways, an ideal colleague and friend. I appreciate the help of the staff of the various libraries and archives, particularly the U.S. National Archives (where, at the time of my research, I had the good fortune of the fine company of the late William Henry Scott, Milagros Guerrero, Ken De Bevoise, Doreen Fernandez, and Bernardita Churchill). I must say, however, that the persons mentioned are not responsible for the views expressed in this study.

Finally, I thank Sally and the children for creating the space within which I could carry out what may have sometimes seemed rather strange work.

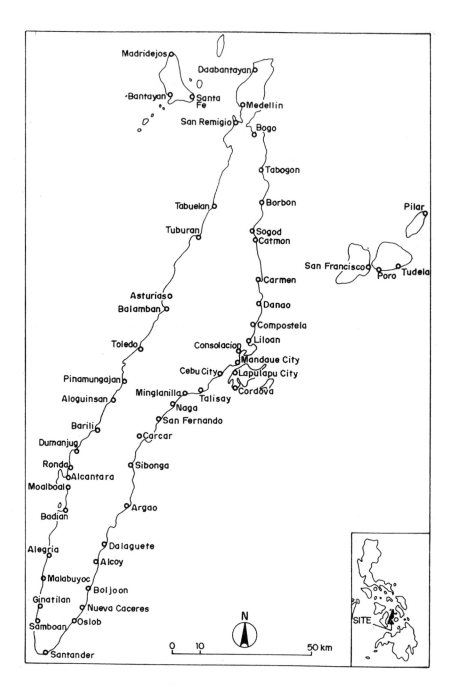

Madridejos
Daanbantayan
Bantayan
Santa
Fe
Medellin
San Remigio
Bogo
Tabogon
Tabuelan
Borbon
Tuburan
Sogod
Catmon
Pilar
Carmen
San Francisco
Poro
Tudela
Asturias
Danao
Balamban
Compostela
Toledo
Liloan
Consolacion
Mandaue City
Pinamungajan
Cebu City
Lapulapu City
Aloguinsan
Minglanilla
Cordova
Talisay
Naga
Barili
San Fernando
Dumanjug
Carcar
Ronda
Alcantara
Sibonga
Moalboal
Badian
Argao
Alegria
Dalaguete
Alcoy
Malabuyoc
Boljoon
Ginatilan
Nueva Caceres
Samboan
Oslob
Santander

N

0   10   50 km

SITE

The Towns of Cebu

1

A Time Between Times

I T WAS the longest year in the history of the province of Cebu, the months from the summer of 1898 to the coming of the rains in 1899. Within the span of a little over a year, Cebu witnessed an armed insurrection against Spain, the establishment of a Filipino Republic, the occupation of the island by troops of the United States, several changes in the local government, and the outbreak of armed hostilities between Cebuanos and Americans. At no other time in local and national history was so much collapsed into so short a span of time. It was truly a "time between times," one that strained the fabric of local society and formed much of the troubled groundwork of Cebuano—and Philippine—society today.

As the nineteenth century came to a close, Cebu City, the provincial capital, was the principal Philippine city outside of Manila. A hub of expanding domestic and foreign commerce, the port city had a population of around 15,000 (over 30,000, counting the adjoining town of San Nicolas) and some 2,000 houses, mostly of light materials, concentrated in the inner barrios of Lutao, Centro, Pampanga, and Ermita, then shading off into the less densely populated outer districts of Sambag, Cogon, and Carreta.

Nineteenth-century urbanism gave the port of Cebu the look and feel of a city exposed to the world: European bazaars, rows of Chinese shops, schools (Seminario-Colegio de San Carlos, Colegio de la Inmaculada Concepcion), printshops, substantial residences of stone and wood, some fine public structures (like the churches and the Episcopal palace), and a crowded wharf where *cargadores* struggled with foreign-bound sacks of sugar and bales of hemp. The city was the economic and administrative capital of a province of some 52 towns, with a combined population of 500,000, dispersed communities into which a market economy and a new order of political ideas, by the year 1898, had made inroads.[1]

In 1898, the casual visitor saw in Cebu a city in the process of building up. Yet, a closer view showed that it was also a society on the verge of a political unraveling. *Independencia*, separation from Mother Spain, was very much in the mind of many Cebuanos. The Tagalog insurrection of 1896 dramatized the possibilities of freedom and a new political order. While Cebu did not join the insurrection, libertarian ideas were in the air in the 1890s, particularly in Cebu City where there was fertile ground for such ideas in a culture increasingly defined by the appearance of books and newspapers, the presence of schools and foreign merchants, and an expanding class of clerks, students, and urban artisans.

Through the months of 1897 and 1898, agents from Luzon and local citizens were busy organizing an underground network of cells (called barangay) of the revolutionary Katipunan society, meeting in small clandestine groups on such occasions as community ferias and family parties, and in such places as private homes in San Nicolas, the *intusan* (native sugar mill) of Paulino ("the Harelip") Solon in the district of Sambag, the woods of Camputhaw, or the bodega of Smith Bell in the port area.

On 3 April 1898, *tres de Abril*, Cebuanos began their armed uprising against Spanish rule.[2] In a disorderly, frenetic encounter, they routed Spanish soldiers and volunteers on Valeriano Weyler Street (now Tres de Abril) in San Nicolas. Organized by the Katipunan, the insurgents quickly seized control of the city streets as, elsewhere, Cebuanos mounted similar actions in various towns of the province. For the next three days, the insurgents controlled the city as the Spaniards and their partisans found themselves bottled up inside Fort San Pedro and a few buildings in the city. The English house of Smith Bell and Company, near the wharf, and the German Botica Antigua (the city's oldest pharmacy, on Calle Legaspi), owned by the Krapfenbauers, flew their national colors for protection. Along Comercio and Magallanes Streets rebels, armed with bolos and bamboo lances, squatted in front of the shuttered shops, seeking shade from the hot April sun, awaiting orders.

With the arrival of Spanish reinforcements from Iloilo and the bombardment of the city on 7 April, however, the revolution was dealt a serious blow. Shelling from the cruiser *Don Juan de Austria* created panic and razed sections of the city to the ground. The Spanish crackdown scattered the rebels and the assassination of Pantaleon Villegas (Leon Kilat) in the southern town of Carcar on Good Friday, 8 April, deprived the local revolutionaries of a charismatic military leader. Troops under Cebu politico-military governor Adolfo Montero tried to run the insurgents to the ground with a brutal campaign of indiscriminate arrests and executions.

Around 13 April, however, the revolutionaries under Luis Flores had started to regroup in the Sudlon mountains and were soon poised to resume warfare. From May to November, armed skirmishes took place between the insurgents and the Spanish soldiers, *cazadores*, and loyalist volunteers in Sudlon, Talamban, Minglanilla, Pardo, San Fernando, and even distant Tuburan and Bogo. By late 1898, insurgents were to be seen moving within the perimeter of the city itself.

A "provisional revolutionary government" had been formed in San Nicolas on 3 April 1898, with Luis Flores as president, Candido Padilla as vice president, and Leon Kilat as general en jefe. The capital of this government moved to Sudlon after 8 April and then to Pardo, closer to the city, as the revolutionaries positioned themselves for the final takeover. This government bore allegiance to the independent Philippine government declared in Luzon by Emilio Aguinaldo and worked under the policies and instructions of this government. In November and December, the Flores government was already engaged in reorganizing municipal governments in the province according to the terms prescribed in Aguinaldo's decree of 18 June 1898.[3]

In the final days, Spain exercised dominion "only over the ground covered by the feet of her soldiers."[4] A large shadow, however, was cast over the struggle for Philippine independence. As the revolution was fought in Cebu through the months of 1898, a larger and more complex war was taking place elsewhere.

On 1 May 1898, less than a month after Cebuanos took up arms against Spain, Commodore George Dewey demolished the antiquated Spanish fleet in Manila Bay in the course of America's own war against Spain. The entry of the Americans gave fresh impetus to the Philippine Revolution and, in many parts of the country, armed Filipinos threatened an end to Spanish power. From his exile in Hong Kong, Emilio Aguinaldo arrived in Cavite on 20 May to rally the Filipinos for the final drive towards freedom. The coming of the Americans stirred anxieties among Filipinos even as it raised hopes of a quick end to Spanish rule through a Filipino-American alliance.

In the beginning, American designs were unclear. In the dead calm of Manila Bay, the triumphant American fleet lay at anchor for weeks. On the forward deck of the flagship *Olympia*, Dewey sat in his wicker chair and awaited fresh orders from Washington.

Residents of Cebu City knew of the developments in Manila soon after the Battle of Manila Bay. Twice-weekly boat mail between Manila and Cebu brought sketchy reports of fast-developing events in Luzon. All sorts of rumors were rife in the city and elsewhere in the province. In May, there were rumors that American gunboats were cruising off the west coast of Cebu, "accompanied by General Aguinaldo and Dr. Jose Rizal, who had not been killed in December 1896 and was on board the American ship heading for Cebu to obtain the surrender of the Spaniards." Late in the year came "news" that the Philippine flag was being paraded by American soldiers in Manila as well as flown by American warships and commercial vessels in the Manila harbor. In Cebu, the Spaniards, besieged, tried to fuel pro-Spanish sentiments with propaganda that the *norte americanos* were barbarians and rapists and that Protestant "infidels" will turn churches into horse stables and use religious images for fuel.[5]

The city was in a high state of anxiety and confusion, with the threat from the Spaniards, the Americans, and the Katipunan revolutionaries. Local Spanish authorities were undertaking a campaign of *juez de cuchillo* ("judgment by the sword") against suspected rebels and Katipunan sympathizers, sending prominent city residents to prison cells at Fort San Pedro and fielding pro-Spanish Muslim volunteers to hunt down and kill insurgents. In the Spanish reprisals, several hundred Cebuanos died and the fires burned for days in Carbon and Carreta where corpses were incinerated.[6] The days of Spanish rule, however, were numbered.

On the national front, the Filipinos were busy installing the apparatuses of an independent state through the months of 1898, installing a Filipino government in Kawit on 24 May, then formally declaring Philippine Independence on 12 June. By July, Filipino troops had ringed Manila and were ready to seize the capital city. Aguinaldo, however, hesitated.

In the meantime, tensions between Filipinos and Americans mounted as the annexationist policy of the United States became more and more evident. In Washington, Pres. William McKinley, musing on the fate of the Philippines, wrote in a private memorandum: "While we are conducting war and until its conclusion we must keep all we get; when the war is over we must keep what we want."[7] In May, several thousand American regulars and volunteers were assembled in California for the armed expedition to the Philippines. On 25 May, the first contingent of 2,500 men embarked for the Pacific and, on 1 July, started landing near Manila. By the end of July, some 12,000 American land troops were in the Philippines, jostling with Filipino soldiers for position outside the national capital. On 13 August, on the basis of secret negotiations with the Spaniards, the Americans occupied Manila and barred Filipino troops from entering the city. It became increasingly apparent that the two "allies" did not exactly have the same image of what should become of the Philippine Islands.

In the Visayas, Gen. Diego de los Rios, who had become Spanish governor-general with headquarters in Iloilo after the surrender of Manila, tried to avert the total loss of the colony by offering reforms and encouraging the Ilongo elite to organize Visayas and Mindanao into a separate government that shall disengage itself from Luzon and resist the Americans. Cebu governor Adolfo Montero supported the plan and two Cebuano delegates, Pablo Mejia and Miguel Logarta, were sent to Iloilo for a conference.

With the insurgents knocking on the doors, however, the Spaniards no longer controlled the situation even in the Visayas. Instead, in an assembly in Santa Barbara, Iloilo, on 17 November 1898, a "provisional revolutionary government of the Visayas" was organized pledging its allegiance to the Aguinaldo government. It was an Ilongo affair with little Cebuano participation. In Jaro, on 17 December 1898, a "Federal State of the Visayas" was established but again without Cebuano participation. An Ilongo, Fernando Salas, was designated "councilor for Cebu." The rapid march of events prevented the materialization of a common Visayan front and the "federal state" was dissolved on 27 April 1899.[8]

With the Treaty of Paris on 21 December 1898, Spain formally ceded the Philippines to the United States. As the American presence in the Philippines at this time was limited to Manila, and with the revolutionaries poised to take Cebu City, Spanish authorities in Cebu were faced with the dilemma of how to effect an orderly withdrawal. Many city residents were concerned about the political vacuum that would ensue with the departure of the Spaniards. It was then that Governor Montero, in consultation with local church authorities, decided to turn over the Cebu government to a caretaker committee of prominent Cebuano citizens led by the Spanish mestizo Pablo Mejia.

At 5:00 P.M. on 24 December 1898, 333 years of Spanish rule in Cebu came to an end when the Spanish flag was lowered at Fort San Pedro. Montero turned over the government to the caretaker "governor" in the person of Pablo Mejia. It was an emotion-charged moment and, in a fit of despair, some Spaniards tore their own flag after it was lowered. In the dusk, the ceremonies over, the Spaniards and their dependents moved out in a lonely convoy of boats bound for Zamboanga, their way station for the final withdrawal to Spain.

On the eve of the Spanish departure, Mejia—in the company of his son Teofilo and cousin Antonio Ruiz—met Luis Flores and Arcadio Maxilom in the southern town of Talisay to discuss the turnover of government to the army of the republic.[9] It was agreed in Talisay that the provisional government would be set up first in Pardo before the insurgents occupy the city. On 26 December, two days after the Spanish withdrawal, Pablo Mejia again conferred with the leaders of the republic at the Pardo convent. With Mejia were Frs. Pablo Singson, Emiliano Mercado, and Ismael Paras, representing the Catholic clergy.

Rumors were rife that the revolutionaries would enter the city "with fire and sword" to avenge the lack of cooperation of the city populace in the revolution. The prospect of fierce, unwashed rebels crowding into the city led Chinese merchants to close their shops, residents to hide their food stores and valuables, and some to seek asylum in the city's foreign commercial houses.[10] Bishop Martin Garcia Alcocer, the bishop of Cebu, sent Frs. Emiliano Mercado and Ismael Paras to meet Flores in Pardo and ask him to "forget the past" and have his troops enter the city peacefully. The priests petitioned Flores not to have his troops enter the city until after he has conferred with the bishop. Flores slipped into the city incognito the following day and assured the bishop he would not allow vengeance or abuses against the population. He also agreed to wait until the twenty-ninth of the month before the insurgents occupy the city.[11]

An orderly transfer was effected from Mejia to Luis Flores, the highest-ranking official of the revolutionary army in Cebu. On 29 December, the Philippine Republic was formally pronounced in the province in festive ceremonies in the city. Two days later, a new provincial government under Luis Flores was duly sworn in. Between 29 December 1898 and 22 February 1899, the Philippine Republic held sway in Cebu. For the first time, a Filipino, Luis Flores, sat in the Casa Gobierno, fronting Plaza Maria Cristina (now Independencia), as head of the government in Cebu.

In a directive dated 24 January 1899, the Aguinaldo government in Malolos thanked the Cebuanos for their "patriotism" and approved as a provisional measure the constitution of the provincial council of Cebu under the presidency of Luis Flores and the members elected in accordance with the Act of 30 December 1898, "until such time as the elections are verified in the manner prescribed by the Decree of 18 June 1898, and the permanent council is constituted and representatives from the province in the National Assembly are elected." The same directive urged the Cebu provincial council to continue the taxes and imposts in force during the Spanish regime and to administer affairs to the satisfaction of the citizenry "until such time as an economic system less hard on the citizens be adopted." It further ordered civil and military authorities to protect "individual liberty and interests" and not fall into "the vices and deceits of the late Spanish Administration." The directive ended by asking the Cebuanos to prevent and repel all foreign invasions at whatever sacrifice "with the assurance that the National Government will not leave unpunished any attempt against any integral part whatever of its territory."[12]

These were months of excitement and dread. Filipinos had seized power by force of arms and yet they were not in full control. They had to face up to the imminence of American annexation. Things came to a head when Spain ceded the Philippines to the United States in the Treaty of Paris on 10 December 1898. On 21 December, Pres. William McKinley issued his "benevolent assimilation" proclamation which declared that "the future control, disposition, and government of the Philippine Islands are ceded to the United States" by virtue of the Treaty of Paris and that an American military government will now be extended throughout the country.[13] An open war became just a matter of time.

The revolutionary government that the Cebuanos established at this time was a makeshift structure. In a sense, there was no breakdown of government. As Spanish power collapsed in the province in the late months of 1898, town governments were reorganized, swearing allegiance to the republic, under the terms of Aguinaldo's decree of 18 June 1898. This decree provided for the election of a municipal chief (jefe), a delegate of police and internal order, a delegate of justice, a delegate of taxes and property, and a headman (*cabeza*) for each barrio. Together, these persons constituted the popular assembly (*junta*). The town chiefs, in turn, were to elect the provincial governor and three councilors who will (with the jefe of the provincial capital) constitute the provincial council.

In many towns, there was minimum disruption not only because the structure of local government remained the same but because, in many towns the local elite, which constituted the town leadership under the Spaniards, remained in office under the republic. It was at the level of the provincial government, formerly the preserve of the Spaniards, that the important power struggle took place. The provincial government under Flores was a "coalition" government, combining the moderate (and even Spanish loyalist) *ilustrados* of the city and the military elements of the revolution. The coalition was, in the main, dictated by the need for a common front in the event of hostilities with the Americans. Its mixed character is to be seen in the composition of the provincial government inaugurated on 31 December 1898.[14]

Luis Flores and Julio Llorente acted as president and vice president, respectively. Completing the provincial council were Arcadio Maxilom as councilor of police, Mariano Veloso as councilor of finance, Segundo Singson as councilor of justice, and Leoncio Alburo as provincial secretary. Only Flores and Maxilom were of the revolutionary Katipunan. The municipal government of Cebu (Cebu City) was even more moderate, with such men as Julio Llorente as municipal president (in addition to being provincial vice president), Pedro Cui as delegate of finance, and Pablo Mejia as "treasurer of the port."

The moderates gained further ground when civil government was established in Cebu on 10 January 1899.[15] The provincial officials were Luis Flores, president; Julio Llorente, "governor"; Miguel Logarta, councilor of justice; Pablo Mejia, councilor of treasury; Arcadio Maxilom, councilor of police and internal order; and Leoncio Alburo, secretary. In the capital of Cebu, Florentino Rallos and Alejandro Valle—both nonparticipants in the revolution—were chosen municipal president and vice president, respectively.

The character of the Cebu provincial government was problematic, its civil component controlled by conservatives even as the military remained in the hands of the revolutionaries. Except for Flores and Maxilom, the provincial government was entirely conservative in composition. It is not clear what powers Llorente exercised as "governor" vis-a-vis Flores. The rapid administrative changes and mixed communications from the Aguinaldo government made for a great deal of provisionality in the power situation.

What is clear is that Llorente, by the beginning of 1899, had eclipsed Flores in the leadership structure. Llorente's claim to primacy was buttressed by recognition from Aguinaldo who presumably knew of Llorente's prestige and early links to the Spain-based Propaganda Movement but was unfamiliar with local politics in Cebu. Prior to the Spanish withdrawal on 24 December, Aguinaldo reportedly appointed Llorente "delegate" with the authority to establish the revolutionary government in Cebu.[16] The eclipse of Flores was also occasioned by the "superior qualifications" of Llorente.

Julio Aballe Llorente (1863–c1955) belonged to one of the wealthiest families in nineteenth century Cebu. His father, Don Ceferino Llorente, owned interisland vessels and a sugar estate in Medellin and dealt actively both with the Spanish government and the English and American merchant houses. The young Julio Llorente studied at Ateneo de Manila (1876–1881) and then was sent to Spain where he took his doctorate in law at the University of Madrid in 1885. In Spain, he was briefly involved in the Propaganda Movement and contributed articles to *La Solidaridad*. A tall Spanish mestizo, Llorente had a background in politics and civil service in the late nineteenth century.[17] He was a "substitute magistrate" in the Audiencia of Cebu in the 1880s and 1890s and served as the city's *teniente alcalde segundo* in 1892–1893. Together with such city ilustrados as Don Pedro Cui and Don Isidro Guivelondo, he was imprisoned at Fort San Pedro in the

Spanish "campaign of terror" after the 3 April revolt for suspected links to the revolution. He was, however, never at the forefront of the struggle.

Luis Perez Flores, on the other hand, had a less distinguished background. A native of Samar who first came to Cebu in 1891 as a steward of Bishop Martin Garcia Alcocer, he went on to acquire some prominence in the local Spanish civil service. With Alcocer's patronage, he served as *procurador* of the Cebu audiencia as well as *regidor* of the Cebu ayuntamiento in the 1890s.[18] He became involved in Katipunan activities as early as 1896 or 1897. In the revolution, he took the nom de guerre Unos and became its head when a provisional revolutionary government was established on 3 April 1898, perhaps less because of his military abilities as the fact that he was the most experienced in politico-administrative matters among the "generals" of the Katipunan. Florencio Gonzales, secretary of the Cebu ayuntamiento, was the most prominent Katipunan organizer in the early days but he was arrested by the Spaniards on 2 April and executed on 7 April 1898. Hence, Luis Flores inherited the leadership.

As provincial president, Flores found himself in the midst of his social betters as well as his patron, the Spanish bishop whom he respected. When Gen. Vicente Lukban (the revolutionary head of Samar and Leyte) sent word to Flores sometime in January 1899 to have Bishop Alcocer put under house arrest, Luis Flores refused. Lukban sent his own armed men to arrest Alcocer in February but the bishop, apparently with the aid of Flores, was able to slip out of Cebu on 1 February 1899, ferried by a banca to the German vessel *Chusang*, off Talisay, for a journey that took him to Colombo, Hong Kong, and then back to Manila.[19]

The militants remained in control of the military. At the beginning of 1899, Cebu was divided into four military zones under Arcadio Maxilom, Pantaleon del Rosario, Nicolas Godines, and Enrique Lorega.[20] On 12 January 1899, a "regiment" was also organized under Emilio Verdeflor, composed of two "battalions" headed by Saturnino Echavez and Fermin Aliño. The other military leaders included such militants as Francisco Llamas, Alejo Miñoza, the Aliño brothers, Lorenzo Eje, Leoncio Alfon, Samuel Maxilom, and Quintin Tabal. At the head of the government, however, were mainly city-based ilustrados, late joiners of the revolution, steeped in the ethos of moderation and compromise. It was only a matter of time before they came into open conflict with the more radical elements of the revolution.

As the year 1899 began, the government was preoccupied with organization and war preparations as Filipino-American relations deteriorated. In the first days of 1899, Cebuano leaders received communications from Iloilo about American attempts to land a force in that Visayan port city. An

American expeditionary force had anchored off the Iloilo harbor on 28 December 1898 but had to sit out at sea because of the refusal of Ilongo leaders to allow the landing of American troops.

Then, in the night of 4 February 1899, shooting broke out between Filipino and American lines facing each other in the outskirts of Manila. With the flare-up of the war collapsed the uneasy alliance between Filipinos and Americans.

On 5 February, Aguinaldo sent the provincial council of Cebu instructions to prepare for war against the Americans. In response, the local government had announcements posted on the streets of the city and the towns. Efforts were redoubled to train soldiers and procure arms and ammunition.

On 10 February, a meeting was called by Luis Flores at the Casa Real (also called Casa Gobierno) for the purpose of discussing war preparations. The meeting was attended by Arcadio Maxilom, Pablo Mejia, Miguel Logarta, and civil and military officers. At this meeting, a decision was reached to place Juan Climaco as "chief of staff" in charge of war preparations with full powers to appoint the heads of the "war department" and other military personnel.

There is no clear record of this 10 February meeting.[21] The appointment of Climaco appears problematic since he was not an official of the provincial government and did not figure prominently in the revolution. Of a wealthy Chinese mestizo family of Cebu City, Juan Faller Climaco (1859–1907) studied at Ateneo de Manila (1873–1875) and had links both to the leading city-based ilustrados, on one hand, and the municipal elites, on the other, as he had served in the 1880s and 1890s as *capitan municipal* of the west-coast town of Toledo where—among other places— his family had large landholdings.[22] His position in the anti-Spanish revolution, however, was ambiguous as he was variously identified as insurgent and Spanish loyalist. It appears that he took the side of the revolution in the outbreak of April 1898 but that, after Leon Kilat's death and in the face of Spanish reprisal, he fled to San Carlos on Negros island. This was a time of confusion and it must have been during this time that his loyalties were held suspect. What is clear though is that he had emerged as one of the leaders of the Cebu government after the Spanish withdrawal in December 1898.

His appointment as "chief of staff" appears to undercut the role of Maxilom as "councilor of peace and internal order" and head of the military. It may have been part of the drama of the ilustrado take-over of the government. Yet Climaco's relations with Maxilom were not adversarial as later events showed. Both were of the municipal elite of the west coast.

There may already have been a symbiotic relationship between the two, the educated capitan of Toledo who became the "brains" of the anti-American resistance and the petty chief of Tuburan who became its military leader.

With Llorente, Flores, and Climaco, Arcadio Molero Maxilom (1862–1924) was one of the principal actors of the events of the time. The least socially prominent of the four, Maxilom was the son of a *gobernadorcillo* of Tuburan and was himself a schoolteacher (1877–1881), secretary to the local justice of the peace (1882–1888), and then capitan municipal of Tuburan (1892–1896). Although he was literate in Spanish, he had little formal education. He neither had the learning nor the kind of status and prestige Climaco had. Even in the small town of Tuburan, Maxilom did not hold complete sway, for the Maxiloms were engaged in a feud with the more economically powerful Tabotabo family.[23]

There were undercurrents of tension between the Llorente-Mejia group and the Climaco-Maxilom faction even before the arrival of the Americans. Sometime around 16 February 1899, a meeting was called by Climaco at the Casa Real to discuss means of defense. Word had been received that the Americans were already poised to invade Cebu. Among those present at the meeting were Climaco, Flores, and Llorente. Climaco rendered a report on the state of Cebu's readiness for war. He reported that instructions had been issued for the organization of local militias; that some trenches had been built in the city; and that all firearms in the possession of the Cebuano army totaled only 200, including rifles, muskets, shotguns and revolvers, while ammunition hardly amounted to 40 rounds per weapon. (Preparations also included the stocking up on petroleum for the burning of the city in case the landing of the Americans could not be stopped.)[24] Climaco recommended that, in the event of an American landing, the Cebuano forces should withdraw to the trenches at the perimeter of the city and from there carry out attacks on the enemy. In what may be a hint of internal struggle, Climaco complained that war preparations had been inadequate because funds had not been made available by the local treasury (which was under Pablo Mejia).

It was the consensus at the meeting that the Americans should be resisted. At this point, the question on whether or not civil authority should now yield to the military in view of the emergency was raised. Invoked was the Decree of 18 June 1898, which provided that "when the province is threatened or occupied by the enemy, in whole or in part, the military chief of the highest rank therein may assume the powers of the chief of the province until the danger has disappeared."[25] Most of those present agreed that this should be so. Llorente inquired about who should then assume both civil and military powers. Climaco argued that Arcadio Maxilom should now hold this office, as he was the supreme military commander. Luis Flores objected, pointing out that he was not only president but also the head of the revolutionary army, which was founded in Sudlon in the days of the anti-Spanish resistance. Many among those present, however, disagreed with Flores and resigned from their offices in the provincial government. Flores accepted the resignations and it was understood that the civil government had been dissolved. This, however, proved to be a matter of controversy in the days that followed.[26]

Cebu had little breathing space. The fierce hostilities in the Tagalog provinces tied down the Americans but, by 11 February, they had brought the war to the Visayas with the occupation of Iloilo. After having been bottled up in their ships in the Iloilo harbor for 45 days, American troops forcibly took Iloilo City as the revolutionaries burned the city and withdrew.[27]

On 16 February, a boat docked in Cebu bringing fresh details of hostilities in Luzon and Iloilo. The provincial council went into a frenzied round of daily meetings. On 20 February, there was a rumor that, midnight of 19 February, the U.S. steamer *Charleston* had tried to land at Dumanjug on the west coast of Cebu but the tide was low and the ship returned to Iloilo.[28] The following day, 21 February, the U.S. gunboat *Petrel* appeared at the mouth of Cebu harbor.

War had come to Cebu.

2

The Coming of the Americans

I N THE early morning of Tuesday, 21 February 1899, the U.S. gunboat *Petrel* entered the mouth of the channel off the Liloan lighthouse. Guided by the launch *Metralladora*, with a pilot from Manila, the gunboat moved into Cebu harbor. The *Petrel*, the smallest ship in Dewey's original squadron, was an 892-ton vessel that had seen action both in the Battle of Manila Bay and the siege of Iloilo.

With the first sighting of the American gunboat, people began to crowd at the Cebu wharf. They were joined by men who had come from neighboring towns as news spread that the battle for the defense of the city was about to begin. At this time, the provincial council convened what turned out to be a marathon session of local leaders at the Casa Real. Heading the meeting were Luis Flores, Julio Llorente, and Juan Climaco. Arcadio Maxilom was out of Cebu at the time, on a mission to confer with Gens. Vicente Lukban and Ambrosio Moxica, leaders of the republican forces in the Leyte-Samar area, to request for arms and ammunition from the Leyte arsenal. A crowd milled restlessly at the plaza while many families, particularly women and children, prepared to evacuate the city. The government began to gather its troops at three locations: Fort San Pedro, the Recollect barracks, and the trenches built in the Cogon district near the house of Doña Isabel Climaco.

The *Petrel* approached the docks unopposed at around 11:00 A.M., dropping anchor 400 yards from Fort San Pedro. John N. Sidebottom, the Smith Bell and Company Cebu agent who was also the local British and American consul, was the first to board the American ship. (He was accompanied by the captain of a British vessel, the *Pigmy*, which was then in the

Cebu harbor.) Sidebottom conferred with the *Petrel*'s commanding officer, Capt. Charles C. Cornwell.[1] Around 3:00 P.M., Sidebottom met with the Cebuano leaders with a message from the Americans. The message—a letter which had to be translated from English to Spanish for the benefit of the Cebuano leaders—read in part:

> Within 34 hours after receiving this letter, the Provincial Council of Cebu must surrender to the United States. If the Cebu government chooses not to surrender or hesitates to do so, the commander of the *Petrel* will be forced to begin bombarding the city in order to impose an American administration on Cebu City.[2]

Sidebottom also conveyed the desire of Cornwell for the Cebuano leaders to meet with him in a conference on board the *Petrel*. In response, the Cebuanos sent a delegation composed of Julio Llorente, Pablo Mejia, Juan Climaco, Segundo Singson, Fr. Pablo Singson, and Fr. Juan Gorordo. Fathers Singson and Gorordo, the ecclesiastical governor and secretary, respectively, of the diocese, were the highest officials of the church in Cebu in the absence of the bishop.

The meeting on board the *Petrel* began around 4:00 P.M. Cornwell gave the delegation a copy of McKinley's proclamation of 28 December 1898 and invoked the terms of the Treaty of Paris, which had ceded the Philippines to the United States. Mejia told Cornwell that Cebu had sworn its allegiance to the Philippine Republic and that the Cebuanos were disposed to defend the republic's integrity. Cornwell, however, was not impressed. He was privy to intelligence reports that the Cebuanos had only "about 100 rifles" and would not be able to mount an effective resistance. Repeating his demand, he assured the Cebuano envoys that Cebuanos would continue running the local affairs of government under his general supervision. Cornwell also tried to impress upon the Cebuanos that they needed American "protection" against foreign powers interested in exploiting the political vacuum left behind by the Spanish withdrawal. It was not entirely a bluff. Anchored in the Cebu harbor at this time were *Kaiserin Augusta*, a big German cruiser; *Higosamashu*, a Japanese merchant vessel; and *Pigmy*, the British gunboat.[3]

Cornwell then announced that the American flag shall be raised at Fort San Pedro at 5:00 P.M. that same afternoon. Mejia asked that this act of possession be delayed to allow the government time for consultations. A delay was granted and the Cebuanos were given 14 hours (or until 8:00 A.M. of the following day, 22 February) to comply before the U.S. flag was raised. If the city refused to surrender, Cornwell said, the Americans would commence bombardment.

After the conference with Cornwell, Cebuano leaders met once more at the Casa Real to discuss their options.[4] After Pablo Mejia relayed to the body what transpired at the conference on board the *Petrel*, a heated discussion ensued between those who favored resistance and those who counseled in favor of a peaceful surrender. Most of those present affirmed that the Americans should be resisted but differed as to the manner, time, and place. The line of division had on one side the older, wealthier, city-based residents who saw immediate resistance futile and the destruction of the city needless and costly. These moderates included Fr. Pablo Singson, Fr. Pedro Julia, Fr. Toribio Padilla, Fr. Juan Gorordo, Julio Llorente, Pablo Mejia, Pedro Cui, and Segundo Singson. Julio Llorente articulated the position of the moderates when he said that, in view of their utter lack of resources for defense, resistance was foolhardy and would only result in the "useless flow of blood." He proposed that the city be surrendered "under vigorous protest." Fr. Pedro Julia, rector of the Colegio-Seminario de San Carlos, commented that their situation could be compared to that of a wayfarer ambushed by a bandit wielding a blunderbuss and demanding either money or life. Since resistance was hopeless, Father Julia said, they should give in and bide for time to recover what shall have been lost. Others who spoke included Escolastico Duterte, Gabino Sepulveda, Leoncio Alburo, and Juan Villarosa. They assailed the legitimacy of the Treaty of Paris and the Spanish cession of the Philippines but acknowledged the dire cost to the city if they resisted an American landing.

On the opposing side were the younger leaders who had, in the year just past, fought in the field against the Spaniards. To this group belonged the *militar* and the *bukidnon* who, while acknowledging that the Americans had superior arms and could not be prevented from landing, proposed that the city be burned as a prelude to armed resistance.[5] The proponents of this view included Juan Climaco and Quintin Tabal.

Luis Flores, caught between the two groups, decided to cast his lot with the moderates. A 1904 article records what Flores reportedly said to the militants in the assembly:

> I am, like you, a *revolucionario*. It pains my heart to see our
> revered flag hauled down from the Fort and replaced by the
> flag of our enemy. My breast seems rent just thinking of
> Cebu's shore stepped upon by the Americans.... But it is my
> duty to let you understand what will surely befall us if we
> resist the disembarkation of those soldiers. Do we have the

weapons sufficient to prevent their assault? No!—even if it is
shameful for us to declare this. The few guns that we have
will not even graze that ship of steel that, even now, has its
big cannons aimed at us. What shall we gain by preventing a
landing? Our town will burn, many will die; we cannot even
address our enemy since it is their cannons that will speak to
us; and, in the end, when Cebu is reduced to ashes, when
nothing is left stirring, it is then that they will land since we
will then be scattered, roaming the hills. Where then would
be the value of the burning of the town? If there is one
among you who can assure me that if Cebu is burned, our
enemies will not be able to land in force, then let us quickly
begin the fight, even if all of us will die, so that this beloved
land of ours will not taste of the boots of the foreign soldiers.
But if there is none, I cannot permit that the word BURN be
spoken since it is not right to endanger the lives of our fellow
citizens. Yonder we have our dense mountains, there the
refuge of Sudlon, the temple of our Freedom, there we will
unfurl once more our flag, there we will wait for the enemy.[6]

In the end, the more moderate elements prevailed. It was finally
agreed around 7:00 P.M. that the city would be peacefully surrendered "under protest." Leoncio Alburo was asked to pen the document of surrender
to be formulated by a committee composed of Llorente, Mejia (taking the
place of Gabino Sepulveda, who begged off), Segundo Singson, and Fr.
Pablo Singson. The finished document read:

In view of the verbal indication to this government given by
the Commander of the gunboat *Petrel* of the Squadron of the
U.S. of America, requiring the surrender of the fort and city
of Cebu, in manifestation of which the flag of his nation is to
be raised over the Fort within fourteen hours, the general
meeting called together, composed of representatives of all
the bonafide citizens of the country, agrees unanimously to
cede to the requirement in view of the superiority of the
American arms, but without failing to make it clear that
neither the government nor all its inhabitants united has
power to execute acts strictly prohibited by the Honorable
President of the Filipino Republic, Señor Emilio Aguinaldo,
our legitimate chief of state, whom we acknowledge in view
of his unquestionable ability to justly govern, and his general

worth. Sad and painful is the position of this undefended city which is forced to act contrary to its convictions, on which account it declares in the face of the entire world that this occupation is based on no law of the many forming the code of all civilized countries, who did not expect such a scene at the close of the century called the Enlightened. One talks of conquests, of protectorates, of cession by the Spaniards, as if the Archipelago and especially our souls were merchandise to be bartered, when a single one of them is worth more than a thousand worlds though they were made of that metal called vile, perhaps because it fascinates like the eyes on a serpent. But be this as it may, the person with whom the claimant must treat is the before-mentioned Señor Aguinaldo, without whose acquiescence cannot be legally valid the act required of this government, being of extreme importance.

CEBU, February 22, 1899
(Signed) LUIS FLORES[7]

The document was delivered to Cornwell by Mejia around 8:30 A.M., 22 February. With Mejia were Sidebottom, Leoncio Alburo, Father Julia, and Father Singson. Cornwell asked the Cebuano officials to continue administering the ordinary affairs of government under his supervision. He announced, however, that he was taking control of the port and appointing an American collector of customs and captain of the port. Cornwell instructed Mejia (as councilor of finance) to submit to him a balance sheet of the accounts of the local government.

The Americans then sent an armed detachment of around 100 "blue-jackets" ashore to raise the American flag over Fort San Pedro.[8] In command of the landing party was Lt. James H. Bull. Present at the ceremony were Cornwell, Sidebottom, Luis Flores, Julio Llorente, Pablo Mejia, and Leoncio Alburo. The American flag was raised at 9:56 A.M. to the sound of a trumpet. Offshore, the *Petrel* fired a gun salute as the day also marked the birthday of "the father of the American nation," George Washington. A U.S. naval officer, present at the time, wryly observed: "It is to be doubted if Washington would have approved of what was done on his birthday."[9]

As the American flag was raised, a large crowd of Cebuanos, many of them still armed, gathered in the plaza and the wharf area spoiling for a fight. The mood was decidedly hostile. As the American soldiers returned to their boat after hoisting the flag they were nearly mobbed and attacked by the restless crowd. Llorente and Alburo, however, moved in to pacify the angry citizens.

The following day, 23 February, Cornwell, accompanied by Sidebottom and officers of the British *Pigmy*, came ashore and raised the American flag on the staff of the Casa Real. After setting up office in the casa, Cornwell conferred with Cebuano leaders and asked that quarters be made available for the American troops. He also appointed Lieutenants J. P. Parker and C. P. Plunkett as collector of customs and captain of the port, respectively.

Outside the building as all these transpired, many Cebuanos, some armed, milled about, angry but unsure about the precise shape of the unfolding events. Inside the huge wood-and-stone structure that was the seat of government, there was the curious situation of an American "governor" and a Filipino governor holding office under the same roof.

Three days later, Gen. Elwell S. Otis dispatched to Cebu the first battalion of the Twenty-third U.S. Infantry, under the command of Major G. A. Goodale, to relieve the navy and furnish "immediate protection" to the inhabitants. Extending their influence over the Visayan islands, the American military organized on 1 March 1899 the "Visayan Military District" with headquarters in Iloilo, under Brig. Gen. Marcus P. Miller, commanding the First Separate Brigade of the Eigthth Army Corps. On 14 March, the "Sub-District of Cebu" was organized under the command of Lt. Col. Thomas R. Hamer of the First Idaho Volunteers. (The Visayan Military District was to become the "Department of the Visayas" on 29 March 1900, with Cebu and Bohol comprising the Second District of the department.)

On 3 April, Lt. Col. Thomas Hamer arrived in Cebu. A 36-year-old Idaho lawyer, Hamer formally assumed command of the Sub-District of Cebu on April 5 and, by June, assumed the role of Cebu's first American military governor.[10]

When Hamer arrived in Cebu, the American occupation force consisted of one battalion (with four companies) of the Twenty-third U.S. Infantry under Major G. A. Goodale. Three companies were assigned quarters in the *cuartel de infanteria* (Recollect barracks, with the Americans taking over part of the Recollect convent, turning the church into "stables" for cavalry horses) and one company in Fort San Pedro, both located in the city proper.[11] The soldiers were mainly engaged in guard duty where they were given quarters. American officers were billeted at the residence of Mariano Veloso (Cebu's best private residence, fronting Plaza Independencia) and the Parian convent was converted into a telegraph office.

In the first days, Hamer himself observed, the situation in the city was "unsettled, possibly threatening." He reported: "Although there had been no open hostilities, yet the general appearance was one of sullen defiance."[12] No American scouting parties were permitted by their superiors to leave the city as a precautionary measure. For the Americans, the condition of the surrounding country was unknown.

In April and May, however, troops of the First Idaho U.S. Volunteer Infantry, the Forty-fourth U.S. Volunteer Infantry, and the Nineteenth U.S. Infantry, started to arrive in Cebu. Hamer now allowed officers to travel beyond the limits of the city. Several availed themselves of the opportunity and visited adjacent towns and the surrounding countryside. They reported that they were not molested but viewed as curiosities wherever they went. On subsequent visits, the officers were met with little attention that indicated—or so some Americans believed—"a desire on the part of the people to be friendly with us when once they became acquainted, and certainly a total lack of hostile feeling of any kind."[13]

Due to a rash of robberies and minor civil disturbances in the city which the 135-man Cebuano police force could not control, the Americans, around 14 May, started a system of night patrols in the city, "without interfering or conflicting with the local police authority." The patrols, Hamer reported, had a positive effect on the peace and order situation in the city. Encouraged, the Americans began on 24 May a series of daily (except Saturday and Sunday) practice marches out of Cebu for the purpose of reconnoitering the adjacent towns and establishing an American "presence." These marches involved one company at a time, reconnoitering three to four miles out, later increased to ten to twelve miles. These marches enabled the Americans to collect useful military information as they did sketch maps and compiled field notes on the areas they had traversed. Mostly, the soldiers met inhabitants about their farm work but they also encountered small squads of Cebuanos, "uniformed, apparently organized, and armed with spears, bolos, and in some instances rifles." Hamer reported that these troops were apparently billeted in the small towns and "inasmuch as they offered no resistance, our troops, conforming to instructions issued by me, did not disturb or molest them in any way."[14]

Of American relations with the local government, Hamer said: "Our relations with the local government still continue to be entirely satisfactory. The President, apparently, cheerfully acts upon any suggestion I make and is in almost daily consultation with me."[15]

American troop strength in Cebu, however, did not allow the Americans to stray too far beyond city limits. Hamer expressed anxiety over the tenuousness of the American position and urged headquarters in Iloilo that American occupation be effectively extended throughout Cebu island as soon as possible. Asking for additional men, Hamer wrote on 6 April: "A display of force on our part will accomplish the whole thing and it seems to me to be worth a trial at this time." Hamer figured that if two battalions were deployed in Cebu he could bring 10 to 12 towns under control "without the loss of a man."[16]

Hamer chafed at the fact that just across the river from the city, in the town of San Nicolas, insurgents under the "feared and hated" insurgent leader Francisco Llamas held sway. He saw that the delay in the effective occupation of the island had undermined the confidence of those who supported American rule, as well as dissipated the fear of those hostile to the American presence. Hamer was convinced that most Cebuanos would acquiesce to American rule if the Americans demonstrated their capability to "protect" those who supported them.

As it stood, a climate favorable to resistance was fostered. Rumors circulated in the city that the insurgents were landing arms on the west coast, which they dominated, and were freely moving from coast to coast by way of mountain passes. There were reports that insurgents were massing in a force of some 2,000 men in the Pardo and Sudlon mountains. Insurgents were spreading the word that the Americans, like the Spaniards before them, will only keep to the city and that an American government will be no different from that of the Spanish, corrupt and exploitative. American intelligence reports also had it that "Aguinaldo's agents" were agitating the people of Cebu with reports of insurgent victories in Luzon. One rumor that circulated was that Aguinaldo's army had driven the Americans from Malolos back to Intramuros and that the victorious Filipino army was now encamped on the Escolta in Manila.[17]

In the first two months and a half after the American landing in Cebu, there was little the Americans could do since the bulk of American troops was tied down in the violent campaign in Luzon. Gen. Elwell S. Otis, commander of the U.S. forces in the Philippines, observed: "We permitted Cebu to drift and foment opposition, careful to hold securely its principal city, an important trading point and one of the open ports of the Philippines."[18]

The limited control exercised by the Americans emboldened even moderate-minded Cebuanos to publicly express opposition to U.S. annexation. On the occasion of the visit of the Schurman Commission to Cebu in the middle part of 1899, Cebuanos presented a memorial in which the signatories declared:

Believing themselves to be the faithful spokesmen of the aspirations of the town of Cebu, they beg that you make known to the Government of your country that the inhabitants of the island of Cebu, like those of the rest of the Philippines, desire the independence of their country; that they have the same ideal just as they have a common flag. Having the pleasure of expressing to you once more our sacred ideals, we further express to you that we gladly accept the temporary protection of your country, but as to its sovereignty never.[19]

The signatories formed a cross-section of the local elite, among them Florentino Rallos, Tomas Osmeña, Luis Flores, Fr. Toribio Padilla, Fr. Emiliano Mercado, Marcial Velez, Leoncio Mansueto, Timoteo Castro, Fr. Alejandro Espina, Juan Velez, Manuel Roa, Pedro Rivera-Mir, Vicente Sotto, Crispulo Rafols, and Alejandro Climaco.

Outside Cebu City, the town governments organized by the republic continued to function. It was the quiet before the storm. Local militiamen spent time with their families and continued to attend fiestas or cockfights as they waited for the Americans to make their move. The situation in Cebu was marked by mutual wariness although there was reserved cordiality between American officers and the local elite. On 7 June 1899, for instance, the Americans gave a *baile* which was well attended by prominent Cebuanos, including all the local officials and "two insurgent generals."[20]

The assassination of Pablo Mejia on 11 June 1899, however, raised levels of tension. It mocked the Americans, agitated local residents, and dramatized the precariousness of peace.

3

A Society Comes Apart

A T AROUND 8:00 P.M., 11 June, Pablo Mejia and Julio Llorente were leisurely walking from Mejia's house on Magallanes Street to the house of Mejia's daughter at the foot of Pahina (Forbes) Bridge when they were suddenly attacked by an unknown assailant. Llorente escaped unhurt but Mejia was fatally stabbed in the chest. He died the following day.[1]

The Mejia assassination brought to the fore the divisions within Cebuano society that American occupation had sharpened. Unity among Cebuano leaders was very fragile and the imperatives posed by the American occupation tore local society apart. At another remove, the assassination was part of an even larger drama. The intra-Cebuano conflict in the period of U.S. occupation is shaped not just by the exigencies of war but also draws out of the political tensions of emergent social formations in Philippine society. It stretches both backward and forward in time.

The plot of this drama was already thick in 1897 when the Katipunan resistance to Spanish rule was organized in Cebu. The key actors in the initial phase of the resistance were a mixed group: Tagalog revolutionary agents, Visayan seamen, dockworkers, clerks, emerging urban proletarians, moderately prosperous merchants and landowners in San Nicolas and other towns, and other personalities marginal to the central elite of the inner city. Many of those who were loyal to Spain were highly educated and truly prosperous city residents. A good number of them enrolled in the roster of the *voluntarios leales*, a corps of loyalists organized by the Spanish authorities in September 1897 to counteract the reported moves of the "Tagalogs" to bring the Katipunan insurrection to Cebu.

There was an emerging class character to the divergence of political loyalties. The local Katipunan leadership gravitated around the lower orders of an urban middle class. It was fluid in the early stages and consisted of such types as civil servants (Florencio Gonzales, the Spanish mestizo from Surigao who was secretary of the Cebu ayuntamiento), skilled workers (Mariano Hernandez, a machine operator at Smith Bell), San Nicolas ilustrados (like the Padillas, Abellanas, and Pacañas), a few Chinese merchants (Lucio Herrera), and migrants and revolutionary agents from Manila and other provinces, including the legendary Pantaleon Villegas of Negros Oriental, Luis Flores of Samar, the Tagalog Gabino Gaabucayan, and Anastacio Oclarino of Laguna (who was an important link between the Manila and Cebu Katipuneros because of his job as a ship engineer on board the steamboat *Bohol*). On the other hand, the elite of Cebuano society (like the Ralloses, Velosos, Osmeñas, Mejias, Cuis, and others) remained either politically uninvolved or loyal to the Spanish Crown.

The elite was late in casting its lot with the revolution. Between the surrender of Manila to the Americans on 13 August 1898 to the arrival of the Americans in Cebu on 21 February 1899—a period of six months—a hiatus in the power situation existed. The entry of the U.S. improved the revolution's prospects of success and the indiscriminate reprisals carried out by the hard-pressed Spaniards alienated prominent citizens in the city. It was at this stage that ilustrado support began to swing in favor of the revolution.

When the Spaniards formally withdrew from Cebu on 24 December 1898, however, they did not directly turn over the government to the revolutionary forces but to a committee of prominent, conservative Cebuanos headed by Pablo Mejia. Mejia and other committee members were of the urban elite that was not actively involved in the revolution.

Pablo Ruiz Mejia (c1838–1899) was a Manila-born Spanish mestizo who came to reside in Cebu in the 1870s, acquired agricultural land and other properties, and was a city official and recognized member of the local elite by the 1890s. An insular and conservative, he was a logical go-between in the transfer of government. He was also the choice of the conservative and influential Catholic hierarchy. His appointment as caretaker was made in consultation with Bishop Alcocer and leaders of the church and the local business community.

The tensions between conservatives and militants were played out in the arguments over the insurgent occupation of the city. The rural militants (pejoratively referred to as bukidnon, or "mountain people"), citing their sacrifices in the struggle, wanted to forcibly seize the city and carry out reprisals against collaborators. It was Luis Flores who held them in

check, acting as the "bridge of reconciliation between the Cebuano revolutionaries and those who chose to stay in the plains" (*taytayan sa paghiusa
sa mga Sugbuanon nga rebolusyonaryo ug sa mga nanagpabilin dinhi sa patag*).[2]
Flores believed that the affairs of government should be entrusted to the
maalam and *dungganon* (learned and honorable) and it is said that it was
Flores who invited such men as Llorente, Mejia, Miguel Logarta, and
Segundo Singson to help him in running the government.

This is not just a local tension. The Malolos Republic was itself be-
set by class division, between what a writer of the time called the "oligarchy of intelligence" against the "ignorant oligarchy" of the military and
"low-class elements" of the revolution.[3] These latter elements were perceived to be volatile and there were anxieties among the propertied about
the dire prospects of mob rule, property confiscation, and a social order
turned "upside down."

Subsequent negotiations laid the ground for a coalition government
in which conservative, city-based ilustrados dominated the provincial leadership. It was a fragile coalition that included Katipunan revolutionary
agents from Luzon, newly empowered military leaders from the countryside, conservative businessmen and property owners, Hispanistas, and
former officials of the Spanish government in Cebu.

The policy of reconciliation and Flores's deference to ilustrados and
church officials did not sit well with some of the revolutionary leaders. An
illustration is the case of Francisco Llamas of San Nicolas. Unhappy with
Flores's policy of tolerance towards "collaborators," Llamas sent his own
armed men sometime around 31 December to arrest Bishop Alcocer,
Florentino Rallos, Escolastico Duterte, and others who served in the Spanish government and refused aid to the insurgents during the revolution.[4]
Llamas's independent move was checked by Flores who put guards at the
bishop's palace where Rallos and Duterte had taken refuge. That the revolutionary leadership's troubles with Llamas did not end here can be seen
in an order issued by Arcadio Maxilom from Pardo on 5 April 1899 calling
for the arrest of Llamas on charges of abuse of authority and gross insubordination.[5]

Political and ethnic tensions are also indicated in a letter to Aguinaldo
which the Tagalog Emilio Verdeflor wrote on 17 January 1899, complain-
ing that although the insurrection was "organized and maintained" by Tagalogs, the government established in Cebu harassed these patriots "in
every way." Verdeflor said that they were being opposed by native priests
devoted to the friars who had Luis Flores "under their thumb." He complained that the leaders in Cebu, instead of preparing for war, "had done
nothing but pay ceremonial visits to each other."[6]

When the Americans arrived in Cebu, therefore, the government in Cebu was newborn, possessed of meager resources to defend itself, and riven with internal contradictions. Luis Flores was, at this time, an ailing man under the sway of city-based ilustrados with largely untested commitments to the cause of revolution and independence.

The occupation of the city by the Americans triggered a crisis in the local leadership. The decision to surrender was not wholly accepted by the leaders of the government. One of them, Arcadio Maxilom, the head of the military, was in Leyte at the time of the surrender. Around 22 February, Maxilom returned to Cebu and learned of the surrender. On 23 February, a meeting was called at the Casa Real with Flores, Llorente, Maxilom, Mejia, Climaco, Segundo Singson, Eugenio Gines, Leoncio Alburo, and other leaders. The meeting was called, according to Flores, to decide on the request of Cornwell for local officials to continue in office to preserve civil order.

Marcial Velez expressed doubts whether persons could be found to serve under the Americans, first, because of dictates of sentiment, and, second, because of fear of incurring the ire of those opposed to American occupation. He suggested that the seat of government be removed away from "the shadow of the American flag." Matias de Arrieta, however, questioned the wisdom of transferring the seat of government, saying it may be taken to mean cession of the territory already occupied by the Americans. Others who spoke were Gervasio Padilla, Leoncio Alburo, and Juan Villarosa. Julio Llorente, once more, counseled moderation. He suggested acceptance of the American offer for the sake of maintaining peace and order. Once more, the issue of whether the basis for a civil government still existed came up, with Llorente arguing for the continued authority of Luis Flores. Juan Climaco, on the other hand, maintained that the civil government ceased to exist upon the surrender of the city and that authority had passed to Arcadio Maxilom as chief of the military. As in the 16 February meeting, the issue of leadership was not satisfactorily resolved.[7]

Maxilom and Climaco refused to abide with the surrender and proceeded to set up their own headquarters in the town of Pardo in defiance of the provincial council. The rumor in the city was that Maxilom had 200 rifles and was gathering men for an assault on the city. The fear of imminent hostilities led many city residents to abandon their homes.

There thus arose two Cebuano "governments"—the Flores-Llorente government friendly to the Americans and the hostile Maxilom-Climaco government.

On 21 March 1899, a council of civil and military officers was held in Pardo to clarify the status of the local government in the light of the American occupation.[8] At this meeting, Juan Climaco set forth the chain of events that culminated in the capitulation of the city to the Americans. He maintained that the Flores-Llorente government had been dissolved as early as 16 February and that authority had passed on to Maxilom as supreme military commander. Launching into an exegesis of the situation, Climaco argued that the Flores-Llorente government had ceased to be a revolutionary government but had become "a North American agent"; that it is an anomaly as it operates in territory occupied by the enemy; that it has tacitly recognized U.S. sovereignty and has abandoned the cause of independence; and that Maxilom is now the rightful head of government, exercising both civil and military powers.

Maxilom informed those present that the military headquarters and the general staff had been transferred to Pardo effective the day the Americans took possession of the city. He stressed that it was anomalous for the Flores-Llorente government to continue to function in a city occupied by the enemy.

Climaco and Maxilom, however, were not prepared to unilaterally establish their government and get on to the business of preparing for war. The indecision is shown in the fact that, at this 21 March meeting, it was decided that the new government be given more "definite and final character" by convening an assembly of town presidents on 10 April.

The struggle between conservatives and revolutionaries over the issue of legitimacy dragged on from February to August 1899 and consumed much of the attention of the local leaders. What was striking in the maneuvers of both groups was their concern (almost excessive, given the conditions) for constitutionality and legal form, with both groups grounding their actions on interpretations of Philippine laws, particularly Aguinaldo's decree of 18 June 1898. The American military chronicler John Taylor remarks: "The attention paid to an appearance of legality by these men is interesting."[9] He goes on to explain that in contesting the people's support the leaders felt it important that their claims to being the "real" government be clothed with the appearance of constitutionality. Over and above the concern for form, however, Climaco and Maxilom may have balked at boldly seizing the initiative because they judged that the support of the wealthy and learned citizens of the capital city was crucial for the success of the anti-American resistance.

Each competing faction deployed both interpretations of the law as well as practical moves to build its position vis-a-vis the other. The Llorente faction tried to undercut the Maxilom faction by taking control of the funds of the government. On 8 March 1899, Luis Flores also ordered Maxilom to bring into the city all rice collected for the supply of his troops.[10] On the other hand, Juan Climaco again issued, on 29 March 1899, an order from Pardo establishing the revolutionary government outside Cebu City.[11] Acting as chief of staff, Climaco announced that Maxilom had assumed both civil and military powers on 16 February and that the Flores-led provincial council had been suppressed. Lt. Col. Arsenio Climaco was directed to take charge of the department of revenues (taking over from Pablo Mejia) and was authorized to withdraw money deposited by the Cebu public treasury with businessman Tomas Osmeña. Juan Climaco charged that Mejia had engaged in illegal and treasonous acts by submitting government books of accounts to the Americans (instead of turning them over to the Maxilom government) and withdrawing $2,000 of public funds deposited with Osmeña.[12] In addition, Climaco charged it was Mejia who urged Llorente to order the collection of all the rice stored at different points outside the city, thus depriving the army of the republic of this supply. Mejia, the memorandum declared, had actively aided the enemy.[13]

On 10 April 1899, Maxilom presided over a meeting of military officers and an undetermined number of town presidents to decide on action to be taken in view of Flores's opposition to Maxilom's assuming command of the army. Those present agreed that the government under Maxilom should be established in the areas not controlled by the Americans. It was the opinion of the body that the members of the Flores government were no longer to be obeyed since they remained in the city and assembled in a building over which the American flag was raised. On 11 April 1899, Mabini sent a message congratulating Maxilom for his patriotism and stating that the Aguinaldo government's policy remained unchanged: "to fight unto death and to reject every American proposition which is not based on the recognition of our independence."[14]

Inside the city, the Flores government was taken over by a more openly collaborationist set of leaders. In the afternoon of 16 April 1899, a popular junta was convened composed of representatives from 40 out of 58 towns in Cebu province. The meeting was held to elect a new set of provincial officials on the basis of the general guidelines set forth in Aguinaldo's Decree of 18 June 1898. The event also marked the resignation of Luis Flores from the position of provincial president.

After the assembly was formally opened, Julio Llorente delivered a short speech in which, in reference to the moves of Climaco and Maxilom to set up a military government, he underscored the supremacy of civilian authority. He invoked the provision of the 18 June 1898 Decree that "the military chiefs will not intervene in the government and administration of the province." In the proceedings that followed, the assembly elected Julio Llorente, president; Segundo Singson, vice president; Florencio Noel, councilor of police matters; Miguel Logarta, councilor of justice; Mariano Veloso, councilor of finance; and Gabino Sepulveda and Juan Climaco, as "Cebu representatives to Manila."[15]

The Climaco-Maxilom faction did not actively participate in the proceedings although Maxilom received some votes for the post of "councilor of police" and Climaco was elected one of the two representatives to Manila. (The *representantes* were supposed to represent the province in a National Assembly, a body which, at this time, had rather uncertain status because of the war). Only around 30 persons—slightly 50 percent of eligible electors—participated in the voting.

Climaco and Maxilom did not mount an active resistance to Llorente's candidacy, first, because the election was held in occupied territory and, second, because (as Maxilom claimed later on) they had hoped Llorente would still find it in himself to see common cause with the revolutionaries.

The election brought the career of Luis Flores to an end. Lt. Col. Thomas Hamer, the American military commander in Cebu, said that the Americans were the ones who pressured Luis Flores, whom he calls "a weak and vacillating man," into retirement.[16] The ailing Flores retired to his house on Basco de Garay (now Juan Luna Street) and died a month later, on 17 May 1899, destitute and suffering from a long and painful illness he contracted in the hills in the war against Spain. A writer of the time said that Flores had wished to take to the field to resist the Americans but his ill health prevented him from doing so, as he did not wish to be an encumbrance to anyone. He refused to accept any wages from the Americans and told them nothing about his old comrades in the resistance.[17]

The 38-year-old Llorente emerged as president and the most prominent supporter of the American presence. (His term as provincial president was short-lived for, with the outbreak of hostilities a few months after, the American commanding officer in Cebu, Hamer, was to take over as military governor.) Llorente was the quintessential ilustrado: aristocratic and highly educated, mestizo, rich, and self-assured about his right to lead. Towering over his colleagues (he was about six feet in height), he cut a dignified figure with his gold-rimmed spectacles and small black moustache. Though he could not speak English, he was, of course, fluent in Spanish.[18] Hamer, on the hand, felt that he was "not a very strong man" but considered him a more acceptable executive than Flores. On the other hand, General E. S. Otis, in April 1900, regarded Llorente "the ablest man of that section of the country."

The Americans were pleased over the new set of provincial officials. Hamer wrote: "The new administration showed every indication of friendship to the Americans and only withheld an open and full recognition of the sovereignty of the United States on the ground that we had not sufficient force on the island to occupy the principal towns and thus protect the person and property of our friends from the lawless element, which would be sure to attack those who declared for American sovereignty."[19]

Llorente moved into an even more adversarial relationship with the Maxilom forces. On 29 April, he informed Maxilom that Maxilom's soldiers would not be entitled to any pay after 1 May, and that warrants drawn for that purpose after said date would not be honored. Invoking legal niceties, Llorente suppressed the town militias which in fact constituted "all the army" of the republic.

Maxilom replied that the provincial council had no right to suppress his army and that the move was patently intended to facilitate American annexation. On 4 May, Llorente reiterated his position by warning the people of Cebu that they were not to furnish money or rations to persons in the military service. He also informed Maxilom that his office had been abolished.[20] On 7 May, the Llorente government repeated the directive of Luis Flores of 8 March 1899 ordering that Maxilom bring into Cebu all rice collected for the supply of the army.

On 15 May 1899, Maxilom reported to Mabini that Llorente and Mejia had become avid partisans of American annexation though they hid under "the cloak of patriotism." He said that at the outset Miguel Logarta and Segundo Singson, "ardent patriots," were opposed to them but, like Luis Flores, they had been brought under the influence of the annexationists. He explained the nomination of Llorente for the presidency by saying that "although he (Llorente) had lost much of the prestige he enjoyed before, on account of the weakness of his character and meanness of spirit which he has demonstrated since the arrival of the Americans," his nomination to the presidency "was necessary, because public opinion had not yet lost the hope that placing him at the front of the government and with a direct responsibility, would cause him to face the difficulties of the situation, knowing his recognized prudence and learning." It was because of this hope, Maxilom said, that Llorente was elected president. However, he has since disappointed the people. Llorente appropriated for his own council the local budget and submitted to the Americans the government's books of account. He suppressed the militias, cut off their supplies, and denied them a separate existence by pretending that Maxilom's army depended upon the provincial council like "a kind of police." In view of the above, Maxilom petitioned the Aguinaldo government to give open recognition to the Maxilom forces. For this purpose, Maxilom said, they had sent an emissary, Aguedo Batobalanos (a capitan of Santa Fe in northern Cebu and a senior aide to Maxilom), to explain to Aguinaldo the Cebu situation.[21]

In his reply, Mabini granted formal recognition to Maxilom as commander of the Cebuano forces and as head of the Cebu provincial government. On the basis of this recognition, Maxilom appealed to his fellow Cebuanos to bear arms against the Americans. At the same time, he instructed the town presidents to draw up an act of recognition for his government.

On 17 May 1899, Maxilom, Saturnino Echavez, and other leaders held a meeting outside Cebu City to denounce the action of the provincial council disbanding the militia. It was argued that the council overstepped its powers as the creation of the militia was provided for by the "supreme authorities" of the republic and its existence was essential in assuring the security and integrity of the province.[22]

In a letter to Mabini on 30 May 1899, Maxilom asked for authority for the military to take over the government in case Llorente succeeded in convincing the town presidents to accept American rule.[23] In his reply, Antonio Luna, the secretary of war, wrote Maxilom on 2 June 1899 that punishment should be meted out to collaborators "without taking into consideration the civil, military or ecclesiastical state" of the person.[24] This letter of Luna, however, still seemed less than explicit to Maxilom on the question of the status of the American-influenced provincial council. In part, the ambiguity in the status of the two "governments" in Cebu derived from confusion over the fast succession of events and the slowness of communications between national and local governments. In the main, Maxilom's repeated appeals for recognition indicated weakness and indecisiveness on the part of the revolutionary leadership.

At the same time that he endeavored to gain legitimacy for his government, Maxilom tried to rally Cebuano support for the cause of independence. In an appeal to Cebuanos, he said:

> You should not, my beloved people of Cebu, believe that you
> are fighting against the whole wealthy and powerful country
> of America. You are only fighting against a party which is also
> hated by their own countrymen. If said party pursues its
> policy of annexation, and if you persevere in the fight, you
> will succeed in casting down from his power its leader,
> McKinley, and the Democratic Party, which is willing to
> recognize our rights and to do us justice, will take his place.[25]

As late as August, however, Maxilom and Climaco were still wrestling with the problem of legitimacy. On 7 August 1899, when hostilities had already begun, Maxilom sent a circular to town presidents, saying that he assumed civil and military powers effective the date "the first shot was fired in defense of our rights." He called the Llorente government illegal. He said that he had previously refrained from assuming full powers as he did not want to disturb the "peace of the towns." Still, he asked that in the coming election of provincial president (September 1899), the delegates of the towns should vote for those who are committed to the cause of independence.[26]

The political and factional differences among Cebuano leaders did not escape the notice of outsiders. The Tagalog Vicente Lukban, who ruled Samar with a tight hand, wrote on 8 July 1899 on the situation in Cebu:

> The origin of all the disturbances here is due to those clerks, lawyers, writers and pettifoggers during Spanish domination.... The tendency of all these men is to sow seeds of discord and friction between families; and to this is due the division of parties. All of them, under the name or pretext of Country, wish to feather their own nests.[27]

He calls the collaborators "barrators and potbellied pretended patriots" and complains that "most of the wealthy and middle class here sacrifice their patriotism in favor of their personal interests and wish to eat when the table is already set, that is to say, they expect us to restore them, but they always offer lives and lands in words and not by acts." He adds: "The Visayans have a tendency to misrepresent things and calumniate, and they consider trifles and not the main issue, which is the war."

There is here the thinly disguised pique of the superior-minded Tagalog over Visayan parochialism. It neither acknowledges the fact that this problem was not peculiar to Cebu or the Visayas nor does it really explain the roots of political division in Cebu. Lukban, however, is correct in that factionalism did undermine the resistance against the Americans.

Even as the Cebuano leaders quarreled among themselves over questions of leadership, the Americans themselves were constrained from quickly consolidating their rule. The support of what the Americans called "the better class of natives," joined to the knowledge that the Cebuano army was hastily conscripted, ill-trained, and poorly equipped, encouraged Hamer in the belief that a swift, decisive show of force would reduce the province to complete submission. In what was the typical American view of the Filipino political situation, Hamer reported to his superiors on 1 May that "the better class of natives here, especially the landed proprietors, are seemingly with us, but the lower classes, in common with their brothers throughout the Philippines, are very susceptible to leadership."[28]

Hamer said that both classes respected armed force as an indication of a strong government.

The situation in the city itself was well under control, Hamer said, and the business situation had normalized. On 13 May, Hamer wrote that Llorente told him that if enough troops are sent to Cebu to protect the people, "he will call the Junta Popular to meet in Cebu and that body will at once acknowledge the supremacy of the United States on this Island and take immediate steps to adopt a constitution similar to that adopted by the people of Negros."[29]

Hamer said that "the more intelligent class" was sympathetic to U.S. rule and only the lack of adequate protection prevented them from openly expressing their sympathies. Hamer chafed at his lack of troops. From Manila, Assistant Adjutant Gen. Thomas Barry wrote Hamer on 21 May on the suggested Negros-type constitution for Cebu: "It is not well that these people act with any great dispatch.... It is not the part of wisdom to hurry up political action in Cebu. Let the people manage their internal affairs for the present as quietly as possible until some definite policy with regard to all the islands can be announced."[30]

Confined to the city proper, Hamer could not do anything but wait.

4

Widening the Orbit

THE MEJIA assassination on 11 June 1899 agitated the city residents and changed the complexion of the situation in Cebu. Together with Llorente, Mejia was the most prominent and visible supporter of American rule. They opposed armed resistance and counseled "moderation" on the part of the people. They were targets of insurgent propaganda that accused them of treason to the Filipino nation. A few weeks before Mejia's death, there were in fact rumors that Llorente and Mejia might leave for Hong Kong because of fear for their lives. Hamer wrote to headquarters in Iloilo: "We cannot afford to lose the active influence of these men on this Island at this time."

In the wake of the Mejia assassination, the word in Cebu was that Mejia's name had been at the head of a "blacklist" of 60 persons to be assassinated and that these men had received warning to this effect. Insurgent elements believed that Mejia was one of those who sold out the revolution to the Americans. Others tagged were those who, with Mejia, were emissaries in the initial talks with Cornwell: Julio Llorente, Segundo Singson, Fr. Pablo Singson, and Fr. Juan Gorordo.

The Americans put up a reward of 1,000 pesos for the arrest and conviction of the assassin. (Sometime in September 1899, an Alipio Bartolaba of Naga surrendered for the killing of Mejia.) Two American soldiers were posted at Llorente's house to secure the governor. Wealthy residents were jittery and some—like Doña Feliciana Enriquez vda. de Carratala, whose husband, Don Enrique Carratala, was hacked to death by insurgents in the 3 April anti-Spanish uprising—formally sought American protection.[1] Llorente himself left Cebu on 26 June 1899 to seek refuge in

Manila, leaving Segundo Singson to take over as acting president. This was apparently the time when he took up the post as associate justice of the Philippine Supreme Court to which he had been appointed on 29 May 1899. (Llorente served in this post until he reassumed the Cebu governorship in April 1901.)

In the wake of the Mejia assassination, Hamer again sent out urgent messages for additional troops. This time, headquarters responded. On 14 June, the American force in Cebu was augmented with the arrival from Iloilo of four companies of the First Tennessee Volunteer Infantry and a platoon of Battery G (with two field guns) of the Sixth Artillery aboard the transport *Aeolus*. The reinforcements, under the command of Lt. Col. Albert B. Bayless of the First Tennessee Volunteers, were initially given quarters in different parts of the city. With the augmentation of the U.S. occupation force, night patrols were increased and the reconnoitered territory expanded. At this point, the decision was reached to extend the limits of occupation to erase doubts on American will.

On 16 June 1899, the town of San Nicolas was occupied by men of the Twenty-third U.S. Infantry under First Lieutenant F. G. Stritzinger, Jr. The Americans took quarters in the San Nicolas tribunal. No untoward incidents occurred during the entry of American troops. Prior to the actual entry, Hamer conferred with San Nicolas presidente Santiago Ferraris. Hamer reported that Ferraris expressed pleasure over the security that the occupation would give to the people of his town.

On 26 June, Pardo was occupied.[2] Pardo had just been abandoned as headquarters of the Maxilom government. Three miles from the city and connected to it by a fairly good road, it was a small town with a population of around 3,000. Except for the church and convent, the houses in Pardo were mostly shacks and even the tribunal was a bamboo-and-nipa affair.[3] Involved in the occupation of Pardo were elements of the Twenty-third U.S. Infantry and the Idaho and Tennessee Volunteers. Offshore support was provided by the gunboats *Charleston* and *Manileño*. Though there was no exchange of gunfire, Pardo was clearly hostile territory for the Americans.

The first American push was southwards, towards the island's most prosperous and populous towns, to Argao and Dalaguete on the east coast and Barili and Dumanjug on the west. By 2 July, the Americans had occupied Talisay, Minglanilla, San Fernando, Naga, and Carcar.[4] By the end of July, the Americans had penetrated Sibonga, Argao, Dalaguete, Barili, and Dumanjug. Small detachments were stationed in the key towns occupied. Sallies even went as far as Alcoy and Santander at the southern tip of Cebu island. No real military resistance was encountered in the occupation of these towns and the only factors that slowed down the American advance were the lack of troops to effectively garrison the occupied towns and the heavy rains that aggravated the poor condition of the roads.

No actual fighting occurred as insurgents, after a few shots in some places, withdrew without engaging the enemy. Only in Sibonga was there a sizeable force of insurgents that attempted to block the entry of American troops to the town. The insurgents, however, abandoned their positions after a brief, desultory exchange of shots that exacted no casualties.

The occupation of some of the towns, however, was protested by the local authorities. On 17 June, the day after San Nicolas was occupied, San Nicolas presidente Santiago Ferraris handed to Colonel Hamer a letter of the San Nicolas junta popular, dated 16 June, protesting the occupation and the raising of the U.S. flag over the town hall. The junta declared that the occupation was contrary to international law and the integrity of the Filipino nation which "only Emilio Aguinaldo, as chief of state, can dispose of in the name of the inhabitants."[5]

In Pardo, the protest was registered by parish priest Fr. Jacinto Ferraris on 27 June.[6] Similar protests were lodged by other towns. In part, these protests were meant by local officials to pacify the insurgents. The Maxilom government had issued instructions to the towns on 20 June 1899, saying that protest must be registered by the occupied towns "within the period of 72 hours fixed by international law." Copies of the protest were to be given to the American military commander in Cebu and the Cebu-based consuls of Germany, Venezuela, and Great Britain.[7]

The protests were ignored by the Americans who dismissed them as the handiwork of the insurgent leaders. The Americans had reasons to regard the protests in cavalier fashion. On 18 June, for instance, the day after the San Nicolas protest, Santiago Ferraris and the San Nicolas delegate of justice called on Hamer and advised him that the protest was merely sent to appease the insurgents as the members of the San Nicolas junta feared they would be assassinated. Ferraris and the delegate told Hamer that they were asked by "the better citizens of their community" to convey to Hamer and the Americans that "the better elements of the town and the island were glad of our occupation and the security it guaranteed the people in the town."[8]

American occupation of the towns was designed to demonstrate American power, bring the population within the American orbit, and impress upon them America's "benevolent" intentions. In the occupation of the towns, American instructions to field officers stated:

> Take down and keep down the insurgent flag wherever
> found; respect the rights of persons and property in the

territory occupied; treat the inhabitants thereof with equal
and exact justice, at all times tempered with kindness, with a
view to establishing friendly relations between the people of
this island and the United States; set a good example for the
natives by enforcing strict discipline in your command;
preserve law and order (but in so doing avoid bloodshed or
trouble of any kind) if possible; and meet such other and
future emergencies as may unexpectedly arise... by the
exercise of that God-given intelligence that an officer is
presumed to possess as a prerequisite to holding a commission in the Army of the United States.

It is not the intention at the present time to interfere
with the local government of the towns occupied as long as
they are honestly and fairly conducted and are not manifestly
unfriendly to the U.S.[9]

On the part of the Maxilom government, it was obviously the policy
at this time to avoid frontal contact since the Cebuano army was ill prepared to stem the American advance. As the Americans advanced into the
towns, the insurgents melted into the countryside.

On 20 April 1899, before the American occupation of the towns,
Maxilom had divided Cebu island into six military zones.[10] The area of
the first zone extended from Cebu to Argao; the second, from Dalaguete
to Samboan; the third, from Ginatilan to Barili; the fourth, from Aloguinsan
to Tuburan; the fifth, from San Remigio to Madridejos; and the sixth, from
Carmen to Tudela. The first and third zones were to be commanded by
major-generals and the rest by brigadier-generals. The staff of each zone
consisted of an adjutant, a secretary, and a judge advocate. The field officers and members of the militia were to be drawn from the towns covered.
In case of officers having the same rank in one locality, the principle of
who was older applied to seniority. The soldiers were exempted from full
payment of personal service obligation and half-payment of the poll tax or
certificate of citizenship (cedula).

The basic unit of the organization was called a sector or *fraccion*, composed of 32 men, commanded by a lieutenant. Three sectors comprised a
company; ten companies a regiment. The total manpower of six regiments
(or 60 companies) would be distributed to the six zones as follows: the
first, twelve companies; the second, eight; the third, eleven; the fourth,
seven; the fifth, twelve; and the sixth, ten. A force of 60 companies meant
that 5,760 men were envisioned for the Cebuano army. At the time the
Americans moved into the towns, however, the insurgent army was still a

fledgling, loosely structured organization. Mired in factional struggles and pressured by fast-developing events, the Cebuano leadership was unable to raise a large and effective army. A low estimate of Maxilom's regular army at the close of July 1899 placed it at only 150 properly armed men.

The Maxilom government faced two problems: Cebuano collaboration and the problem of getting enough manpower and logistical support. Collaboration eroded mass support for the cause of the republic. As early as 15 May 1899, Maxilom wrote to Apolinario Mabini about the problems posed by "the Americans who are continually trying to intimidate us into recognizing the rule of their nation with ample autonomy, and the active part the provincial council is playing, especially its president, Señor Julio Llorente, who openly sympathizes with the invaders, placing difficulties and stumbling blocks before the military element with the object of weakening their strength."[11]

Even as American troops moved into the towns, the Maxilom and Llorente governments were still contesting the loyalty of the municipal governments. Llorente had suppressed the bulk of Maxilom's army by not authorizing salary payments from public funds. In response, Maxilom had asked the Aguinaldo government for written authority to take over the provincial government. Yet, a great deal of indecisiveness marked the Maxilom leadership during this period.

As late as August 1899, the struggle between the Maxilom and Llorente camps for legitimacy was still going on. In a letter of 2 June 1899, Antonio Luna, the secretary of war of the Aguinaldo government, directed Maxilom to oppose to his utmost the full autonomy offered by the Americans.[12] He must impose severe punishments upon such persons as proclaim the advantages offered by the Americans without consideration for their positions, whether civil or ecclesiastical. Luna wrote that if the provincial council and the officials of "autonomist tendency" incline toward the Americans, hostilities must ensue for "we cannot permit any flag except the Filipino one on that Island [of Cebu]."

Lacking the military force, however, the insurgents could only resort to harassment when the Americans moved to occupy the towns. Apart from the Mejia assassination, there are references to the liquidation of Justice of the Peace Isidro Guivelondo and of a brother of Florentino Rallos. Guivelondo was assassinated in his own house in the presence of the woman to whom he was to be married the following day.[13]

In the weeks that followed the American advance, several cases of harassment were reported.[14] On 27 June, the Tagalog cook of an American officer stationed in Pardo was kidnapped and manhandled, his right ear slit by insurgents, before he was released. Sometime in mid-July, a man who furnished labor to the Americans was kidnapped and kept prisoner for two or three days before he escaped. Inscribed in bluestone on his forehead were the words *Traidor a la patria* and on his chin the word *Amigo* (literally, "friend," but meaning "collaborator" in popular usage). In early July, Juan Melgar, the presidente of Dumanjug, was arrested and jailed by insurgent chief Nicolas Godines for Melgar's support of the American occupation. Around October, Francisco Rodriguez, the chief of police of San Nicolas, was abducted by the insurgents and taken to the hills though he was subsequently released.[15]

The reception of the Americans in the towns was mixed. The Americans found many villages and towns virtually deserted. Residents, forewarned of the Americans' approach by the blowing of conch shells, stayed out of sight as the Americans marched in. In places like Sibonga, Argao, Naga, and Dumanjug, the town presidents received them in a friendly and cordial manner. Argao officials declared that the town would fight the insurgents at the side of the Americans. In Sibonga ("the president here is very friendly"), which the Americans entered on 12 July, the situation was tense as Nicolas Godines—said to be at the head of some 200 men with 20 Mausers and as many pistols—was operating in the hinterland of Sibonga and Dumanjug. However, the townspeople were friendly, according to the American report, and welcomed the Americans as "they have much fear of robbers" and were worried over a recent raid on Dumanjug by Godines's band in which the insurgents carted away $16.000.[16]

In Pardo, the presidente did not present himself to the Americans and was nowhere to be found. Captain W. H. Allaire of the Twenty-third U.S. Infantry said: "There is no doubt about the hostility of the natives here. I can see and feel it in the air."[17] American troops were billeted in the Pardo convent and in tents on the convent grounds. The Americans enforced a curfew in the town, prohibited gatherings, and arrested anyone caught carrying a bolo. The tense situation in Pardo was occasioned by its proximity to the mountains where Maxilom and his men were reportedly massed.

While there were town leaders who received the Americans with open arms, the general attitude of the population was one of wariness and suspicion. To fend off American control, civilians resorted to silence, avoidance, dissimulation, and other forms of passive resistance. The Maxilom government itself encouraged the use of these tactics. Maxilom ordered that upon the entry of U.S. troops into a town, the local police should appear friendly to the Americans, gain their confidence, and elicit information. "The presidentes and the residents of the pueblo should not show their feelings."[18] Attitudes of avoidance and denial were in particular evidence in the later occupation of the northern Cebu towns. When San Remigio was entered in early March 1901, the Americans found a deserted town. The American commanding officer in northern Cebu reported:

> The people of San Remigio have either left that pueblo in a body or fled at the approach of American soldiers. Everything in my power had been done to show these people the benefits of American control. The place had been garrisoned and apparently great confidence had been created, but very suddenly the whole population left in much the same manner as did the people of Maravilla and to occupy San Remigio now would be simply to occupy a town filled with empty houses. I recently entered that town about daylight and found it empty and captured about a dozen insurgent flags; also some powder and ammunition.[19]

The officer wrote that insurgent tax collectors did their work in the towns but could not be caught "because the citizens will not give the necessary information." He added: "Although the towns are filled at times with strangers, the inhabitants thereof say these strangers are not insurgents but simply buyers."

In Pinamungahan in August 1900, an American officer reported: "The people as a whole seem perfectly cowed and afraid to show any signs of friendship and during our stay carefully avoided the troops. It was also impossible to buy anything in the shape of fish, eggs, chickens, cigarettes, etc., all such being carefully concealed or ownership disclaimed."[20]

In the first push into southern Cebu, American troops stationed in the towns were not large in number. Two companies occupied Pardo but in places where there were no reports of significant insurgent presence, only a few soldiers were stationed. Talisay was occupied by only 12 men and 2 noncommissioned officers, Minglanilla was occupied by 20 men and 4 noncommissioned officers, and Carcar was garrisoned by only 21 men. The main body of American troops that advanced into the towns had offshore support from the gunboats *Charleston* and *Manileño*. The naval guns, however, were silent in the absence of active resistance. The insurgent army kept out of the way as the Americans advanced into the southern towns.

At the start of the American push southwards, U.S. authorities issued orders through the Llorente government for the arrest of Maxilom, Godines, and other insurgent leaders. The Maxilom government, however, had decided to wage its war from the hinterland.

5

The Siege of Sudlon

T HE FIRST battle took place in the country beyond Pardo on 24 July 1899. In the early hours of 24 July, a contingent of 61 American soldiers of the Twenty-third U.S. Infantry left camp in Pardo on a reconnaissance mission.[1] The Americans split into two groups, a smaller unit of 16 soldiers going towards Mananga Valley and the main group of 45 men striking towards Labangon River. The main group reached the small settlement of Buhisan around 5:40 A.M. and proceeded to search the houses. The Americans rounded up 15 persons, "many armed with bolos," whom the Americans' Filipino guide had called *gente malo*. At this moment, a bugle, horns, and conch shells were sounded in the neighboring hills where, in the early morning light, the Americans could discern men in "white or bluish clothing" gathering. The Americans took the 15 prisoners with them and moved across the valley, hoping to rendezvous with the American soldiers who had separated from the main group over an hour earlier. Seeing what appeared to be new earthworks at the top of a ridge, the Americans decided to scout the area, slowly moving up steep cogonal ground until they reached the top of the ridge. It was around 10:00 A.M. It was at this point that the Americans were fired upon. One American was instantly killed. In the sudden gunfire, the Cebuano prisoners attempted to escape by rolling down the steep hillside. The Americans fired on the fleeing prisoners, killing five. Pinned by fire from a well-positioned enemy and exhausted from their hike, the Americans decided to cautiously retreat towards Jacupan (Jaclupan) Valley and, finally, back to Pardo where they arrived at about 2:00 P.M. The Americans estimated that what they had run up against was an insurgent force of around

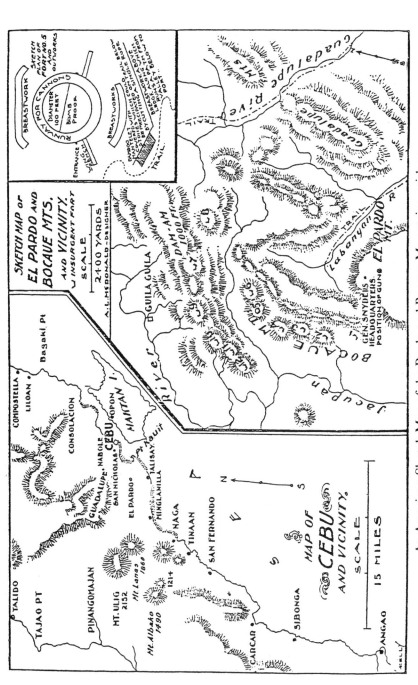

An American Sketch Map of the Pardo and Bocaue Mountains, with an Inset Showing the Plan of an "Insurgent Fortification"

100 men with 20 rifles, Remingtons and Mausers, and "some kind of field piece."

The insurgent account of this battle (circularized by Gen. Potenciano Aliño to the presidentes of San Fernando, Carcar, Sibonga, Argao, and Dalaguete) said that the Cebuanos battled the Americans for two hours and killed two Americans.[2] In the wake of the battle, Maxilom issued a call to arms to his fellow Cebuanos on 29 July 1899. He called the attack on Cebuano lines the final provocation. He said:

> The hour has already sounded when the Mother Country, in the midst of her tortures and countless sufferings, calls to us, Cebuanos, with a sorrowful and pleading voice, so that we, her sons, may without hesitation or dismay, raise the war cry throughout our fields.... Independence or death—this is our theme.... Let us fight then without hesitation or dismay, because God is in us, and His power is great, and however powerful the American nation may be, He can overthrow its power, destroying it as He did the giant Goliath, by the hand of the boy, David, with no weapon but a sling.
>
> Let us fight, I repeat, and trust in God, the God of armies, who is watching over us.[3]

American intelligence reports of July 1899 indicated that there were two or three sizeable insurgent "bands," one in the mountains behind Pardo, another in the mountains back of Carcar and Sibonga. These bands had a limited number of rifles and some ammunition. Reports said that they "terrorized" the people and impressed them for the purpose of constructing fortifications of various kinds in the mountain passes; sent small squads down to the coastal towns to levy tribute on individuals; punished traitors; and had spies reporting on American movements. Hamer judged: "If these marauders are exterminated promptly and without delay you will find this island submissive, ready, willing and anxious to acknowledge the sovereignty of the United States."[4] He complained that he had only enough men to hold important positions on the east coast and a few to spare for field operations. If he had 200 men to deploy under command of officers experienced in "Indian fighting," Hamer said, he was certain he could subdue the whole island. He stressed that a decisive campaign against the enemy was important before the situation worsened.

From July 1899 to January 1900, the focal area of the war was the island's central zone, with Sudlon as the base of resistance as it was here that the leading insurgent generals had set up camp. There were scattered actions in some towns at the periphery of this zone. On 17 September 1899, for instance, American troops of the Twenty-third U.S. Infantry and the First Tennessee Volunteers were ambushed in Moalboal. Two Americans were killed and two others wounded. On 23 September, Dumanjug was occupied by insurgents under Gen. Emilio Verdeflor with the aid of Barili policemen. They collected some 14 rifles, ammunition, and a large sum of money.

The Pardo and Sudlon mountains, however, were the epicenter of the war as there was a concentration of armed insurgents in the area. Situated some 34 kilometers west of the city, Sudlon is surrounded by a sharply dissected terrain and a complex of hills (bearing such names as Lumbang, Bitlang, Budlaan, Alemagahon, and Butong). Two rivers—Mananga and Guadalupe—course irregularly down from this highland to the coastal plains. The country leading up to Sudlon is characterized by steep ridges and narrow valleys with little cover but coconut trees and tall cogon grass. In this rugged upland area were scattered houses and farms growing corn, rice, and coconuts.[5]

An army based in Sudlon (near Camp 7 of the Cebu-Toledo road, northwest of the city) had the advantage of access to stores of food since the area had both livestock and upland farms. Moreover, there were only two approaches to its highest peak (called Sip-ak): Bitlang Pass in the rear and, in front, a narrow pass along Bagakay Ridge. Hostile forces approaching from the direction of Cebu City or Pardo could be detected long before they entered the Sudlon area.

Maxilom had armed units stationed at various points in this central mountain zone. A Cebuano account says that these included the men of Alejo Miñoza in Hibuyo (a mountain above Buhisan), Potenciano Aliño in Acan, Enrique Lorega in Sam-angan, and Nicolas Godines in upper Lahug.[6] It appears, however, from the battle reports that the two main lines of defense were a range of hills near Pardo, called Bocaue, and then the mountain range of Sudlon itself.

On 23 August 1899, a force of two officers and 25 men of the Twenty-third U.S. Infantry went into this rugged area and again made contact with an insurgent force of around 30 to 40 men.[7] After an hour-long battle, the insurgents retreated, leaving behind one man dead. One American was wounded and two were reported missing. The Americans found five or six earthworks and captured two field guns. On 25 August, three men of the Twenty-third U.S. Infantry were waylaid and killed by insurgents in the Guadalupe Valley and their bodies mutilated.

Again, on 28 August, men of the Twenty-third U.S. Infantry moved into the Pardo mountains, this time with one gun of Battery G of the Sixth

U.S. Artillery. Reaching the site of the enemy fortifications, the American field gun started firing, destroying two "forts" and forcing three "blockhouses" to hoist the white flag. The insurgents retreated and the Americans, finding no one, torched the huts they found in the area.[8]

In September, the Americans began a concerted effort to sweep the hills beyond Pardo free of insurgents. On 12 September 1899, from 2:50 P.M. to 5:30 P.M., the U.S.S. *Monadnock* bombarded insurgent fortifications in the Pardo mountains. Firing was resumed the following day, from 2:20 P.M. to 5:10 P.M. The target were forts and breastworks that insurgents had built at elevations of from 800 to 1,200 feet to command the various roads and trails from Buhisan. Naval bombardment was intended to soften insurgent positions preparatory to a ground assault by the U.S. Army. The Americans moved towards Cebuano positions in the central highlands but were met with heavy enemy fire. Bombardment from *Monadnock* was ineffective as most of the shots fired fell short of their targets. Only two shots did damage to the Cebuano fortifications, blowing up what appeared to be a magazine in one of the forts. American ground troops called off their advance on 13 September, as their force of around 300 men was not considered sufficient to meet an insurgent army estimated at between 800 to 1,200 men. A total of 31 ten-inch cannon shells was fired by the double-turreted *Monadnock* during the two-day bombardment.[9]

On 18 September, a battalion of the Nineteenth U.S. Infantry, commanded by Col. Simon Snyder, arrived in Cebu on board the transport *Indiana*. The new force had come to relieve the First Tennessee Volunteers in Cebu. Snyder took over from Hamer and assumed command of Cebu on 19 September.

In transit at the Cebu port at this time were two battalions of the First Tennessee Volunteers from Iloilo who had come to pick up their comrades in Cebu for the trip back to Manila. (At this time, the state volunteers were in the process of being mustered out of service.) There was then a heavy concentration of American troops in Cebu at the time when the situation in the island had apparently worsened. Americans received reports of some 2,000 to 3,000 insurgents holding strongly fortified positions in the Bocaue mountains, a range of hills rising to a maximum elevation of about 1,500 feet, near Pardo.

The Americans resolved to avail of the presence of the Tennessee Volunteers to mount a massive offensive.[10] Colonel Snyder, the new military commander in Cebu, inspected American troops near Cebu City in the company of Col. Gracey Childers, commander of the First Tennessee Volunteers, Lt. Col. Thomas Hamer, the outgoing Cebu commander, and other officers. After surveying the situation in the field, they decided to launch a large-scale offensive.

Reconnaissance indicated that the insurgents had built up a front of about four miles along the crest and slope of very steep hills in Bocaue (in upland Sapangdaku, Pardo). They had a number of detached forts and entrenchments covering all approaches to their central camp. As to the armament and the number of the Cebuano troops, reports were conflicting and estimates varied widely. Reports indicated that the Cebuanos had six or eight field guns, supposed to be old brass smooth bores, but their effectiveness was questionable.

With monitor *Monadnock*, anchored in the bay, firing shells into the mountain forts, Colonel Snyder quickly deployed his men. Fifty-three officers and 747 men participated in the offensive that began in the early light of 21 September. [11] It was the biggest American offensive of the war in Cebu.

The Americans brought up two field guns. A press dispatch of the operation said that the day was "fearfully hot." The process of hauling up steep terrain the heavy field pieces "killed eight buffaloes, or carabaos... and finally the men had to haul them themselves for four miles over about as bad a country as can be imagined." [12]

In the multipronged attack, position "A," about 2,000 yards from the nearest enemy fortifications, was occupied by a large attacking force composed of men of the Nineteenth and Twenty-third U.S. Infantries, the Sixth Artillery, and the First Tennessee Volunteers. At the same time, three companies of the Nineteenth U.S. Infantry, under Capt. William P. Evans, marched to Guadalupe and thence by trail up the Guadalupe Valley in an encircling movement to attack the rear of the enemy position.

The main force at position "A" was led by Colonel Snyder and Colonel Childers. The Americans were divided into four columns. Column A was composed of four companies of the First Tennessee Volunteers. Column B comprised four companies of the First Tennessee and one company of the Nineteenth U.S. Infantry. Column C consisted of two companies of the First Tennessee and one company of the Twenty-third U.S. Infantry. Column D was made up of the three companies of the Nineteenth Infantry dispatched for the encircling action in Guadalupe.

Actual hostilities began in the afternoon of 21 September and lasted until the morning of 23 September. With largely ineffective rifle and cannon fire from their fortifications and ridges, the Cebuanos tried to stem the American advance for hours. The roar of small-arms fire washed back and forth between Filipino and American lines. From gullies and ridges, shouts of command punctuated the sound of Mauser bullets spatting into the tall grass and the louder noise of the ancient Springfields. The press dispatch about the battle said that the Cebuano cannons, "loaded with scrap iron," had little effect, as Cebuano marksmanship was atrocious.[13]

The Americans systematically moved their men to the flanks and rear of the insurgent fortifications but were slowed down by the steep terrain, the lack of natural cover, and the heavy front and crossfire from the insurgent positions. The Americans overran fortification after fortification (12 "forts" were subsequently identified). As evening fell, the Cebuanos slowly dropped back from their forward positions. The exchange of fire lasted until 10:00 P.M., 22 September, and resumed the following morning as the Americans mounted a final attack on the remaining forts. The conquest of Bocaue was completed around 10:00 A.M. of 23 September. After destroying the insurgent works, the American forces returned to Cebu City on 25 September, leaving behind two companies of the Nineteenth Infantry to garrison the abandoned insurgent positions.

The Americans were not able to engage a large body of insurgents in face-to-face combat since the insurgents withdrew from their positions before they could be completely overrun. The Cebuanos' familiarity with the terrain allowed them to slip out as the American dragnet drew close.

One American was killed in the battle and four were wounded. Cebuano losses were not determined although 27 bodies and 12 graves were reported found. Local residents, however, estimated that insurgent casualties totaled 300. No Cebuano prisoners were taken.

Insurgent arms captured included one 3.2-inch rifled brass muzzle loading cannon, one 3-inch brass muzzle loading cannon, three small smooth-bore cannons of seventeenth-century vintage, fragments of one brass cannon (which had evidently burst from an excessive charge), and 200 cannon canisters. The Americans also found an arsenal comprising three large bamboo shacks. Buried near the arsenal were 15 gun barrels, 6 gun stocks, 2 pistols, 2 revolvers, a lot of Krag-Jorgensen projectiles, several hundred other shells, large quantities of bullets, lead, and 2 bullet molds. In the arsenal were a lot of reloading and reworking tools. A bamboo shack was found equipped with charcoal, saltpeter, and a complete powder-making outfit. Not far away was a corral with seven heads of cattle and a number of hogs and goats.

The elaborate insurgent network in Bocaue was called by one of the Americans a "Philippine Gibraltar." An American military chronicler wrote: "No battle in the Philippines was fought under such difficulties and disadvantages as the one of 23 and 24 September in Bocaue Mountains." This was a self-congratulatory assessment. Though the terrain worked against the Americans, there was no doubt that the Cebuano insurgents were grossly inferior in a large positional battle. Outmaneuvered and ill trained, they were poorly equipped with homemade firearms and the assorted remnants of an outmoded Spanish armory.

The Battle of Bocaue was an important point in the war. It was the biggest engagement of the war in Cebu and it demonstrated American military superiority. Despite their defeat in Bocaue, however, the insurgents were still bent on denying the Americans control of the central highlands. Maxilom sent out orders to his leaders to hold on to their positions and defend the approaches to Sudlon. In a series of letters to Justo Cabajar in September-December 1899, Maxilom instructed Cabajar's detachment in Ga-as, Talamban, to defend their position, "to die on your feet in the trenches" before yielding to the enemy even a "hand-breadth (*palmo*) of land."[14]

The Bocaue-Sudlon area remained disturbed as a considerable number of insurgents continued to hold out in the area. On 14 October 1899, men of the Nineteenth U.S. Infantry, on reconnaissance in Jacupan Valley, were fired upon by insurgents near the Compensa mountain (near Mananga River) somewhere between Cebu and Toledo.[15] Although there was a heavy exchange of gunfire, no physical contact was made.

After Bocaue, the insurgents put up one more important stand in the heart of Sudlon. In December, American troops began operations to completely dislodge the insurgents from the troubled mountainous zone. They took insurgent positions along Guadalupe trail, Bocaue, Compensa Range, Mananga Valley, Jacupan Valley, moving beyond the positions the Americans took in Bocaue, towards Sudlon. The siege of Sudlon began on 7 January 1900 under the command of Col. Edward J. McClernand.

In the early morning of 8 January 1900, an American force, comprising three companies of the Nineteenth Infantry, under the overall command of Colonel McClernand, began a multipronged assault on insurgent strongholds in the Sudlon mountains. As in the battle of Bocaue, the terrain worked against the Americans as they had to do a lot of climbing and clambering up steep, exposed hillsides. The Cebuanos tried to slow down the Americans, firing their odd assortment of guns and field pieces, and even rolling rocks down the steep hillsides.[16]

At past 9:00 A.M., the Americans reached the main insurgent "forts" or earthworks. By about 10:40 A.M., the battle was over, resulting in the complete rout of the defenders. The Americans found eight dead insurgents. On the American side, four were wounded and none killed. The Americans demolished seven forts, captured 11 smoothbore cannons and 33 small arms of various calibers.[17]

Four companies were dispatched to reconnoiter the surrounding areas for the presence of the retreating army. American soldiers fanned up and down mountain trails east and west, scattering small bands of Cebuanos. On 15 January 1900, men of the Twenty-third U.S. Infantry captured six small arms and dispersed an insurgent band near Talisay. At around the same time, men of the Nineteenth U.S. Infantry surprised the enemy west of Danao, captured Gen. Leoncio Alfon and four of his men, one rifle, ammunition, and important papers.[18]

Sheer American superiority scattered the Cebuano army in the central highlands. The lopsided war could be seen in the slight American losses in the field. Despite an active war service in Cebu from June to September 1899, the First Tennessee Volunteer Regiment lost only one man in Cebu, a Cpl. Lucien Price of Company A who was killed in Pardo in the night of 12 September. Prone to nightmare, the young corporal had jumped from his bed, rushed from his tent, and sped out in the darkness past the picket line. Mistaken for a fleeing insurgent, he was shot down by an American sentry.[19]

6

Fire in a Field of Dry Grass

$$I$$

T WAS clear to Maxilom that the Americans were determined to end the war quickly. It was only at this point that Maxilom decided to shift to a strategy of guerrilla warfare. In Luzon, this strategy was adopted as early as 12 November 1899 when a war council held by Aguinaldo at Bayambang, Pangasinan, adopted a resolution calling for a shift to guerrilla warfare by breaking up the Filipino army into small, mobile bands.

On 16 January 1900, as a result of the Sudlon debacle, Maxilom abolished the military zones and created six guerrilla bands. The shift was dictated by American firepower superiority and the Cebuanos' lack of war materiel. The shift ushered in a protracted war of small, scattered encounters throughout the whole island that, for the Americans, "putting down the insurrection was something like putting out a fire in a field of dry grass."

The lay of Cebu province was, at least for a time, supportive of guerrilla warfare. A narrow island, Cebu has an area of 1,762 square miles, length of 139 miles, and is only 24 miles at its greatest breadth. A mountain chain runs from northeast to southwest throughout the island's entire length. This chain becomes wider or narrower according to the configuration of the island. While human occupation had stripped a large part of the island of primary forest cover, a rugged terrain and lack of roads made for an environment hospitable to guerrilla activities. Seventy-six percent of the island's total land area is constituted of hills and mountains. Meridianal ridges have an average elevation of 400 to 900 meters, and maximum elevation of the island is 1,034 meters.

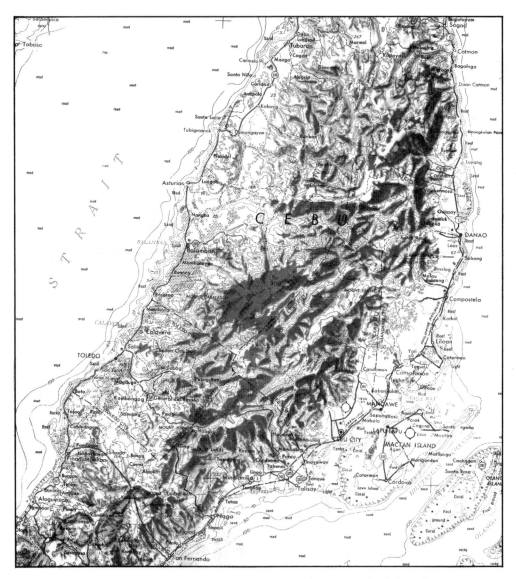

Central Cebu, Locale of the Heaviest Fighting in the Anti-American
War in Cebu

In 1900, many towns of the province were not yet connected by wagon roads, there being simply bridle paths between them. Travel from the east to the west coast, across the mountain range, was slow and difficult as there were only two roads ("which ought properly to be termed bridle paths") running across the island, one of them connecting Sibonga with Dumanjug and the other Carcar with Barili. It took five or six hours by pony to cross the island from Carcar to Barili. Outside of these two arteries, access by land from coast to coast had to be made by winding footpaths and mountain passes.

The towns on the west coast and the farther ends of the island were practically inaccessible from the city except by boat. Communications and supplies moved slowly. Mail from Cebu to Daan Bantayan (a distance of 128 kilometers) took eight or nine days. Even the town governments exercised limited influence within their own jurisdictions. A military report in 1906 said: "There is not one municipality that pretends to govern the people living over seven miles from the coast line. Once the *tao* established himself beyond this approximate line he was out of touch with all forms of government."[1]

In his order of 16 January 1900, "General-in-Chief" Maxilom said: "It not being possible to construct any position, however fortified, that can resist the powerful arms in the possession of our enemies, and considering the very deficient warlike resources for defense possessed by us, it becomes necessary for us to adopt guerrilla tactics which is the system best suited to our condition." The order set forth the following provisions:

Art. 1: The force will be divided into a number of groups.

Art. 2: The first group will have 10 riflemen and 10 bolomen with 2 spies and 2 couriers, commanded by a chief or officer. Its territory will extend from the extreme town of the north to the boundary between Catmon and Carmen on the east coast and that of Tuburan and Asturias on the west coast.

The second group will have 20 riflemen and 20 bolomen with 4 spies and 2 couriers, commanded by chiefs one and two. Its area will be between the boundary of Catmon and Carmen and that between Consolacion and Mandaue on the east coast and the line that separates the towns of the west coast from those of the east.

The third group will consist of 20 riflemen and 20 bolomen, 4 spies and 2 couriers, commanded by first and second chiefs,

having for boundaries the line separating Mandaue and
Consolacion and that separating Pardo and Talisay and the
line between towns of the east and west coasts.

The fourth group will be composed of 10 riflemen and 10
bolomen with the same number of spies and couriers as the
first group, having for boundaries the line separating
Minglanilla and El Pardo and the road to Barili.

The fifth group will be composed of the same strength as the
fourth group, its territory limited to that between the Barili
road and the extreme town in the south on both coasts
including all to the south of Barili and Sibonga.

The sixth group will be of the same strength as the second
and third groups with 4 spies and 4 guides, being limited by
the boundary of Asturias and Tuburan on the north and
Aloguinsan and Barili on the south to the center of the Island.
For lack of definiteness in the line separating the western
and eastern towns, the direction of rivers and streams will be
considered, i.e., whether their water flows to the eastern or
western coast.

Art. 3: Groups will have no fixed positions but the chiefs will
keep themselves near the enemies' detachment with a view
of attacking them continually and surprising scouts and
convoys.

Art. 4: The Headquarters and General Staff will have no
fixed place but will move in the province according to
circumstances.

Art. 5: Guerrilla chiefs will keep a daily register of their
operations and will send a literal copy of this weekly to the
chief of staff, giving in addition the condition of their arms
and ammunitions.

Art. 6: All orders and regulations from the Headquarters will
be promulgated through the general staff except in cases of
greatest urgency.

Art. 7: Depots will be established in towns to be selected
according to circumstances. From these depots, chiefs of

groups will draw every 15 days in advance the pay for their forces. Depots will also contain rations and ammunitions.

Art. 8: Guerrilla chiefs of adjacent areas will agree on signals for recognition and must agree on cases of joining forces for operations.

Art. 9: Said chiefs will avoid, as far as possible, attacking the enemy in inhabited districts but will attack them on trails and roads in uninhabited places.

Art. 10: The first and second groups will form the first column under its own chief. The third and fourth groups will be the second column under a chief.[2]

The chiefs of the groups (called fraccion) were as follows:

ROSTER OF UNITS, 16 JANUARY 1900

Group	First Chief	Second Chief
1	Nemesio Maxilom	Ramon Allego
2	Enrique Lorega	Leoncio Alfon
3	Lorenzo Eje	Mateo Luga
4	Potenciano Aliño	Martin Cabuenas
5	Hilario Aliño	Sulpicio Aliño
6	Emilio Verdeflor	

The first and second groups composed the first column under the command of Pantaleon del Rosario, while the third and fourth made up the second column under Alejo Miñoza. The third column was led by Emilio Verdeflor. There were, of course, subsequent changes in the leadership and composition of the units owing to reassignments, desertions, capture, surrender, or death. Some fracciones were dissolved and others created. For instance, Gervasio Padilla took over as second chief of the second fraccion on 12 February 1900 after Leoncio Alfon was captured near Danao on 15 January 1900. Troadio Galicano served as chief of the fourth and sixth fraccion and took over as head of the third column after Verdeflor died in action on 7 December 1900. Nicolas Godines succeeded Miñoza as head of the second column sometime in 1900 after Miñoza was stricken ill. The number of fracciones later increased to ten but, in the later phase of the war, the size of some fracciones dwindled to a low of 10 or fewer men.

With the abolition of the old zones, a supplementary decree on 17 January 1900 charged the presidentes locales (town mayors) with the responsibility for the governance of the towns. They were given military ranks and integrated into the army.[3]

A later, more expanded roster of "the Army of the Republic," drawn up around December 1900, gives us a better picture of the organization and personalities of the anti-American resistance (see table following).

In the aftermath of Sudlon, the Cebuano generals scattered to set up camp in their various areas of operation. Maxilom and his staff moved north to set up headquarters in the mountainous area of Capayas in the interior between Tuburan and Catmon. With the shift to guerrilla tactics, however, the Cebuano fighters were largely *ambulante*. The new strategy called for decentralized bands that gravitated around American detachments and harassed small exposed American units. The Cebuano term for this style of stealth and sudden ambush was *kamang* or *pangamang* (literally, "crawling towards an object"). Secret storehouses were established in selected towns so that soldiers could draw supplies twice a month and chiefs could draw salaries for their men every 15 days in advance. Insurgents sought refuge in the towns by blending into the population whenever pursued.

The shift in strategy is indicated in the small encounters that took place in various parts of the province in the months that followed. On 27–28 January 1900, Gervasio Padilla and his men tracked down a group of five American soldiers that had passed through Sogod. They killed one American in the Sogod convent, captured another who had stayed behind to eat in the churchyard of Catmon, then later killed two and captured one more in Luyang, Carmen.[5]

On 4 February, men of the Nineteenth U.S. Infantry engaged a small band near Consolacion, killing four and wounding two. One American was wounded in the skirmish. On the same day, insurgents fired upon American soldiers searching some houses near Sogod. Capt. Edmund D. Smith was wounded and died the following day.[6]

On 5 February, an American outpost in Talamban was attacked by heavy rifle fire from 8:00 P.M. to 12:00 P.M. The attackers had an estimated 40 guns and were believed led by Mateo Luga, Lorenzo Eje, and Enrique Lorega. The insurgents were driven back and there were no American casualties.[7] On 6 February, an American outpost in Consolacion was also fired upon in the early dawn by an estimated group of 30 to 40 insurgents.[8] No face-to-face engagement, however, took place.

On 8 February, men of the Twenty-third U.S. Infantry engaged insurgents in a battle near Pardo. The Americans, who suffered no casualties, killed three, dispersed the rest, and captured some ammunition, bolos, and documents.[9] On 27 February, a detachment of 25 men of the Nineteenth Infantry was ambushed on the road at Guimbal near Compostela. In the firefight, lasting from 4:00 to 6:00 P.M., one American died and another was injured. The attackers, under Pantaleon del Rosario and Gervasio Padilla, had what Americans reported were around 40 to 50 rifles. In the insurgent account, the Americans were routed "with numerous losses to them" while the Cebuanos had no casualties. The Cebuanos picked up many haversacks and canteens left behind by the Americans.[10] The American report, on the other hand, said the insurgents were led by three persons, who seemed to be whites, "apparently Americans as they had blue shirts and used the English language repeatedly."[11]

On 15 March, men of the Nineteenth Infantry attacked a group of Cebuanos on the road outside Talisay, killing two and wounding one.[12] The party was reportedly carrying a supply of meat and corn from Talisay to a place beyond Bitlang in the Sudlon area. Earlier, the Americans noticed an exchange of colored lights between Bitlang and a point between Sudlon and Mt. Uling. Then on 22 March, a detachment of the Twenty-third U.S. Infantry surprised insurgents in Guadalupe, killing one, scattering the enemy, and capturing three Mausers. There was no American casualty.[13]

Surprise encounters continued all throughout 1900. With the shift to guerrilla warfare after 16 January 1900, the Americans themselves adapted to the situation by fielding small columns of soldiers from their stations in the towns. As early as 4 October 1899, American military authorities had issued General Order No. 5 that provided: "To insure from surprise and ambush, hereafter no party consisting of less than eight men will be sent on duty, or permitted to go, for any purpose, more than a mile beyond the outposts of any camp or garrison in the Sub-District (of Cebu)."[14] The Americans established a network of stations and camps throughout the island of Cebu. From these camps, they sent out patrols to track down and engage the insurgents.

Through the months of 1900, Americans scouted the countryside, moved from coast to coast, arresting men they considered "hostile" (often anyone caught carrying a bolo or acting suspiciously), setting to the torch houses they considered "insurgent lairs," and gathering military information. American units of from 20 to 50 men were in insurgent-hunting expeditions in the environs and hinterlands of Dalaguete, Argao, Dumanjug,

ROSTER OF OFFICERS OF THE ARMY OF THE
REPUBLIC, PROVINCE OF CEBU, DECEMBER 1900

GENERAL STAFF

General-in-Chief	Arcadio Maxilom
Chief of Escort	Samuel Maxilom
Major Adjutant	Gervasio Ledesma
	Remberto Roa
	Sabas Estrella
	Apolinar Cabibil
Escort Officer	Jose Agasan
Chief of Staff	Juan Climaco
Assistant Chief of Staff	Marcial Velez
Auxiliary	Arsenio Climaco
First Adjutant	Ciriaco Alburo
Second Adjutant	Andres Jayme
Judicial Corps	
Auditor	Godofredo Lago
Assessor	Hilarion Buhay
Examining Magistrate	Eduardo de Roda
Auxiliaries	Florentino Borromeo
	Rufo Masocol

FIRST COLUMN (NORTE)

Chief of Column	Arcadio Maxilom
Military Administrator	Graciano del Mar
Auxiliary	Mariano Jayme
Manager of Armory No. 1	Pedro Abarca
Chief of the First Fraccion	Melquiades Lasala
Chief of 1st Guerrillas	Melquiades Lasala
Chief of 2nd Guerrillas	Recaredo Gonzales
Chief of Second Fraccion	Nemesio Maxilom
Chief of 1st Guerrillas	Nemesio Maxilom
Chief of 2nd Guerrillas	Ramon Allego
Chief of the Tenth Fraccion	Felix Aliño
Chief of 1st Guerrillas	Felix Aliño
Chief of 2nd Guerrillas	Gregorio Rosetes
Officers of the First Fraccion	Macario Ornopia
	Ulpiniano Pastilla
Officers of the Second Fraccion	Anastacio Montebon
	Catalino Alarde
	Restituto Bragat
	Sabas Rello
	Fabian Calonge

Officers of the Tenth Fraccion	Miguel Severino
	Federico Rosales
	Joaquin Conde de Villamar
Factor	Tomas Alonso
Artilleryman	Quintin Tabay

SECOND COLUMN (CENTRO)

Chief of Column	Pantaleon del Rosario
Manager of Armory No. 2	Fulgencio Vega
Chief of the Third Fraccion	Lorenzo Eje
Chief of 1st Guerrillas	Lorenzo Eje
Chief of 2nd Guerrillas	Justo Cabajar
Chief of the Fourth Fraccion	Mateo Luga
Chief of 1st Guerrillas	Mateo Luga
Chief of 2nd Guerrillas	Raymundo Rizarri
Chief of the Fifth Fraccion	Enrique Lorega
Chief of 1st Guerrillas	Enrique Lorega
Chief of 2nd Guerrillas	Claudio Lopez
Chief of the Sixth Fraccion	Troadio Galicano
Chief of 1st Guerrillas	Troadio Galicano
Chief of 2nd Guerrillas	Maximino Abatayo
Officer of the Third Fraccion	Benito Aves
Officers of the Fourth Fraccion	Leopoldo Libre
	Damaso Tablada
Factor	Marcelo Tomolas
Concierge	Fausto Durano
Hospital Agent	Dionisio Novicio

THIRD COLUMN (SUR)

Chief of Column	Nicolas Godines
Auxiliary	Jose Veloso
Military Administrator	Anastacio Bello
Manager of Armory No. 3	Lino Abadia
Chief of the Seventh Fraccion	Hilario Aliño
Chief of 1st Guerrillas	Hilario Aliño
Chief of 2nd Guerrillas	Angel Libre
Chief of the Eighth Fraccion	Macario Godines
Chief of 1st Guerrillas	Macario Godines
Chief of 2nd Guerrillas	Guillermo Suarez
Chief of the Ninth Fraccion	Saturnino Echavez
Chief of 1st Guerrillas	Saturnino Echavez
Chief of 2nd Guerrillas	Francisco Rodriguez[4]

Badian, Tuburan, Balamban, and other towns.[15] Small units of American troops were posted in such towns as Alegria, Toledo, and Tuburan. The civilian population stayed out of the Americans' way and in some places houses were deserted. The municipal halls (*municipios*) of Badian, Moalboal, and Dumanjug displayed white flags.

On 7 April 1900, at 1:30 P.M., four American soldiers of the Twenty-third U.S. Infantry attacked a group of 11 native "bolomen," killing two and capturing one.[16] This happened in the northern outskirts of Cebu City. In the evening of 19 May, American soldiers engaged insurgents in the poblacion of Boljoon. The insurgents, believed led by Nicolas Godines, were driven out of town and the Americans captured some arms.[17] On 21 May, Americans also made contact with a band of insurgents in Recerril (Becerril) and drove the group towards Malabuyoc and Ginatilan.[18]

On 19 June, a unit of the Nineteenth Infantry, out on reconnaissance, captured two "bolomen" and later attacked without warning a group of men and women (because they were seen carrying bolos). The Americans killed four and captured several men.[19] This was in the area of Binaliw River in Mandaue. On 20 June, an American detachment in Minglanilla was attacked by insurgents at around 8:30 P.M. The firing lasted for 30 minutes before the insurgents withdrew, leaving behind two Americans wounded. The Americans suspected that the town presidente and residents knew of the attack beforehand. The presidente was known "to be friendly both to us and to the insurgents."[20]

On 27 July, men under Nicolas Godines and Troadio Galicano were attacked in Malabuyoc. After fighting for half an hour, the guerrillas withdrew toward Dumanjug. One Cebuano was killed and four wounded. The insurgent report claimed, for propaganda effect, that 14 Americans were killed and 9 wounded.[21] On 7 August, an American patrol struck a large band of insurgents in Naga, killing three and capturing two. The insurgents were said to be selling cedulas and collecting money for the resistance.[22]

The insurgents were active in ambushes and sniping attacks. Sometime in September 1900, an American unit was ambushed in the barrio of Bugas (near Manduyong, between Badian and Moalboal) by Cebuanos under Gen. Hilario Aliño. Though Aliño's men were armed only with rocks, bolos, spears, four rifles, three revolvers, and a brass cannon, they sent the Americans on a retreat towards Dumanjug.[23] On 20 October, a fierce fight took place in the mountains of Barili between men of Troadio Galicano and an American force. Armed with three small field pieces, the Cebuanos staged a surprise attack on an American encampment in the early dawn of

20 October. The fight lasted the whole day until the two groups disengaged and the Cebuanos withdrew towards Pinamungahan.[24]

On 21 October, a camp of the Nineteenth Infantry in Guadalupe, Cebu, was fired upon at 8:25 P.M. Two American soldiers were wounded before the attackers withdrew. In retaliation, the Americans burned down about 20 houses in the vicinity where the attackers' fire came from. In further retaliatory action, the Americans struck a band of suspected insurgents near Talamban on 24 October (believed to be the same group that attacked the Guadalupe camp) and killed four and wounded eight.[25]

The Americans were particularly interested in tracking down the insurgent leaders but information on their whereabouts was either scarce or conflicting. This was due to the dispersed and highly mobile position of the insurgent bands and the obvious support given to them by the rural population. Sometime in February 1900, Pantaleon del Rosario was in the mountains of Danao but, by May 1900, he was reported to be somewhere in the vicinity of Naga. Juan Climaco was reported to be in the hinterland of Carmen and then later in Carcar. Nicolas Godines was reported to be somewhere in Boljoon and then the environs of Moalboal. Troadio Galicano moved through the hinterlands from Carcar to Malabuyoc. The insurgents often avoided direct contact.

On 4–6 May 1900, Americans launched an operation to capture Maxilom who was reported to be in the vicinity of Tuburan, in a place called Marmol Mina.[26] More than 100 men of the Forty-fourth Infantry under Capt. James L. Malley struck out for Tuburan from Balamban. They spent the night in Colonia, a barrio of Tuburan, then resumed the march at 3:30 A.M., 5 May, reaching Tuburan at 6:00 A.M. The local officials appeared unfriendly and said that no insurgents were in their area. Taking the presidente and vice presidente with them, the Americans marched into the interior. Crossing Tapon River and moving into a gorge, the Americans surprised Maxilom's outposts. An exchange of volleys followed. The Americans found a hastily abandoned camp made up of around five houses including storehouses, barracks, and Maxilom's house, on a high and sheltered location. There the Americans found 200 Remington shells and a few Krag-Jorgensen shells. The Americans occupied the abandoned camp and then burned it before withdrawing the following day, 6 May.

In still another expedition in the first week of December 1900, Capt. James L. Malley led his men of the Forty-fourth U.S.V. Infantry from Balamban to Toledo, Pinamungahan, and Aloguinsan.[27] At the coastal barrio of Ibo, within the jurisdiction of Toledo, they nearly came upon a band of insurgents but arrived only to see them rowing away in boats. Along the road, the Americans found that the telephone poles the U.S. Army had put up had been cut down and the wires carted away. In the areas where they found the telephone lines cut, Malley ordered all the neighboring houses burned. Passing through Toledo, he also had the houses of insurgent leaders Juan Climaco and Angel Libre put to the torch.

Among the more significant engagements in this phase of the war took place on 7 December 1900 and 30 January 1901. On 7 December, an American force under Major H. B. McCoy of the Forty-fourth U.S.V. Infantry surprised Gen. Emilio Verdeflor and his men near Balamban. In the encounter, Verdeflor and several of his men died. This was a blow to the Maxilom government as Verdeflor was one of its more able generals.[28]

Then on 30 January 1901, the insurgents delivered their own blow. On this day, 30 men of the Forty-fourth U.S.V. Infantry under Lieutenant E. J. Hincker, left Balamban in search of insurgents reported to have been in the vicinity of Guinabasan River. While crossing the river, the Americans were ambushed by guerrillas under Felix Aliño and Recaredo Gonzales. Surrounded by what the Americans estimated, in an overblown report, to be 130 riflemen and 150 bolomen, the detachment retreated to Balamban. Lieutenant Hincker and five of his men were killed, four were wounded, and two were reported missing in action. There was no report of Cebuano casualties. The insurgent report of this battle, however, said that in the three-hour engagement, 14 Americans were killed and insurgents captured 4 rifles, 2 revolvers, 302 belts of ammunition, and other supplies.[29] Popular recollection of this battle underscores Cebuano bravado. A local account says that the battle was initiated by the Cebuanos who had dug in at Sitio Macalbang of Santa Lucia, Asturias, and then sent word to the American detachment in Balamban to come and get them. "More than a hundred Americans" fell to the bolo-wielding guerrillas.[30]

A clear image of the movement of insurgent bands can be drawn from the captured diaries and "reports of operations" of Lorenzo Eje, Gervasio Padilla, and Troadio Galicano.[31] Written in the aftermath of the Sudlon debacle, when the Cebuano army shifted to guerrilla warfare, these documents show guerrilla bands constantly on the move, occasionally merging with other groups, avoiding large American formations, attacking smaller American units, and skirting the town centers. They collected taxes and contributions, performed sabotage work (like cutting telegraph wires), rallied people to support the insurgent cause, and organized clandestine "revolutionary committees" in American-occupied towns. They established their "presence" to instill fear among collaborators and avoided armed encounters in populated areas so as not to compromise inhabitants.

Lorenzo Eje's diary covers the period from 8 January to 15 May 1900. At this time, he was *general de brigada* and chief of the "thirteenth zone" of the province. On 8 January, the day Sudlon was lost, Eje's men retired from their entrenchments in Lobo, Sudlon, and withdrew to a place called Sabon where they spent the night. In the days that followed, the group marched through Lahug and reached the mountains of Catmon, where they awaited orders. From 20 to 27 January, Eje's group reconnoitered the mountains of Cebu and San Nicolas. On orders from Pantaleon del Rosario, Eje's men moved to Consolacion where they consulted with the chief of the second fraccion, Enrique Lorega. The joint force of Lorega and Eje then set out in the night of 1 February toward the town of Mandaue, seeking the enemy. Failing to find the enemy, they proceeded to Cogon District, Cebu City, before withdrawing back to Consolacion. On 4 February, in the vicinity of Sogod, they ambushed a group of American soldiers. In the hour-long firefight they killed two Americans and had one wounded on their side. In the days that followed, Eje and his men were again on the move, reconnoitering the hinterlands of Mandaue, Talamban, Guadalupe, and Lahug, and probing into Banawa, Cogon, and the city's perimeter.

The daring of the group is indicated in a raid into the heart of the city on 2 March. In the afternoon of this day, Pantaleon del Rosario, Eje and his men, "clothed like the Americans," slowly moved into the district of Pajo, near Colon Street (Calle Teatro), just a few blocks away from the American headquarters. Their target was the bawdyhouses maintained by a woman named Aning (*maestra* of prostitutes and *berdugo*, possibly spy) that were frequented by American soldiers. The guerrillas set fire to three whorehouses and such was the suddenness of the fire that some of the American soldiers jumped out of the windows "without trousers" and ran in the direction of their camp. American soldiers quickly responded to the alarm and an exchange of gunfire ensued before the Cebuanos withdrew toward the barrio of Cogon.

In the succeeding days, the guerrillas continued to prowl in the outskirts of San Nicolas and Guadalupe. They marched to Talamban on 8 March having received orders to arrest the "American spies" Juan Borres, Juan Bontuyan, and the brothers Anatalio and Quintin Tabal. The Tabals, however, were able to detect their approach and succeeded in escaping. Eje then ordered houses in the area burned. Later, they captured Juan Borres "and his carabaos." On 11 March, Eje's men set out toward Napo, San Nicolas, and surrendered Borres to Pantaleon del Rosario. They then continued reconnaissance work in the mountains of Guadalupe, Lahug, Talamban, and Consolacion. On 17 March, they linked up with Mateo Luga and his men and attacked the American outpost in the town of Consolacion. They then withdrew to Guadalupe where they rested until 30 March. Through the large part of April, they were again in Talamban in search of the Tabal brothers. They also tried to win over the inhabitants who had been "threatened and robbed by the bandits Adoy and Quintin."

From 28 April to 2 May, they linked up with other guerrillas and rested in Lahug, cleaning their guns. In the morning of 3 May, they watched an American company move through Lahug, Napacpac, and Tamagan. The Americans were burning houses near the old insurgent trenches. The outnumbered guerrillas kept themselves hidden from view. The following day, they set out towards Labangon in compliance with orders. Apparently, it was decided that the central zone had become too hot because of an intensive American military campaign. On 8 May, with Pantaleon del Rosario and chiefs of the second fraccion, Eje and his men marched southwards, skirting the towns of Minglanilla, Naga, San Fernando, and Carcar. They reached Sibonga on 15 May. Here the diary ended.

Cebuano resistance did not prevent the Americans from extending their control throughout the whole length of the island. In the early months of 1900, the Americans moved to bring about the pacification of northern Cebu. Sometime in January 1900, an American gunboat loaded with troops anchored off Bogo. The Americans landed at Nailon Point, marched to the poblacion, and took possession of the town. In February 1900, a "subdistrict of Bogo" was established, with Sogod as the initial base for operations in the northern part of Cebu island.[32] By April 1900, detachments of American troops were stationed in Mandaue, Consolacion, Compostela, Liloan, Danao, Sogod, and Bogo. American troops crisscrossed the northern district in reconnaissance missions, tracking down guerrilla bands, arresting suspected insurgents, and burning houses and suspected insurgent "storehouses" of rice, corn, and other crops. The arena of warfare had widened.

In 1900, the subdistrict of Bogo encompassed such places as San Remigio, Maravilla, Malagasi (Managasi), Lambusan, Maraat, and Cawit (renamed McClernand, after the American military governor). (As of December 1900, 117 American soldiers were stationed in this subdistrict.) Bogo was the center of U.S. military operations in northern Cebu. It was the first Cebu town where the municipal government was reorganized by the Americans by virtue of U.S.-supervised local elections held on 31 July 1900 under General Order No. 40. The Americans set up stations at Malagasi and Maraat, reorganized municipal governments, collected taxes, improved roads and constructed bridges. To facilitate communications among the strung-out American stations, they laid out telegraph lines connecting Danao, Bogo, San Remigio, Medellin, and Daan Bantayan.

The subdistrict of Bogo was under Capt. Andrew S. Rowan of the Nineteenth U.S. Infantry, a colorful military officer who had seen action in Cuba in the Spanish-American War. Rowan virtually ruled the area and the local *principales* had to deal with him in the conduct of government affairs.

The inhabitants were either hostile or wary of the Americans in the early phase of the northern occupation. Rowan expressed his first impression of the people of Bogo thus: "The people are very much like children, are easily terrorized."[33] He analyzed the initial hostility of the town as the handiwork of the four men who wielded influence in the district. The four were Pedro Rodriguez (a big landowner and Bogo presidente), Leoncio Mansueto (reputed "Aguinaldo agent" who served as Bogo teniente alcalde*)*, and the parish priests of Bogo and San Remigio (whom the Americans suspected were "spies" for the insurgents). If these four persons were removed, Rowan reported, the area could be quickly pacified and an "American Party" established in northern Cebu.

Eventually, Rodriguez collaborated with the Americans. Mansueto— who reportedly agitated against the Americans by saying that those who will take the oath of allegiance will be assassinated—was arrested sometime in March 1901. The parish priest of San Remigio was banished from the district. By 1901, much of the hostility against the Americans had dissipated. Northern Cebu was slowly absorbed into the American order.

Of the town of Daan Bantayan, Rowan said: "The people of Daan Bantayan appeared not only willing but anxious to go ahead with the new order of things."[34] Of the people of the island of Bantayan, Rowan observed: "I am sure that the people are not inclined to make war against us, although I am not sure that they are anxious for our sovereignty."[35]

The reduction of the people was, in large measure, wrought through force or the demonstration of force. Wearied by the Cebuano war of attrition, the Americans adopted mailed-fist tactics in enforcing their rule in northern Cebu. Northern Cebu sustained the worst damage in the course of the Cebuano-American War. In 1900–1901, the towns of Tabogon, Sogod, and Catmon were utterly destroyed, with only the church and convent left standing in Catmon and only the church in Tabogon. Sogod was completely leveled by fire. The town of Carmen was spared but was left deserted as its residents fled to the mountains. Inhabitants left their homes in Mandaue, Consolacion, Opon and Cordoba, due to the threat of indiscriminate killing. The word spread that the Americans were burning "everything from Bogo to Cebu."[36]

On 8 February 1900, for instance, the Americans entered the town of Consolacion and proceeded to search the houses, destroying household properties and laying to waste cultivated plots. Residents fled from the town as soldiers fired randomly into surrounding groves. The presidente of the town was arrested and carried off by the Americans.[37]

The burning of Sogod was tragicomic as it was also illustrative of the cavalier way in which the Americans regarded Cebuano life and property.[38] A unit of the Nineteenth Infantry (28 men, 1 guide, and 9 carriers), under Lt. Cromwell Stacey, had left station in Bogo to investigate the reported presence of insurgents under Maxilom in Sogod and to free a Filipino messenger of Bogo commanding officer Captain A. S. Rowan reported to be "spread-eagled" in the convent of Sogod. Tensed up for a fight, the Americans entered Sogod at 8:00 A.M., 13 September 1900, and immediately shot down one man seen carrying a bolo. They found Sogod almost entirely deserted. The Americans interrogated prisoners in the abandoned police station and learned that Maxilom had been in Sogod earlier but had gone to Carmen.

The Americans decided to bivouac at the convent and church for the night. Thinking that the insurgents could flush them out in the night by burning the houses close to the church, the young and edgy Lieutenant Stacey ordered his men to burn the houses surrounding the church. It was about 1:00 P.M. While the fire blazed, he had his unit's Cebuano carriers climb to the inflammable roofs of the church and convent to beat out the sparks that might fall on them. The fire, however, spread uncontrollably and before long the whole town was burning. At 4:30 P.M., the convent itself caught fire. The Americans were driven out by the flames and found themselves without shelter for the night. In the dark, Lieutenant Stacey had to march his men from Sogod to the town of Borbon, reaching Borbon close to midnight. Reviewing Lieutenant Stacey's report of this case, Colonel McClernand concluded that the burning was unnecessary and, in dark humor, reported to his own superiors: "Lieut. Stacey has been informed that the desire to obtain a good night's rest in a convent is not sufficient justification for the destruction of a town."[39]

7

Running a War

F OR THE Maxilom government, the war was not going well. The government had reversed the disastrous policy of fighting a war from fixed positions. It tried to whittle away at American strength through scattered, harassing guerrilla actions but, though these caused the Americans much trouble, they neither inflicted serious damage nor did these actions prevent the Americans from slowly extending and consolidating their sphere of influence.

The Americans had a wealth of military experience derived from the U.S. Civil War, the suppression of the American Indians, and the Cuban campaign. Except for the crash course they had in the rising against Spain, Cebuano military leaders had limited experience in the science of war. Moreover, the Maxilom government faced three major problems: lack of manpower and logistical support, problems of leadership, and Cebuano collaboration with the Americans.

To raise revenues, the government collected direct and indirect taxes.[1] The towns were required to pay a monthly contribution to the Maxilom government for which a certificate of payment would be issued. Fixed monthly contributions were based on the size of the population and the resources of the town, ranging from a high of $150.00 for Cebu City to a low of $10.00 for Pardo and $15.00 for Alcoy, Santander, Ronda, and Alcantara.[2] The raising of contributions by the town depended on the municipal councils, which passed resolutions to comply with the monthly quota dictated by the Maxilom government. For instance, the popular council of Opon passed a resolution on 27 January 1901 imposing fixed amounts of contribution for male taxpayers, headmen, and women, prescribing penalties for nonpayment and requiring payment even if the town should fall to the enemy. Failure to comply was deemed treason.[3]

Basically, these contributions were in the form of personal taxes (cedula) levied on citizens. These assessments were about 75 or 80 U.S. cents or its equivalent. In addition, the Maxilom government attempted to collect business taxes, particularly from Chinese merchants. A complaint was raised by the Chinese consul general in Manila who reported that Chinese residents in Cebu City were being forced to pay a cedula assessment of $9.80 in addition to being forced to get special books of account from the insurgent government so that their business earnings could be monitored for taxation purposes.[4]

Revenues were also raised through the levy of customs duties in areas controlled by the insurgents. For instance, on 26 November 1899, "Special Commissioner" Pantaleon del Rosario issued a circular providing for the establishment of a Philippine Customs House throughout the island. A collector of customs was to be appointed in the towns to appraise all interprovincial goods, collect duties, and remit money to the military government. This was to be carried out in secret in places occupied by the Americans. Apparently, duties were also imposed on intermunicipal trade. On 12 December 1899, Maxilom and Climaco issued instructions to the town presidents for the collection of a 3 percent ad valorem tax on all exports and imports, except on corn and rice. This was to be paid at the town of origin or destination and applied to goods transported either by land or by sea.[5]

In collecting money from the population (in the form of cedulas, licenses, and other taxes), the insurgent government was, in its view, simply laying claim on revenues that properly belonged to it as the legitimate government. Moreover, because of the state of war, it was the view that it could impose a "war tax" on property holdings and so-called voluntary contributions on wealthy citizens.[6] The Maxilom government also carried out such measures as the seizure of properties, such as livestock, belonging to pro-American Cebuanos. Contributions of food and military supplies were solicited from the townspeople. American reports in late 1899 indicated that rice and guns were being taken up to the mountains from the Talisay area, eluding American outposts, and carried out under cover of darkness.[7] Insurgents' relatives in the occupied areas—such as Felicidad Climaco and the Velez sisters—also helped the cause by sending clothing, food, and other supplies to the hills.[8]

We have a sense of insurgent finances in a statement of the budget of the Maxilom government, dated 1 August 1899, indicating total expected revenues of 158,478 pesos. Revenue sources included direct taxes valued at 25 percent of the personal cedula tax and other receipts collected by the towns of the province. Other sources were indirect taxes in the form of voluntary subscriptions, confiscated properties, imposed fines, and fees for civil court proceedings. A corresponding statement of expenditures showed that much of the funds went to the maintenance of personnel: the officers and 665 soldiers, as well as laborers, smiths, a physician, a "director of saltpetre works," and others. An outlay was also marked for supplies and the purchase of weapons and tools.[9]

There were also reports that indicated that the republican movement in neighboring provinces also procured supplies from Cebu. Cebu also collected contributions from Bohol and other provinces in an attempt to purchase guns from abroad.[10] With the American control of the port of Cebu City, underground traffic was carried out at coastal points like Cordova where, in September 1899, for instance, a two-mast banca was reported to have weighed anchor for Misamis with a hundred or more sacks of rice, canned meats, and insurgent papers.[11] American gunboats, meanwhile, were also busy cruising Visayan waters to interdict smuggling or what the Americans imagined to be insurgent traffic. In late 1900, for instance, the U. S. S. *Panay*, an American gunboat, destroyed off Camotes Island an "insurgent banca carrying among other cargo 160 gallons of tuba."[12]

More unorthodox means of raising the resources for war must have been employed. We have a reference to how insurgent elements in Cebu were collecting cash contributions to be invested in a trading company, part of the profits of which will go to the insurgent treasury. Insurgent chiefs were reportedly cornering supplies of hemp and other products in the countryside at fixed prices for this business.[13] Apparently, this method of setting up trading firms to raise money for the war by exercising monopolies in insurgent-controlled areas was practiced in other places.[14] In the disorder of the war, however, it cannot be determined whether, and to what extent, these activities were legitimate efforts of the republican government or the self-interested schemes of war profiteers.

Military manpower was a major problem of the Maxilom government. The government provided for the enforced conscription of inhabitants aged 18 to 50, excepting only those who were mentally or physically disabled. Penalties were provided for those who either refused to bear arms or discouraged others from doing so. This was, however, never effectively carried out.

It is difficult to get at the exact number of armed Cebuano combatants as the army of the republic included part-time fighters and civilians in the barrios and towns who provided support services (such as collecting contributions, gathering intelligence information, or acting as couriers). The size of this force fluctuated according to shifts in the fortunes of war. The existence of part-time fighters is referred to in an American intelligence report which accused San Nicolas policemen of being in league with the insurgents. These policemen were on "shore duty" when they stayed in San Nicolas as policemen or noncombatants, recuperating, attending the fiesta, or visiting family and friends. They were on "sea duty" (*molawod*) when they were out in the hills fighting as insurgents.[15]

Throughout much of the war, Maxilom must have had under his formal command around 200 properly armed men, corresponding to the estimated number of guns in insurgent possession, with probably several hundred (200 to 500) irregular troops armed with bolos, spears, and other weapons. American estimates of insurgent strength ranged from 200 to 3,000 men. Extant insurgent records indicate that, at top strength, the army of Maxilom during the hostilities must have consisted of only around 1,000 men enrolled in its rosters. This army was organized into fracciones and included *artilleros* (artillerymen), *tiradores* (shooters), and *macheteros* (bolomen). Auxiliaries were buglers, couriers, carriers, and spies. Two to four fracciones constituted a column *(columna)* and each fraccion consisted of two bands of guerrillas. After Sudlon, we have no report of a full column engaged in a single operation. The basic operating unit was either the fraccion (of 20 to 40 men) or a guerrilla band (of 10 to 20 men). Bands merged or split up according to the mission or situation.

As of 23 December 1900, Maxilom's army consisted of 283 men, 242 rifles, revolvers, and assorted weapons, and 6,035 shells and cartridges. The following is a breakdown of the strength of the army.

The first column, under Arcadio Maxilom, was deployed in the north. The second column, headed by Pantaleon del Rosario, covered central Cebu, while the third column, under Nicolas Godines, operated in the south.

Despite conscription and efforts at organizing a formal army (with ranks, commissions, salaries and regulations), the Maxilom army remained a loose organization, particularly at the edges. The leaders had to contend with men who went on prolonged "absences," as well as with the problem of defections. On 15 March 1900, for instance, Maxilom had to issue a circular threatening punishment, on one hand, and granting clemency, on the other, to soldiers who deserted the army for such reasons as grievances against their chiefs or commanders.[17] While there were decrees that provided for compulsory military service, it is doubtful whether these were seriously enforced to a wide extent. Those who decided to bear arms against the Americans must have been motivated by a range and mix of motives now difficult to specify with precision: personal and familial ties, love of

ROSTER OF THE CEBUANO ARMY, 23 DECEMBER 1900

First Column	Men	Weapons
1st Fraccion 1st Chief: M. Lasala 2nd Chief: R. Gonzales		4 cannons 25 rifles 1 shotgun
2nd Fraccion 1st Chief: N. Maxilom 2nd Chief: R. Allego	66	6 revolvers 4 bladed weapons
10th Fraccion 1st Chief: F. Aliño 2nd Chief: G. Rosetes		

Second Column	Men	Weapons
3rd Fraccion 1st Chief: L. Eje 2nd Chief: J. Cabajar		
4th Fraccion 1st Chief: M. Luga 2nd Chief: R. Rizarri	114	7 cannons 65 rifles 8 shotguns, 5 revolvers
5th Fraccion 1st Chief: E. Lorega 2nd Chief: C. Lopez		16 bladed weapons
6th Fraccion 1st Chief: T. Galicano 2nd Chief: M. Abatayo		

Third Column	Men	Weapons
7th Fraccion 1st Chief: H. Aliño 2nd Chief: A. Libre		
8th Fraccion 1st Chief: M. Godines 2nd Chief: G. Suarez	86	2 cannons 37 rifles 3 shotguns
9th Fraccion 1st Chief: S. Echavez 2nd Chief: F. Rodriguez		

General Staff General-en-Jefe: A. Maxilom		4 cannons 9 rifles
Jefe del Estado Mayor: J. Climaco	17	9 shotguns 17 revolvers 20 bladed weapons[16]

adventure, fear of punishment, patriotism, or a sense or vision of a better order of things.[18]

Networks of kinship and friendship played an important role in the shaping of loyalties. Clusters of relatives and friends helped constitute the Cebuano army. We have the cases of the Aliños (the brothers Hilario, Felix, Potenciano, and Sulpicio, and then Gervasio and Fermin, possibly cousins), the Tabals (the brothers Rafael, Anatalio, Quintin, and Serafin), the Miñozas (Alejo, Bonifacio, Pedro), the Pacañas (Jacinto, Felipe, Dalmacio), and the Maxiloms (the brothers Arcadio, Nemesio, and Samuel). Among other relatives, Arcadio had a cousin, Sabas Estrella, as a "major adjutant" in his staff. Then we have the Climacos. Juan Climaco had in his own staff his nephew Arsenio (as "auxiliary") and a cousin, Marcial Velez (as "assistant chief of staff"). The family of Jacinto Velez, husband of Josefa Climaco (Juan Climaco's aunt), supported the insurgent cause with contributions. Another Climaco relative is Jose Veloso, who served as auxiliary to Nicolas Godines (who also had a brother, Macario, as one of his officers). In Bogo, we have the cousins Pedro Rodriguez, Leoncio Mansueto, and Melquiades Lasala heading the local guerrillas.

Additional cases can be cited. Three men active in the anti-American war were sons of Katipunan organizers executed by the Spaniards in April 1898: Gervasio and Severo Padilla (sons of Candido Padilla) and Recaredo Gonzales (son of Fortunato, brother of Florencio Gonzales).

Kinship, however, was one variable among many and does not explain, by itself, patterns of recruitment. One notes, for instance, that the Climacos were also related to the Osmeñas and Noels, families that cooperated with the Americans.

Not much data exist on the ordinary Cebuano combatants. The fighters who formed the core of Maxilom's army were generally young men. One roster of a guerrilla unit yields the following profile: The average age of the 19 soldiers in the unit is 23, with the oldest at 35 and the youngest at 15. Only two are married. Another roster, with 117 names, has an average age of 28, with the oldest at 45 and the youngest at 16. Of these 117 guerrillas, 64 are married, 52 single, and 1 a widower.[19]

The problem of raising an army was also occasioned by the fact that the Maxilom government did not have the weapons for all those willing to fight. The insurgents were direly lacking in armament. On 8 November 1898, prior to the American landing in Cebu, Cebuano revolutionary leaders sent a message to Aguinaldo asking for 1,000 rifles, saying that they had 7,000 men in their ranks. However, no shipment of arms was received from Luzon. The Maxilom government had to resort to buying arms and ammunition in small quantities from private persons, manufacturing guns, and recycling shells. Native forges were also used to manufacture the "war" bolos (*pinuti*) needed by the insurgents. In October 1900, for instance, there is a reference to the Americans destroying forges in the outskirts of San Nicolas as these were suspected of providing bolos for insurgents.[20]

In their dire need for weapons, the insurgents established makeshift munitions factories *(maestranza)* in different parts of the province.[21] Cited as *fabricantes* of insurgent arms and ammunition were Angel Libre in Toledo, Fulgencio Vega in Pinamungahan, Tiburcio Quijano in Carcar, and Solomon Abarca in the Zapatera district in the city. So hard pressed were the insurgents for war materiel that they experimented with the use of resin of various plants and trees *(guisok, lawaan, kulitis)* and *carbon del tronco* for the manufacture of gunpowder.[22]

An insight into the insurgent arsenal can be had from a military report on an American expedition to the hinterland of Toledo in early January 1901.[23]

On 4 January 1901, a unit of the Forty-fourth U.S.V. Infantry stationed in Balamban marched out in response to intelligence reports of a native arsenal in the vicinity of Tajaljo River, back of Bato (in the hinterland of Toledo), in the hacienda of Mariano Veloso. When the Americans arrived in the target village, they found that the place "had been stripped of everything." In an initial search of the houses, they found a bag of shells and pistol balls, cut strips of telegraph wire, some blank receipts for contributions to the insurgent cause, and "ammunition or shells in almost every house of the community." The village was deserted but the Americans managed to round up five boys who initially refused to talk but were later so threatened that they led the Americans to a coconut grove some 300 yards from the main village cluster, where was found a major insurgent armory. The workshop included one charcoal oven, one bellows-and-forge, one pig-iron anvil, one bullet mold for making balls of assorted calibers, files, rasps, 30 Remington and Krag-Jorgensen shells, some of which had been reloaded, and several pistol balls. All in all, the Americans confiscated 104 rounds of ammunition, 4 bolos, 2 spears, and some papers and documents. The Americans were told that insurgent chief Mateo Luga had been in Masaba a few weeks earlier and had taken away some rifles. The Americans burned the workshop and around 12 houses in the area.

Insurgent arms, therefore, were largely raised within the island, from the arms left behind by the Spaniards, those captured or stolen from the Americans, those sold by small-time gunrunners, and those made by local artisans. A limited number of arms and ammunitions passed between Cebu and neighboring provinces.[24] U.S. Army intelligence estimated that the

Republican Seals in Cebu Province

total insurgent arsenal on the island of Cebu in March 1901 was around 200 to 225 guns. Other estimates in 1901 ranged from 100 to 300 rifles.[25] The insurgent arsenal was an irregula: collection of Spanish cannons, rifles (mostly Remingtons and Mausers, with some Colts, Winchesters, and Muratas), shotguns, and revolvers (Smith, Colt, and Bulldog).

The extreme difficulties in the procurement of arms are illustrated in the narrative of Melquiades Lasala's mission to Leyte and Samar to solicit arms and ammunition from Generals Lukban and Moxica. Lasala's narrative covers the period from 12 November 1899 to 23 February 1900.[26] Lasala traveled by sailboat from Camotes Island to Merida, Leyte, and then hiked the greater part of the way to Palo, where he presented himself to Moxica. After much haggling, he could only get 13 rifles and 325 *municiones* (shells or cartridges) from Moxica who said that the Leyte insurgent government itself was in dire need of arms. Subsequently, Lasala lost 4 rifles and 20 cartridges to one of his escorts. He had to hike from town to town, stay out of the sight of American gunboats plying the coast of Leyte, procure transportation, weather a storm at sea, before he arrived back in Bogo, Cebu, on 14 December. On 18 December, he turned over 7 rifles and 175 municiones to Gervasio Padilla and, on 21 December, conferred with Pantaleon del Rosario, who gave him fresh orders to contact Lukban in Samar. Once more, Lasala left Bogo on 29 December, arriving in Palompon, Leyte, the following day. From Palompon, he traveled by boat and hiked much of the way until he reached Catbalogan, Samar, on 21 January 1900. He presented himself to Lukban who inquired about the situation in Cebu and the loyalty of its prominent residents.

Lukban had a well-run maestranza in his command but could not give more than 20 rifles and 4,000 cartridges for the Cebuanos. Lasala then set off on the return journey; found himself in Ormoc at the time of the American landing; continued to move from place to place until he arrived in the vicinity of Daan Bantayan on 8 February. He learned that the Americans had started to occupy northern Cebu and he had to stay out of sight as the Americans occupied Bogo on 12 February. From this point on, Lasala linked up with the American deserter Fred M. Baker and other local residents in preparation for the guerrilla war that had just commenced.

The insurgents maintained makeshift camps and they disguised the locations of their bases by using code names (San Mateo, Santo Rosario). In the early phase of the war insurgents built fortifications or earthworks of packed soil and bamboo revetments.[27] The central fort at Sudlon, before its fall, was made of well-laid sod, measured about 12 feet high and 40 feet square, with embankments from 5 to 10 feet thick. In the later phase of the war, however, the Cebuanos operated mainly as mobile units that lived off the land.

Cebuano insurgents employed bamboo traps *(balatik)* to slow down or kill the enemy. They supplemented their small arsenal with long knives, spears, and bows-and-arrows. They also devised a cipher, or code, for communications although this was not used systematically.[28]

The Maxilom government yeomanly tried to function as a government. It passed and circularized laws and directives governing the conduct of its men and relations with the general population. On 1 August 1899, Maxilom issued an order (reissued on 8 December 1900 and 5 March 1901) imposing punishment on those who destroyed private property, collected war contributions without proper authority, spied for Americans, maltreated prisoners, illegally detained persons, usurped authority, or refused conscription into the army of the republic.[29] The government also cautioned its chiefs against conducting military operations that would compromise the civilian population. Noting how the unsettled conditions had given rise to criminality, the government also issued instructions for its men to arrest criminals.[30] That the government tried to enforce discipline and order is shown in extant documents pertaining to the investigation and arrest of persons for acts of criminality or treason.[31]

The government's sometimes-excessive attention to legal and bureaucratic form is profusely illustrated in the insurgent documents captured by the Americans. It was as though the Cebuano leaders believed that maintaining the appearance of government would help create the substance of rulership. The government expected monthly statements of revenues to be submitted, vouchers accomplished, and receipts issued.[32] Seals and stamps were used by Cebuano insurgents.[33] A letter from Maxilom to Filemon Sotto, dated 29 October 1899, asked the latter, who was then editor of the newspaper *El Imparcial*, to help arrange for the printing of a few thousand copies of some forms, including a certification by the "Superior Military Commander and General-in-Chief of Operations" attesting to membership in the "Republican Army."[34] The form indicated registry number, seal, and personal description of the recruit or soldier.

Secret revolutionary committees were organized in the towns occupied by the Americans. On 11 December 1900, for instance, American soldiers uncovered a "shadow government" in Danao when they raided the barrio of Pangdan in that northern town.[35] The Americans rounded up 32 men, including insurgent leader Graciano del Mar, and collected 2 revolvers, 36 rounds of ammunition, 3 bolos, 1 U.S. army blanket, money, and personal effects. In the wake of this raid, the Americans arrested Candelario

Cuizon, a local landowner, said to be the presidente revolucionario de la comite de Danao.

The Maxilom government was in communication with the national organs of the republic, as indicated by the large number of circulars and memoranda from the Aguinaldo government copied and circulated in the field.[36] While Cebu was not represented in the Malolos Congress (except by Tagalog proxies in the persons of T. H. Pardo de Tavera, Ariston Bautista, Felix David, and Francisco Macabulos), it was clear that Maxilom and Climaco placed themselves under the authority of Aguinaldo.[37] Even proindependence propaganda from Hong Kong found their way to the field in Cebu. On 28 December 1899, for instance, Maxilom issued a proclamation relaying a manifesto from the Comite Filipino Central in Hong Kong (dated 14 November 1899) urging Filipinos to continue the anti-American struggle. Maxilom's proclamation also relayed news of the death of Gen. Henry W. Lawton in "the battle of San Mateo" and the imprisonment of "General Weler" [Joseph Wheeler] and four American officers in Pangasinan.[38] The insurgents circularized another statement of the Central Filipino Committee in Hong Kong, dated 15 May 1900, exhorting Filipinos to resist the enticements of the Taft Commission:

> McKinley vacillates; Bryan and Dewey are gaining strength. The future Commission will use all means like a merchant to make the best possible bargain. For us the line of defense is firm, firm and firm![39]

While communications were exchanged between the Aguinaldo government and the Cebuano leaders, and agents and commissioners from "the Center" were sent to Cebu from time to time, the Cebuanos largely worked independently of Malolos and Aguinaldo. Much of the revenues collected locally stayed in Cebu and the leadership remained largely in the hands of Cebuanos. While Climaco and Maxilom saw their resistance as part of a "national" effort, the actual management of the war—in contrast, for instance, with the case of Leyte-Samar where leadership was in Tagalog hands—was carried out by Cebuanos.

The Maxilom government actively engaged in propaganda to support its war effort and shore up the morale of the Cebuanos. After the Sudlon debacle, an attempt was made to buoy up Cebuano spirits with a circularized letter from Manila, dated 20 January 1900, saying that because of "massive losses" on the part of the Americans—"10,000 killed and wounded, and 500 prisoners, including 2 generals, 10 colonels, and 50 field and line officers"—President McKinley had been forced to resign. "In spite of the efforts of the imperialistic party to conceal this defeat from being known by the popular masses in America, who are crying against the campaign in the Philippines, the triumph of our soldiers cannot have been kept in shade." The letter announced that William Jennings Bryan has succeeded McKinley and a Democratic Party representative has relieved General Otis. It went on to say that peace had been declared and the Philippine Republic would be proclaimed on 4 February.[40] Psychological warfare included releases sent to local Cebuano newspapers about insurgent successes, fabricated communications about positive political developments in the U.S., and circulars to *jefes locales* to alert them to expect landings in their area of arms and ammunitions by a vessel of a "friendly nation" and to instruct them to forward this cargo to insurgent headquarters.[41]

Psychological warfare was waged by Filipinos elsewhere in the country, and often carried to somewhat preposterous limits. A person who claims to be an Aguinaldo agent, for instance, writes to Ambrosio Moxica in Leyte, on 2 March 1900, that hundreds of Americans (including Gen. Arthur MacArthur) have been captured with their weapons and many towns recovered from the enemy; that because of disenchantment over the terrible cost of the war ($200 million and 40,000 men killed), four states in the U.S. have revolted against the McKinley government; that the Cubans have risen up in arms against the U.S.; that other nations are poised to join the war—in Chinese ports, the Russians are readying 39 war ships and 300,000 troops; in Saigon, the French have 18 ships and 80,000 troops; in the Carolinas, the Germans are massing 26 men-of-war and 40,000 soldiers; and in Formosa, the Japanese are preparing 15 ships and 26,000 men.[42]

The Maxilom government used a combination of suasion and force to discourage collaboration with the Americans. On 14 March 1900, Maxilom issued a circular providing for the execution of traitors after a summary trial.[43] In a strongly worded warning, Maxilom threatened that the republican army will destroy all towns that recognize U.S. sovereignty "and without any consideration whatsoever [to] kill all males, even the poorest, and set fire to all the houses." Available evidence, however, indicates that insurgents burned down houses on a much smaller scale than did the Americans.

On 22 June 1900, Maxilom gave instructions for the creation of a "secret avengers" corps known as Magdudukot (Snatchers) or Agocoy (Ghost Crab) to seek out and punish traitors as well as enforce discipline within the ranks of the republic.[44] On 8 December 1900, Maxilom issued a memorandum providing guidelines for judging who may be considered traitors, namely: (1) any person who does damage to the well-being of persons or property; (2) one who demands contributions from others without proper authorization; (3) one who furnishes information to the enemy; and (4) one who offends or ill-treats people in any manner. It adds other cases in which a person can be hailed as traitor before a military court: (1) anyone in the 18-to-50 age range who refuses to bear arms against the enemy, excluding the physically and mentally disabled; (2) one who discourages others in the defense of the national honor; and (3) any person of authority who refuses to publicize this edict. The memorandum also enumerated cases for which an officer may be removed from his command (1) if he usurps authority and impedes civil officials from performing their lawful duties; (2) if he arrests any person without a just cause; and (3) if he uses threat in a lawsuit.

It is not completely clear to what extent these edicts were enforced. We have reports, however, that they were applied. Felix Aliño, chief of the sixth guerrilla faction, reported to Maxilom on 17 October 1900 that the Magdudukot had arrested in Toledo one Ciriaco Legaspi, an ex-policeman of Tuburan, who had actively conspired with the enemy. Maxilom instructed revolutionary officer Florentino Borromeo to have Legaspi tried for treason.[45] In another instance, there is an instruction from Maxilom urging Gregorio Escario, the police commissioner of Bantayan, to apprehend and execute spies when necessary information on their espionage activities shall have been forwarded and approved by the Maxilom headquarters.[46]

On 6 September 1900, at 10:00 P.M., a guide and interpreter of Lieutenant J. L. Bond of the Nineteenth U.S. Infantry, stationed in Mandaue, was murdered in the municipio.[47] On 14 October 1900, Nicolas Godines, insurgent chief in southern Cebu, wrote to the Dumanjug mayor warning him against collecting taxes for the Americans.[48] Godines warned the mayor that he was "sucking the blood" of his fellow Filipinos in behalf of the Americans. Godines informed the mayor that the teniente of Barrio Bulak had been arrested for being an Americanista and was being held in Godines's headquarters in the mountains of Sibonga. Then, in early July 1901, there was also the report that the teniente of Barrio Lamakan in Sibonga and two policemen were snatched and murdered by the insurgents.[49]

The Maxilom government also tried to shore up local support by offering amnesty to collaborators. On 21 August 1900, Maxilom issued a circular providing that from 21 August to 24 September 1900, there will be "absolute and unconditional" amnesty for those who have directly or indirectly aided the Americans but will now profess allegiance to the republic, with persons who have violated the laws of war or engaged in banditry excluded. Cash rewards were also offered for arms surrendered by those who were fighting on the American side.

As the fighting wore on, however, it became evident to the Cebuanos that they were fighting an increasingly hopeless war. Both Cebuano insurgent leaders as well as those who remained uninvolved hoped for a peaceful settlement. They looked towards a satisfactory termination of the conflict through a change of U.S. policy on the Philippine question. In this regard, the insurgent leadership kept close track of developments in the White House and the U.S. Congress and hoped for an ascendancy of the Democrats (who mainly opposed the annexation of the Philippines) over the Republicans (the party of McKinley).[50] Hopes for a negotiated peace were fanned in 1899 and 1900 with the prospect of the pacifist and populist William Jennings Bryan winning over McKinley in the U.S. elections of 1900. Hopes, however, were dashed when Bryan went down in defeat by close to a million votes.

Many felt that Philippine independence could not be won militarily. Too many problems hampered the resistance. It was, for one, difficult to raise money from an impoverished population. In tax-collecting visits to northern Cebu towns in November 1899 and February 1900, insurgent chief Melquiades Lasala could only collect 70 pesos in San Francisco in Camotes, 28 pesos in Medellin, and $3.43 in San Remigio.[51] As a consequence, the guerrillas were woefully provisioned and often had nothing but their weapon and the shirt on their backs. Something of the travails of the fighter could be seen in a communication from Justo Cabajar, head of a detachment in the hills of Talamban, to Arcadio Maxilom on 17 October 1899. In a plaintive letter, Cabajar told the commander-in-chief that he was suffering from chills and would like to have a blanket to protect his sore stomach at night. He also asked if there was any positive news of developments from Manila. In his reply, Maxilom sent the requested cloth, apologizing that he could only send one of dimity (a thin cotton sheet), as none of flannel was available. As for Manila, Maxilom said, news was "good" and it would not be long before they would all have a well-deserved rest.[52]

The straitened circumstances of the insurgent government could be gleaned from an American military circular of 10 December 1900 which indicated that insurgents tried to build up their meager arsenal through such means as the theft or purchase of guns and cartridges from American soldiers themselves. There were even cases of people collecting American cartridges dropped on the ground and of children asking friendly American soldiers for cartridges as playthings or in exchange for tobacco or trinkets. These cartridges later found their way to the hands of the insurgents.[53]

8

Cracks in the Resistance

PROBLEMS OF cohesion and leadership also plagued the resistance against the Americans. An immediate explanation for such problems lies in the fast-changing conditions of the war. The Cebuanos raised an irregular army in the armed struggle against Spain in the months of April to December in 1898, then worked to consolidate and institutionalize this army in the first months of 1899, and then had to contend with internal dissension as the fighting against the Americans raged in the late months of 1899. The army of the republic in Cebu was an army hurriedly welded together under conditions of war.

In essence, however, the lack of cohesion is determined by the inchoate, fragmented Cebuano polity on the eve of the war. The fissures in the resistance point to what was the important internal drama of the anti-U.S. war, the contradictions of emerging classes. To understand these contradictions requires an understanding of social forces in motion long before the coming of the Americans.

The resistance against the Americans was, in a real sense, a continuation of the anti-Spanish revolution. The revolution itself was expressive of the buildup of social forces, which restrictive Spanish rule had bottled up. Such buildup did not only widen the gap between colonizers and colonized, it fractured the relative homogeneity of local society, creating new social formations and cleavages among groups and classes.

A class analysis of the leadership of the resistance affords us with a sense of this social drama. Though there were changes in the composition of the leadership because of the exigencies of war, the men who led the struggle constituted a fairly definable social formation. The leadership of the revolution in Cebu suffered its first blow at the hands of the Spaniards in the crackdown of April 1898. Many of the original Katipunan leaders were murdered or executed. These included Pantaleon Villegas (Leon Kilat), Florencio Gonzales (the secretary of the Ayuntamiento), Mariano Hernandez (a Smith Bell and Company, abaca press operator), Candido Padilla (former San Nicolas capitan municipal), Teopisto Cavan (an employee of the Cebu audiencia), and Luis Abellar (a Smith Bell and Company bodega foreman and long-time cabeza de barangay of Pasil, San Nicolas). The Spaniards also caused the execution of such leaders as Solomon Manalili (a prominent city intellectual) and Bonifacio Aranas (a student at San Carlos).

However, there were others, led by Luis Flores, who quickly moved in to assume the leadership of the struggle. These included Emilio Verdeflor, Arcadio Maxilom, the Pacañas, Eugenio Gines, the Tabal brothers, the Aliño brothers, Nicolas Godines, Alejo Miñoza, Francisco Llamas, Lorenzo Eje, Gervasio Padilla, Telesforo Salguero, Justo Cabajar, Troadio Galicano, and Leoncio Alfon. These men also figured prominently in the war against the U.S. that followed.

Who were these men?[1] They were a mixed group, mostly in their thirties, members of the municipal gentry of the province, lower civil servants, students, and figures outside of "the wealthiest and best-educated" of Cebuano society at the time. They were generally a literate group, inhabiting the interface between town and city, mobile and exposed to developments in the wider colony.

Arcadio Maxilom, 38 years old, was a propertied citizen and one-time capitan (1892–1896) of Tuburan. He received his commission as captain in the revolutionary army on 2 April 1898 and was active in the anti-Spanish hostilities. Another municipal capitan was Jacinto Pacaña (b. ca. 1850), of San Nicolas, who was involved in the Katipunan from the very beginning. Already advanced in years at the time of the revolution, he brought men into the army, including his sons Felipe and Dalmacio (who was killed in Sudlon) and other family members. He helped provide leadership as well as resources (like food) to the insurgents in Sudlon after the Leon Kilat assassination, and then from his base in Consolacion during the American phase of the war.

Alejo Miñoza (1867–1925), of a Talamban family of modest means, studied at San Carlos and, briefly, at San Juan de Letran in Manila. On the eve of the revolution, he worked as *escribiente* for the city court in Cebu and the lawyer Don Francisco Matheu. Miñoza was recruited into the Katipunan in 1897 by Mariano Hernandez. Potenciano Aliño (1865–1907), the son of a municipal employee in Talisay, worked as a part-time teacher and directorcillo (municipal secretary) of Talisay (1888). At one time, he also clerked for Judge Segundo Singson (1891). Restless and independent minded, he came into conflict with the Augustinians who owned an estate in the Talisay-Minglanilla area. It is suggested that he may have come into contact with the Katipunan in Manila in the 1890s while on a trip to secure legal representation for Talisay residents in their complaints against the Augustinian Order. When the tres de Abril uprising broke out, he helped lead insurgents in taking over the Guardia Civil station in Talisay. Like Miñoza and Aliño, Saturnino Echavez (1866–1933) had a civil-service background. A native of Ginatilan, he studied at San Carlos and taught school in San Fernando, Barili, and Aloguinsan. He also served briefly as *juez de paz* (1888) of Barili. He was a resident of Aloguinsan at the time of the revolution.

Enrique Lorega (1855–1941) was a native of the district of Tinago in Cebu City. A Spanish mestizo, he served as *cantor* in the Cebu cathedral. Troadio Galicano (b. 1870) studied at San Carlos (1884–1890) and came from a landowning family in Carcar. He became prominent in the resistance only during the anti-American phase of the war. Gervasio Padilla (b. 1872) also studied at San Carlos. The son of Capitan Candido Padilla of San Nicolas, Gervasio was already active in the revolution as of April 1898. Another Sanicolasnon was Justo Cabajar (Kabahar), born ca. 1870, a composer, musician, and organist in the San Nicolas parish church.

Nicolas Godines came from a propertied family in Opon but, by the time of the revolution, had moved to Dumanjug where his cousin was a parish priest. He was a leading general in southern Cebu in the fight against the Americans. An American intelligence report disparagingly and inaccurately dismisses him as "a very ignorant man and unable to write." Godines's occupation is cited by the American report as "grass cutter and general laborer."[2]

The other leaders were not natives of Cebu. Emilio Manalo Verdeflor, a Tagalog from Cavite, served as a corporal in a Spanish native regiment in Luzon but appears to have lived in Cebu prior to the revolution and had a family in Balamban. In the fighting against Spain, he headed a force of several hundred men in the west coast. The importance of Verdeflor in the revolution is indicated by how, on 25 November 1898, he was commissioned by Luis Flores to reorganize the municipal governments in the west coast of Cebu. Like Verdeflor, Telesforo Salguero (b. 1872), a native of Capiz and a *jornalero* (laborer), was a corporal in the Spanish army. He left the service in 1894 and eventually came to settle down in Cebu where, at the outbreak of the revolution, he was employed as a jail warden. Verdeflor and Salguero were involved in the Katipunan, together with three other Tagalogs who were prominent in the early phase of organizing the secret society in Cebu: Mariano Hernandez, Anastacio Oclarino (a *maquinista* in a boat owned by Smith Bell and Company), and Gabino Gaabucayan (an employee of Singer and Company).

In the war against the Americans, two other Tagalogs became prominent. The most important was Pantaleon Estuard del Rosario (1878–1930), a native of Imus, Cavite, and relative of Emilio Aguinaldo. A strongly built mestizo, he was educated at Ateneo de Manila and came to Cebu towards the end of 1898 as a "commissioner" of the Aguinaldo government. For a time, he used the alias Pedro del Rosario.[3] Another Tagalog who figured prominently in the war against the Americans was Mateo Luga who came to Cebu in April 1899 as an Aguinaldo agent.

Of the other personalities, even less is known. Eugenio Gines, a native of Pinamungahan who used the nom de guerre Lindol, sustained a gunshot wound in the leg during the uprising of 3 April 1898. He was still with the army at the beginning of the resistance against the U.S. but we have no information about what happened to him. Lorenzo Sedeña Eje, said to be a native of Negros, had little formal education but was reputed to be a brave fighter. An American report refers to him as "formerly a cook."[4] Leoncio Alfon is said to be from Naga, and like Eje, was already involved in the early Katipunan movement in Cebu.

There are other names that appear in the records, but about these men we know practically nothing and we can only deduce that most of them must have come from various towns or villages in Cebu.

On the eve of the Spanish withdrawal, the acknowledged leaders of the republic in Cebu were Flores and Maxilom. They headed an army, however, which was rather loose and decentralized, its men recruited by local leaders and hurriedly pressed to action in the field. Within the army, therefore, the potential for fragmentation existed.

Shortly before the revolutionaries occupied Cebu City, a gathering of revolutionary officers in Pardo on 22 December 1898 established an interim republican government and named Arcadio Maxilom "governor." This gathering included Alejo Miñoza, Eugenio Gines, Nicolas Godines, Potenciano Aliño, Pedro Miñoza, Felix Aliño, Fausto Durano, Arcadio Cabreros, Baldomero Buyug, Floro Echivarri, Ramon Enriquez, Dionisio Sabay, Epifanio Balsamo, Atilano Lopez, Venancio Tabada, Moises de la Espana, Rufo Abella, Felipe Seco, Victor Cabellon, Telesforo Bayo, Guillermo Nacurada, Isidro Tuburan, Valentin Caballero, Mateo Sabellano, Leocadio Lopez, and Telesforo Caballero.[5] When the republic, however, was inaugurated in Cebu City on 29 December it was Luis Flores who was recognized as the new Governor although Maxilom held the title of comandante general de ejercito.[6]

After the cooptation of Luis Flores by the city ilustrados, Maxilom once more emerged as leader of the republican army. At this time, the complexion of the leadership of the resistance also changed with the emergence of such men as Juan Climaco, Pantaleon del Rosario, and Mateo Luga. While Del Rosario was involved in the final days of the anti-Spanish resistance, he was, in the early days, regarded more as a "commissioner" from Luzon rather than a local leader. Luga joined the fighting in Cebu only during the American phase of the war.

Climaco brought in a more ilustrado element into the anti-American resistance. Allied with Climaco was Marcial Velez, the son of the wealthy city resident Jacinto Velez (married to Josefa Climaco, daughter of Juan Cuico Climaco, Juan Climaco's grandfather). Velez studied at Letran (1878–1883), served as regidor of Cebu City (1892–1893, 1896), and was a *delegado de policia* (chief of police) of the city when he joined the insurgents. There is an undated (possibly December 1898) appointment extended by Aguinaldo to Marcial Velez as "chief of the revolutionary forces of the province of Cebu."[7] Because of his involvement in the war, his father was held at Fort San Pedro. His two sisters were also accused of soliciting money for the insurgents and were compelled to take refuge in Hong Kong. The Velez family house was taken over by the U.S. military authorities.[8]

The socially prominent Juan Climaco also had around him such peers and personal associates as Arsenio Climaco and Angel Libre, who both held the rank of "colonel" and served in Climaco's general staff. Arsenio Climaco (b. 1870) was a graduate of Ateneo de Manila (1891) and regidor of Cebu City (1896–1897). Libre was the twenty-year-old son of a Toledo capitan and landowner. Others in the Climaco staff were Tomas Alonso and Andres Jayme, both students of the Colegio-Seminario de San Carlos at the inception of the hostilities.

In the early phase of the war against the Americans, there were also leaders of an ilustrado background like the cousins Pedro Rodriguez and Leoncio Mansueto of Bogo. Both Rodriguez and Mansueto studied at the Ateneo de Manila, and the latter was finishing a course in medicine at the University of Sto. Tomas when the anti-Spanish revolution broke out in Cebu in 1898. Their involvement in the resistance, however, was brief.

With some exceptions, the leaders of the anti-American resistance were of a quasi-elite. Moderately educated and propertied, they were exposed to the vitalizing influences of "modern" ideas and rapid economic change in the nineteenth century, yet barred from fully participating in political and economic power by a colonial order controlled by Spaniards and a very small Filipino elite that had more direct access to the privileges of this order. They were outsiders to the "central elite" of Cebuano society. It is not surprising that the members of this central elite regarded these leaders with suspicion as potentially subversive of the social and economic order. American and local elite sources viewed Maxilom as an "ignorant coward" whom the more-ilustrado Climaco allowed to have the title of "general-in-chief." The reputation of such mavericks as Francisco Llamas and Leoncio Alfon fostered an image of the militants as violent men. Moreover, the involvement of non-Cebuanos must have been a disturbing element for the city's wealthy and conservative citizens.

Within the republican army itself there were fault lines owing to rural-urban tensions, class contradictions, personal and factional loyalties, ethnic bias, and suspicions directed at "outsiders" and "latecomers" to the movement. Available rosters of the Cebuano army indicate a certain fluidity in leadership, particularly in the early stage of the war. This is to be explained not just by mortality, communication problems, and the successive reorganizations dictated by battle conditions. It is also indicative of factionalism within the army.

The first full *plantilla* of the Cebuano army leadership that we have was drawn up on 10 November 1899 (see succeeding pages).

This plantilla was drawn up in a meeting in Sudlon on 10 November 1899 by a group of officers that included Alejo Miñoza, Leoncio Alfon, Potenciano Aliño, Nicolas Godines, Felix Aliño, Saturnino Echavez, Telesforo Salguero, Lorenzo Eje, and Francisco Llamas. In this meeting, these men declared their adhesion to the Maxilom leadership and cited their sacrifices in the war against Spain and the U.S. One deduces that there must have been, at this time, rivalries over the highest commissions in the army. We do not know to what extent this plantilla, which was presented to Maxilom and Pantaleon del Rosario (in the latter's capacity as "commissioner" to Cebu of the Army in Luzon), was put into effect.

Of the fourteen persons listed as "generals" in this plantilla, seven disappeared from the army's roster as of December 1900. These were Alejo Miñoza, Francisco Llamas, Telesforo Salguero, Potenciano Aliño, Pascasio Dabasol, Leoncio Alfon, and Martin Cabueñas. We do not have the full story on how this came about.

Miñoza was stricken ill in the days after the Sudlon debacle. As the Americans pressed their offensive, Miñoza had to be bodily carried to Ronda. He then found his way to Badian, then Oslob, where he crossed over to Calape, Bohol. Around mid-1900, he returned to Cebu, settling down in Opon before rejoining the insurgents in the hinterland of Carmen in the final days of the war.[10]

Leoncio Alfon murdered in cold blood a woman in Mandaue on 7 April 1898 during the anti-Spanish revolution. He was captured by the

Americans on 15 January 1900 and was tried and convicted on 20 July 1901 for the murder. His appeal to the Supreme Court was denied. He escaped from prison in Cebu in August 1901, and was reported to have drowned while on his way to Samar to join the resistance there.[11]

The case of Francisco Llamas and Potenciano Aliño was different. They bolted the ranks of Maxilom's army, gathered their own men, and operated independently of the Maxilom-Climaco command. Martin Cabuenas might have also broken away from Maxilom's army since he resurfaced only in 1904 when he surrendered to the Americans, one of the last of the original "generals" to surrender.

Francisco Llamas (1854–1901), a propertied mestizo of San Nicolas, was one of the original initiators of the Katipunan in Cebu. He was a maverick who largely operated on his own throughout much of the anti-American war. Sporting the alias Manghuhusay (Arbiter), Llamas was implicated in a case of "piracy" around March 1899 but escaped the Americans. He was reported to have confiscated the boat *Tres Hermanas*, owned by Florentino Rallos, using it to tour Bohol towns to sell cedulas of the Katipunan. Another report said that he collected not only cash but also a piano, a harmonium, and other "contributions." Llamas's associate in this piracy case, Gabino Gaabucayan, was arrested and imprisoned by the Americans. Gaabucayan, alias Juan Pozos, was a Tagalog Katipunan leader in the anti-Spanish uprising in Cebu. Gaabucayan was also arrested by the Americans as a suspected combatant, together with insurgent officer Gregorio Padilla and some others, but he was released for lack of evidence.[12] Llamas led a shadowy existence and was, for a time, hunted by both the American authorities and the Maxilom government. The Maxilom government accused him of abuse of authority and gross insubordination and issued an order for his arrest on 5 April 1899. He was under American custody in early 1900 as records cite his taking the oath of allegiance to the U.S. on 18 April 1900.[13] Apparently, he was again back in action after this time as he is reported to have surrendered in 1901, the year he died.

Potenciano Aliño must have split up from Maxilom's command sometime in mid-1900. An order issued by Pantaleon del Rosario on 10 January 1901 called for the arrest of Aliño, saying that Aliño had rebelled against the Maxilom government by "raising bands of seditious persons" whose "criminal acts defame the sanctity of the cause."[14] On 26 March 1901, the Maxilom government also issued orders for the arrest of "ex-generals" Potenciano Aliño and Francisco Llamas for rebellion and brigandage. Little is known of the activities of Aliño. He surrendered to the Americans sometime in October 1901, but continued to have trouble with the authorities until 1903.

Position	Name and Rank
General Headquarters	
Military Headquarters	
Supreme Chief	Gen. Arcadio Maxilom
Adjutants	Capt. Aguedo Batobalanos
	Capt. Gervacio Ledesma
Second Supreme Chief	Col. Juan Climaco
Adjutant	1st Lt. Bernabe Climaco
General Staff	
Chief of General Staff	Capt. Arsenio Climaco
Adjutants	1st Lt. Lope Pacaña
	2nd Lt. Ciriaco Alburo
War Commissioner	Commandant Samuel Maxilom
Military Court	
Judge	Commandant Troadio Galicano
Corps of Engineers	Commandant Francisco Largo
	Capt. Tito Estrella
	1st Lt. Segundo Jayme
	2nd Lt. Mariano Isidro Samson
Artillery	Commandant Godofredo Lago
	Capt. Apolinario Cabibil
	1st Lt. Bernardo Tabar
	1st Lt. Jose Alonso
	1st Lt. Tomas Alonso
	1st Lt. Abdon Gonzales
Munitions	Commandant Lino Abadia
	Capt. Pedro Cardenas
	1st Lt. Filomeno Lopez
	1st Lt. Marcial Acasio
Field of Operations	
Generals	Alejo Miñoza
	Francisco Llamas
	Nicolas Godines
	Telesforo Salguero
	Potenciano Aliño
	Enrique Lorega
	Lorenzo Eje

Generals (*continued*)

Pascasio Dabasol
Hilario Aliño
Felix Aliño
Leoncio Alfon
Martin Cabuenas
Saturnino Echavez

First Regular Battalion

Chief of Battalion	Lt. Col. Gervasio Padilla
Chief of Arms	Commandant Hilarion Buhay
Chief of Detail	Commandant Jose Veloso
Adjutant	1st Lt. Gregorio Rosetes
Color-bearer	2nd Lt. Angel Libre
Administrative Officer	Graciano del Mar
Medical Officer	Capt. Fulgencio Vega
Master Gunsmith	Marcial Acasio
First Company	Capt. Mateo Luga
	1st Lt. Francisco Rodriguez
	2nd Lt. Melquiades Lasala
Second Company	Capt. Sulpicio Aliño
	1st Lt. Pelagio Bacus
	2nd Lt. Jose Gerra
Third Company	Capt. Pastor Ruiz
	1st Lt. Marciano Abatayo
	2nd Lt. Jose Agasan
Fourth Company	Capt. Floro Echevarri
	1st Lt. Victor Reyes
	2nd Lt. Tomas Delgado
Fifth Company	Capt. Martin Solo Peste
	1st Lt. Wenceslao Peñalosa
	2nd Lt. Paulino Durano
Sixth Company	Capt. Justo Cabajar
	1st Lt. Rufo Alfon
	2nd Lt. Sulpicio Ylaya

Second Regular Battalion

Chief of Battalion	Lt. Col. Pedro Abarca
Chief of Arms	Commandant Andres Abellana
Chief of Detail	Commandant Anastacio Bello
Adjutant	1st Lt. Candido Pacaña
Color-bearer	2nd Lt. Severo Arandia
Administrative Officer	Perfecto Enfasis
Medical Officer	Capt. Pedro Molina
Master Gunsmith	Abdon Samson

First Company	Capt. Felix Cuison
	1st Lt. Bruno Maniago
	2nd Lt. Anastacio Pacaña
Second Company	Capt. Silvestre Cañeda
	1st Lt. Serapio Cabing
	2nd Lt. Gavino Bestig
Third Company	Capt. Andres Sosobrado
	1st Lt. Claudio Guerrero
	2nd Lt. Honorato Cabreros
Fourth Company	Capt. Dionisio Sabay
	1st Lt. Rufo Llamas
	2nd Lt. Rufino Pacaña
Fifth Company	Capt. Baldomero Matag
	1st Lt. Brigido Tabada
	2nd Lt. Agustin Ylaya
Sixth Company	Capt. Bartolome Campo
	1st Lt. Ciriaco Llamas
	2nd Lt. Adriano Sabay

First Reserve Battalion

Chief of Battalion	Lt. Col. Nemesio Maxilom
Chief of Arms	Commandant Ramon Allego
Chief of Detail	Commandant Anastacio Lapinig
Adjutant	1st Lt. Nicomedes Bacalla
Color-bearer	2nd Lt. Leopoldo Libre
Administrative Officer	Pastor Corro
Medical Officer	Capt. Isidro Ortiz
Master Gunsmith	Tiburcio Quijano
First Company	Capt. Eduardo de Rosa
	1st Lt. Anastacio Rama
	2nd Lt. Fausto Durano
Second Company	Capt. Miguel Abad
	1st Lt. Miguel Cabarrubias
	2nd Lt. Laureano Enfasis
Third Company	Capt. Catalino Alarde
	1st Lt. Nicolas Abarquez
	2nd Lt. Isabelo Echivarri
Fourth Company	Capt. Macario Godines
	1st Lt. Basilio Cabarrubias
	2nd Lt. Isabelo Sabate
Fifth Company	Capt. Severo Padilla
	1st Lt. Benito Tevez
	2nd Lt. Gregorio Abellana
Sixth Company	Capt. Roberto Rafael
	1st Lt. Crispin Echevarri
	2nd Lt. Basilio Reyes

Second Reserve Battalion

Chief of Battalion	Lt. Col. Daniel Padilla
Chief of Arms	Comm't. Guillermo Sanchez
Chief of Detail	Comm't. Eugenio Fernandez
Adjutant	1st Lt. Anacleto Ferraris
Color-bearer	2nd Lt. Joaquin Clavano
Administrative Officer	Basilio Quijano
Medical Officer	Capt. Maximo Abarquez
Master Gunsmith	Abdon Samson
First Company	Capt. Hipolito Mariscal
	1st Lt. Vicente Maurillo
	2nd Lt. Arsenio Familar
Second Company	Capt. Tomas Labrador
	1st Lt. Segundo Enriquez
	2nd Lt. Balbino de la Paz
Third Company	Capt. Melencio Peñalosa
	1st Lt. Gregorio Enriquez
	2nd Lt. Epifanio Enbino
Fourth Company	Capt. Pedro Miñoza
	1st Lt. Domingo Ababon
	2nd Lt. Eleuterio Cañeda
Fifth Company	Capt. Gregorio Padilla
	1st Lt. Dionisio Novicio
	2nd Lt. Dionisio Ramonada
Sixth Company	Capt. Emiliano Maxilom
	1st Lt. Claudio Maxilom
	2nd Lt. Juan Pacaña

There was no homogeneous Cebuano army in the field. Orders issued by the Maxilom government on 7 January 1901 and 5 March 1901 indicate that there were armed groups operating outside of the Maxilom-Climaco command.[15]

This is not surprising since, to begin with, the state of Cebuano political development on the eve of the war was such that an organized provincewide polity did not exist. There was, as yet, little basis for people to feel themselves a single community and, on this basis, to act in concert. It was only in the second half of the nineteenth century that Cebu towns were effectively linked together, and to the Cebu port area, due to the expansion of cash cropping and trade. Economic changes engendered a greater mobility of men. They created social and business networks of patrons and clients, allies and agents, and partners and dependents across the island. Such networks were still in an early stage of formation when the war began. Local factions, kin alliances, clientilist networks, and new economic groups were still imperfectly welded together into a Cebuano or Filipino polity.

Combatants were recruited and mobilized along varied lines. Leaders brought in relatives, friends, dependents, and townmates into the struggle. Such sets were the building blocks of the Cebuano army. While the ideology of nationalism was the important glue that held the army together, the state of political development at the turn of the century was such that unity based on broad ideological principles was highly problematic.

An analysis of the 141 names in the plantilla of 10 November 1899 suggests something of the kin-and-locality groupings that constituted the army.[16] The largest set is made up of residents of the town of San Nicolas. There are at least twenty-five of them in the plantilla, led by the Pacaña, Padilla, and Llamas families. There are twelve men from the town of Talisay and eleven from the Tuburan-Asturias area, led by the Aliños and Maxiloms, respectively.

These sets suggest something of the geography of the resistance. The old town of San Nicolas, adjacent to Cebu City, was the seat of the Katipunan in Cebu. It supplied many of the leaders and participants of the tres de Abril uprising. From the beginning of the Spanish colonial period, when a policy of the residential segregation of the races was put into effect, San Nicolas had the character of an indio district, the "Tondo of Cebu," vis-a-vis the Spanish and Chinese mestizo-dominated city of Cebu. South of San Nicolas, Talisay also had the same indio character and was, in addition, a scene of peasant ferment in the nineteenth century because of the presence of the Talisay-Minglanilla estate of the Augustinian Order. In the depressed *contracosta* (west coast) of the island of Cebu, the stretch of land from Toledo to Tuburan was a focal area of sugar cultivation in the nineteenth century. Here, commercial exploitation in a backwoods environment made for a climate of social volatility that gave rise to the appearance of prophets, bandits, and rebels.

The Cebuano army, however, drew men from all over the province, particularly the zones of active military operations. The plantilla carries the names of persons from the west-coast towns of Toledo, Aloguinsan, Barili, and Dumanjug, and from the northern towns of Mandaue, Danao, San Remigio, and Santa Fe.

While islandwide, the army was a loosely structured organization, more real at the level of bands and fracciones than that of "companies" and "battalions." An understanding of how the army was raised and organized provides us with part of the context for assessing the leadership exercised by Maxilom and Climaco during the war.

The weakness of the Maxilom-Climaco leadership was demonstrated in at least two instances. At the onset of the occupation, it failed to respond boldly to the defection of the city ilustrados, cherishing the hope of a common front even long after the basis for such hope had disappeared. Then, at the onset of the fighting, it decided to face the Americans in a set-piece war from "forts" in Sudlon instead of adopting a policy of guerrilla warfare. Though Aguinaldo's forces had switched to guerrilla tactics by November 1899 (a change that was itself disastrously late), it was not until January 1900 that Maxilom ordered a change to guerrilla warfare.[17]

There is an explanation for both errors. In the case of the first, Maxilom and Climaco must have judged that it was difficult to mobilize provincewide resistance without the help of the city elite. The situation in 1899 was such that a provincial "citizenry" organized around republican ideals did not yet exist. (The republic was established in Cebu only a scant two months before the American arrival.) What existed, in large part, was a coalition of city and municipal leaders whose spheres of influence were largely limited to their respective towns and villages. Of these leaders, the most prominent and influential were the city-based ilustrados who, by virtue of their superior learning, vaster wealth, proximity to the centers of state and trade, were on their way towards becoming a *provincial*, if not *regional*, elite. Their landholdings in various parts of the province, extralocal business networks, and corps of allies, clients, tenants, and dependents, gave them a reach of influence wider than that which men like Maxilom, Godines, or Lorega had. That Climaco and Maxilom bent backwards to accommodate them is an acknowledgment of the realities of power formation at the time.

The second error was occasioned by the effort of the Maxilom-Climaco leadership to create the semblance of being a part of a "national" army. This is shown in the excessive attention given to ranks, commissions, and procedures, and in the decision to fight a positional war from forts and entrenchments. (The decision may have also been occasioned by the symbolic value that Sudlon had acquired in the anti-Spanish revolution.) The desire to sustain the fiction that there was a "real" army in the field—instead of roving, ragtag bands—was to prove costly.

In both, the errors of the leadership were not just a matter of calculations on the part of individuals. They provide us with a sense of the political weakness at the heart of the anti-American resistance.

9

Fire Above, Fire Beneath

CEBUANO COLLABORATION also undercut the resistance. American occupation resulted in two competing Cebuano "governments," the insurgent Maxilom government and the pro-American Llorente government. The two governments—one based in the interior and the other in the city—vied for the loyalty of town officials and populace. When the Americans decided to exercise direct control of provincial affairs—and the Llorente government was superseded by a military government under an American officer—pressures for defining loyalties increased.

In 1903, Mariano Albao Cuenco, an American-appointed clerk of court in the city, analyzed the political situation by dividing the population into three classes: ilustrados, *medio* ilustrados, and *ignorantes*.[1] He said that, at the onset of U.S. occupation, there was general suspicion of American intentions. In time, however, the ilustrados saw that American motives were "benevolent" and thus lent their support to U.S. protection and tutelage. The medio ilustrados, on the other hand, were the prime movers of the anti-Spanish revolution and the war against the Americans. Resistance, however, broke down because it did not have the support of the ilustrados who condemned the war as "counterproductive" and argued that *libertad* could not be won through brute force. Cuenco said the medio ilustrados eventually modified their views as they came under the ilustrados' influence. The ignorantes, incapable of judging the totality of the situation, were manipulated by their leaders and stirred to anxieties and war by such immediate problems as excessive taxation. Cuenco concluded his analysis by saying that though active support of U.S. rule was focused on a small segment of the population, this segment was the most influential. This class ("the better elements") believed that independence was premature and was a goal to be attained only when the Filipinos were "ready."

This elite analysis of the political disposition of classes is mirrored in the views of U.S. officials themselves. In an interview with an American writer, Cebu Military Governor Thomas Hamer also analyzed Cebuano society as a three-class system. He said that "the rich and intelligent" favored U.S. control. Those against were "ambitious fellows without property interests, looters and highwaymen and pirates by nature." He called the third class the "hill-folk," an even lower class "in intelligence and property," easily led and impressionable.[2] "The better class are shrewd enough to see that sooner or later the Americans will take possession of the archipelago, and have quietly changed their political belief without exciting unfavorable comment." On this basis, Hamer offered a theory for governing the islands:

> I do not believe the native government should be general at first. I think it would be better to begin at the bottom and organize upward; for example, organize the town first, and not the Provincial government. Preferably, let the Americans appoint a president of the town, let the natives elect and make a selection, subject to the American approval; leave the qualifications of voters for future consideration; elect a president and justice and clerk from the natives; but let their records and official acts pass under American inspection. Make the towns "kindergartens" to give the people a chance to learn the art of self-government; divide them into wards, some to be American wards absolutely. Permit the people to elect aldermen and councilmen, and make the city council a "kindergarten" in which to give these people a chance to learn the American system of self-legislation. I would give the president, or mayor, of the towns the absolute veto right, supervised by the United States authorities. My impression is that these officials should be required to report all their acts in writing to some Central American Supervisor or Governor of the islands.[3]

While elitist and colonialist in bias, the analyses of Cuenco and Hamer draw the attention to the important social drama in the war. They simplify however the political disposition of the varied social groups in Cebu.

It is difficult to gauge the sentiment of the great mass of the population. However, the assertion that the "overwhelming majority of the peasants were essentially indifferent to the conflict" is demonstrably false if only because the war was of such scale that it could not have left even rural dwellers unaffected. The assertion that many of those who joined the fighting were simply following their landlords, patrons, or leaders (like the contrary assumption that they did so out of nationalist or republican sentiments) also oversimplifies peasant behavior.[4]

There seems little doubt that, at the beginning of the American occupation, the organized citizenry of the province had already professed allegiance to the Aguinaldo government and the ideal of political independence. However, this government, in both institutional and political terms, was inchoate in many places when the Americans came. It was held together less by a clearly defined commitment to republican and democratic ideals as by networks of racial and ethnic sentiments, certain shared political and moral notions, and patron-client ties that varied in degree and kinds of refraction as one moved from city to countryside or ascended from class to class.

How did the leaders and the mass resisters perceive the cause of their struggle? Independencia—the concept of a *Filipinas Libre*—was the main organizing idea; yet, there were clearly discordant interpretations of the concept since, to begin with, one finds it shared both by resisters and "collaborationists." Undoubtedly, there were collaborators (like Matias de Arrieta) who saw independence as undesirable either because, steeped in European racism, they viewed the "natives" congenitally incapable or because, taking themselves to be realists, they were convinced independence was untenable in the face of foreign powers, such as Germany and Japan, who were on the prowl for Asian colonies. Yet, there were collaborators (such as Julio Llorente)—and they constituted the greater number of the ilustrados who supported the Americans—who adhered to the goal of independence but saw it as desirable only "in the future" after a period of apprenticeship during which the Philippines submits herself to the United States as a ward or protectorate.

Among resisters themselves, there was no common image of independencia. Juan Climaco and other leaders—as their written proclamations indicate—were heirs to nineteenth-century liberalism. They were wide-aware participants in an emerging national community that was becoming conscious of itself as a nation and of its place in the world. Yet, there were other leaders (the Tabals, for instance) and many mass participants who probably held different notions of independence, interpreting it as a condition of social egalitarianism, of a more radical transformation of social relations than was envisioned by such men as Climaco.

Perceptions and motives constitute a field difficult to map, particularly in the case of ordinary men who do not leave behind written records of their actions or thoughts. There is moreover, in our case, a paucity of oral texts on the war (songs, narratives, and other items of oral traditions). Something can be inferred, however, from what is known of what men did and of the language they spoke. Of the latter, it can be noted how the Cebuano vocabulary problematizes the interpretation of such a concept as independencia. A Spanish term that came into general circulation in the late nineteenth century, it was collapsed in popular usage into notions of *kaugalingnan* ("selfhood"), probably a turn-of-the-century coinage, and the more primary notion of *kagawasan* ("freedom," derived from the concept of gawas or "outside"), which has a register of social and moral meanings richer and more ambiguous than statist concepts of political independence.[5]

In general, however, it can be said that American intrusion into the islands was perceived as a violation. Even if not quite achieved, the moral reality of nationhood existed. No matter how inchoate or filled with contradictions, a Filipino government existed. American occupation violated the moral fact of nationhood as well as the political integrity of a native government. The violation was rendered even more immoral by the naked use of superior military force.

Bereft of resources to militarily defend themselves and their state, the civilian population adopted other forms of resistance: flight, silence, subterfuge, and other varieties of sabotage and noncooperation. Such forms of resistance, while not easily documented, are important since they are the most available for an unarmed population. An appreciation of these forms and practices provides us with a broader view of popular resistance to enemy occupation than simple inventories of troop strength and battles.

The forms of sabotage and subterfuge varied and were encouraged by the insurgent government itself. Civilians fled from the Americans and denied them access to labor, supplies, and information. On the other hand, they supplied the insurgents with food and shelter and provided intelligence on the movement of American troops. In Cebu City in December 1900, for instance, a combined force of American soldiers and local policemen went out in search of Pantaleon del Rosario and Mateo Luga who were reported to be in the Zapatera district but were unable to find them as these men had many "spies" in Zapatera and Cogon who forewarned them.[6] Local officials and citizens also adopted various propaganda and legal measures to undermine the American presence. Under adverse conditions, they tried to sustain the semblance, if not substance, of a working Filipino government.

Numerous local officials and town residents could openly support the Maxilom government in the early stage of the war, but as the Americans occupied the towns and embarked on their own program of "pacification," many found themselves like the proverbial Visayan rice cake or *bibingka*, heated by fire both below and above.

The Americans kept a tight lid on the territories they occupied. They secured the ports, both to prevent the flow of supplies to the insurgents and control the collection of customs duties. In 1899, as part of the blockade on hostile territory, only vessels bound for ports "in United States possession" were cleared by the American captain of the port in Cebu City. Gunboat patrols were conducted; shipping vessels (and even bancas) going from Cebu to nearby Opon had to secure permission from U.S. authorities; and records were kept even on the movement of fishing boats in the Pasil-San Nicolas area, the major fish-landing point in Cebu City.[7]

The display of the Filipino flag was prohibited on pain of imprisonment for 24 hours. Permits were required for the transport of rice and other food supplies.[8] Curfew was imposed. From 1899 to 1900, residents in Cebu City and San Nicolas were prohibited from being out in the streets beyond 8:00 P.M. and those who needed to be out on the streets at this time had to give prior notice and carry a lamp (*farol*).[9] In late 1899, residents needed a military pass to move between Pardo and Cebu. Surprise searches were conducted and persons found without residence certificates (cedulas) or with certificates bearing a different place of residence were detained.

American intelligence authorities compiled confidential dossiers on inhabitants.[10] These included "descriptive cards" on each individual, containing his name, residence, place of birth, description, distinguishing marks, names of kin, occupation, financial condition (including location of real properties), and "attitude toward the U.S." The card indicated whether the person was ever held prisoner and whether he took the oath of allegiance to the United States. This card file (also called "Book of Individual Histories") apparently focussed on persons of some prominence and those who had participated (or were suspected of participating) in the "insurrection." American intelligence also systematically collected, analyzed, and archived captured insurgent documents. The Americans collected detailed information on the towns—terrain, demographic and economic features, prevalent diseases, ports, water supply, bridges, and even data on the number of horses, carabaos, and cows in the town.[11]

American authorities exercised censorship on cablegrams and publications.[12] Local printing presses were directed not to print circulars, papers, or statements of a political nature without prior approval from the American commanding officer in Cebu.[13] American censors kept close watch on the city newspapers. On 30 December 1901, for instance, American soldiers searched the offices of *El Nuevo Dia* and *El Pueblo* and closed them for 24 hours as the books of these publications were examined for possible insurgent connections.[14]

No one could carry firearms without the proper license from U.S. military authorities and permits were granted only in a few cases (such as in the case of big businessmen or government officers like Nicolas Guivelondo and Martin Llorente).[15]

Pressures and claims on loyalty were then exercised from both the republican and American sides. There were those who decisively cast their lot with one or the other, either out of principle or personal consideration, but most tried to "play the game" of political survival, moving according to the shifting circumstances of power. The problem for many was (as an American scholar puts it) determining "the minimum level of contact with the Americans necessary for survival" and "the maximum cooperation that could be offered short of betraying the Revolution."[16]

Collaboration is a complex response. It may be motivated by notions of patriotism, estimates of present or prospective personal benefit, perceptions of class interest, factional and family ties, or demands of plain survival. It may be short-term and tactical or it may issue from deeply held principles. It ranges from passive accommodation to active support though, clearly, the distinctions between the two may be difficult to judge.[17] The diverse range of loyalties can be illustrated by looking at the positions taken at various points in time by various groups and individuals in Cebu.

The Catholic hierarchy in Cebu took a conservative position. This hierarchy was represented by Bishop Martin Garcia Alcocer (until his forced departure on 1 February 1899), then by Vicar-General Pablo Singson, and then, in 1904, by American Bishop Thomas Hendrick. The portly Bishop Alcocer was a strong defender of church interests as well as a person of influence. He interceded in behalf of some of the prominent Cebuanos arrested in the Spanish pogrom after 3 April 1898 and persuaded Governor Montero into releasing all political prisoners prior to the Spanish withdrawal. Montero had urged Alcocer to leave Cebu together with the other Spaniards but Alcocer chose to stay to look after the interests of the church and his loyal parishioners. In the days after the establishment of the republic in Cebu on 29 December 1898, he cooperated with the new authorities in reestablishing order. Alcocer maintained good relations with the city ilustrados and had the confidence of Luis Flores as well. He also had the support of staunchly Catholic elements in the city. On 3 February

1899, a number of women in Cebu sent a petition to Aguinaldo asking that the bishop be allowed to stay in Cebu. When another group of women sent a counterpetition on 10 February 1899, saying the first petition did not represent the views of Cebuano women, still another petition was sent on 7 April 1899 urging the retention of the bishop.[18]

Fr. Pablo Singson, a native of Samar, was the highest-ranking church official after Alcocer's departure. Singson mainly looked after Church interests, avoiding explicit political commitment and stressing that the mission of the church was the "mission of peace."[19] In effect, however, the position of the hierarchy favored the government that was in place, whether Filipino or American. Singson cooperated with American authorities in investigating the complicity of priests in guerrilla activities. He denounced excesses on the part of the officials of the Republic. In a letter to the Holy See on 8 February 1899, he complained that "the government of the republic is not yet well-organized, abuses are not lacking, and even misbehavior on the part of those who ought to be models of morality and culture."[20] In many ways, the church officials shared in the ethos of the ilustrados with whom they had links of education, social status, and kinship.[21]

However, individual priests actively aided the insurgent cause. One of them was Fr. Francisco Blanco (b. 1866), parish priest of Liloan (15 kilometers north of the city), who aided the guerrillas by hiding them, sending word of American troop movements, and contributing supplies. He was found out when some documents he allegedly penned were found in a bag captured by the Americans during a battle with men under Mateo Luga. Father Blanco was briefly imprisoned and interrogated by the Americans in Fort San Pedro.[22] Another case was that of Fr. Francisco Latorre (b. 1857) of Malabuyoc who was arrested by the Americans on 2 August 1900 for providing aid and intelligence information to the insurgents. Latorre was subsequently barred from acting as a parish priest in Cebu province.[23]

Other citizens' responses to U.S. rule were often shaped by perceptions of personal and group interest. There is the case of Matias de Arrieta, a Manileño physician who took up residence in Cebu in the late nineteenth century. As early as 1 July 1899, he sent a letter direct to General E. S. Otis in Manila in which he offered his services to the Americans. Arrieta boasted: "I know how to crush the mad ambition of the stupid revolutionists of these islands."[24] Of Maxilom and other insurgent leaders, he said: "I know them all and I know what should be done with them, i.e., make them work, for they are nothing but a lot of vagabonds." He said he was not afraid (this in the wake of the Mejia assassination) though he knew he was one of those most "hated and threatened" by the insurgents. "The dagger of Pablo Mejia is hanging over me." To Otis, he declared:

I offer myself to you now for the complete occupation and
pacification of these islands, without fear of stiletto or anything else.... Dissolve this false government and declare
autonomy here as the people wish and send down a good big
shipment of handcuffs and chains to fasten up the rebels, and
also another Regiment of troops. I assure your Excellency
that Cebu will then acknowledge the sovereignty of America.

Arrieta did not disguise his contempt for the insurgents whom he
called tulisanes who should be "hunted down like wild beasts, for that is
what they really are." He singled out Francisco Llamas in his diatribe:
"The only man who will be shot or executed is that thief and murderer
Llamas for there is no salvation for such a monster of wickedness. The
others should only be forced to perform the public work which is so necessary here, for I am not a bloodthirsty man."

The cantankerous and arrogant Arrieta fancied himself the only bold
man among the American sympathizers. He considered Llorente a "very
pusillanimous fellow." He also reported on men he suspected to be involved in insurgent activities.[25] It is clear Arrieta had his ambitions. On 20
October 1899, he wrote to the military governor of Cebu seeking appointment as "secretary of interior" in the provisional government proposed to
be organized in Cebu.[26] He did not get any such appointment. In the middle
of 1900, as an offshoot of his removal from the junta popular of Cebu due
to a feud with other officials, Arrieta noisily waged a campaign against
Florentino Rallos and the junta of Cebu which he wanted to see abolished.

Arrieta was an extreme case. Other men of his class were more dis-
creet in their support of the United States. The presidente of Cebu,
Florentino Rallos (1854–1912), actively cooperated with the Americans.
His cooperation was a mix of principle and personal interest as he was, as
early as the 1880s, a major landowner in Carmen and Danao with business
dealings with Smith Bell and Company and other foreign houses. A U.S.
intelligence officer sized up Rallos thus: "He was shrewd enough to see
very early that the United States intended to keep the islands and that his
best opportunity lay with the Americans." The officer went on to say that
Rallos was an Americanista who had reasons to be wary of the insurgents
as they had his brother assassinated.[27] Of Rallos, Hamer wrote on 8 June
1899: "The President, apparently, cheerfully acts upon any suggestion I
make and is in almost daily consultation with me." Rallos and the city's
junta popular cooperated with the Americans. On 8 March 1900, for instance, Rallos forwarded to U.S. military authorities information supplied
by the jefe of Barrio Sambag to the effect that insurgents under Lorenzo

Eje were meeting in the house of Paulino (Bungi) Solon near the McLeod house on Guadalupe Road, just a half-hour away from Calle del Teatro (Colon).[28] Rallos asked that American troops be sent. Such was Rallos's closeness to the Americans that the insurgents had him targeted for assassination. We have a document dated 7 December 1900 suggesting an insurgent plot to kidnap Rallos.[29]

Other mayors who extended cooperation to the Americans at the beginning of the U.S. occupation were Juan Melgar of Dumanjug, acting presidente Segundo Singson of Cebu, Alejandro Ruiz of Argao, Antonio Ruiz of Sibonga, and Teofilo Mejia of Naga. Melgar, for instance, led a posse of local policemen on 27 July 1899 in a bid to capture insurgent leaders in his area.[30] Captured was a Tagalog colonel named Macario A. Nicomedes, an adjutant to Nicolas Godines. Seized with Nicomedes were 13 rifles and a quantity of ammunition. Nicolas Godines, his brother Macario, and Jose Veloso (cited as Godines's "brains" in U.S. reports) escaped. Melgar reported to the Americans that he undertook the mission, "it being no longer possible to suffer the many abuses (of) the military men of (this) pueblo." It was not surprising that Melgar welcomed the American occupation of his town. Before the entry of the Americans into Dumanjug on 31 July 1899, Melgar had been briefly jailed by Godines for his American sympathies. The American report said: "We were well received. The Dumanjug president is cooperative."

Teofilo Mejia, the son of Pablo Mejia, was active in the campaign against the insurgents.[31] In October and September 1899, he and his policemen arrested and imprisoned four suspected insurgents. He asked for U.S. troops to be stationed in his town and rifles supplied to his men. The Naga police joined American troops in anti-insurgent operations such that they came to be called Macabebes Nagueños (after the Filipino mercenaries from the town of Macabebe in Pampanga who gained notoriety as scouts for the Americans).

The brothers Alejandro and Antonio Ruiz, who were cousins of Teofilo Mejia, also cooperated in the American occupation and were described by the American reports as "very friendly." Under Alejandro Ruiz, the Argao town council, on 31 July 1901, ordered that the male residents in the poblacion be organized into a vigilante force to defend the town against the insurgents.[32] The Ruiz brothers were Tagalogs who settled in Cebu in the 1870s, built up their wealth and became the most prominent citizens of southeastern Cebu by the time of the revolution. Alejandro Ruiz was educated at the Colegio-Seminario de San Carlos, served in the Spanish civil service and was capitan municipal of Argao for several terms, and was an agent in Argao for the Compania General de Tabacos de Filipinas and Smith Bell and Company.

It is difficult, however, to calibrate the sympathies of many Cebuano leaders. Other mayors, such as Pascual de la Cerna of Opon, were reported as giving aid and shelter to insurgents.[33] For the most part, perhaps, people were moved by pragmatic considerations of existing realities. For another, it is not too difficult to understand the local ilustrados' lukewarm or distrustful attitude towards the Maxilom forces as many of the insurgent leaders were either non-Cebuanos or belonged only peripherally to the Cebuano elite. The insurgent army, on the other hand, was made up largely of "mountain people."

Such men as Presidente Florencio Noel of Carcar tried to appease both insurgents and Americans during the uncertain days of the occupation. Noel received the Americans cordially when they occupied Carcar on 2 July 1899 but on 25 September 1899, a letter of Naga presidente Teofilo Mejia complained that Noel had just sent two cases of ammunition to the insurgents in the mountains.[34] Brinkmanship was required since both Americans and insurgents often moved within the same territory and had the capability to mete out reprisals. Something in the situation of the towns is indicated in a letter Pantaleon del Rosario wrote to Troadio Galicano on 6 February 1901 that complained of Carcar leaders' collaboration with the Americans. Del Rosario said that the policy should not be to break with the town authorities but to maintain secret relations with them and cultivate the services of agents for the collection of contributions and information. He instructed Galicano:

> The forces under your command will ostentatiously appear
> within the confines of the town, inspiring the inhabitants
> with respect and at the same time with fear, in order that
> through fear the people may preserve their respect for the
> revolution in addition to becoming convinced that we are not
> intimidated by any change in the policy of the towns.[35]

Other local officials, unable to stand the pressure from both sides, abandoned or tried to abdicate their offices. On 17 July 1900, presidente Santiago Ferraris of San Nicolas resigned from his post.[36] On 30 June 1900, Hilarion Alquizola asked to be relieved as presidente of Barili for reason of ill health. The American officials, however, surmised that the request was caused by "political pressure."[37] On 3 October 1900, Presidente Elias Espina of Mandaue, who had earlier asked for the stationing of American troops in his town, resigned on grounds of poor health and advanced age.[38] Also on 3 October 1900, Florentino Rallos submitted to the military governor his resignation as Cebu presidente on grounds of poor health, his wish to attend to his family and business, and the difficulties in carrying out his functions due to the "obstacles and troubles" put on his path by uncooperative persons.[39] Even the pro-American Teofilo Mejia of Naga complained in September 1899 that he was disheartened by the lack of adequate American protection. Mejia was reported to have said that he will "pack up and go to Hong Kong."[40]

Several ilustrados in the municipalities actively supported the revolutionary cause in the early stages of the war. A prominent example is Don Pedro Lasala Rodriguez (1869–1932), hacendero and presidente municipal of the northern town of Bogo. He was the acknowledged jefe of Bogo and the northern end of the island in the last days of the Spanish regime, the republican interregnum, and the early days of the war against the United States. In this capacity, he is said to have contributed money and supplies to the Maxilom government in Sudlon. After the fall of Sudlon, he participated in a meeting in Danao, together with Juan Climaco, Pantaleon del Rosario, and others, which decided on the transfer of the republic's headquarters to the interior of Sogod and Catmon.

After the Americans occupied Bogo in January 1900, Rodriguez was still active in the republican cause. He is said to have maintained a guerrilla band of forty soldiers—called Guerrilla Rodriguez—under Melquiades Lasala and the American deserter Fred M. Baker whom Rodriguez harbored in his own house. Rodriguez was arrested by the Americans and made to choose between cooperating with the Americans or leaving the country. Rodriguez reportedly left for Europe and returned to Cebu only several months later. Upon his return, he was ordered to stay in Cebu City so his actions could be monitored. At this time, however, Rodriguez was already convinced of the futility of the armed resistance and he was active in the efforts to bring about the surrender of the insurgent army.[41]

City-based ilustrados, who lived in frequent contact with the Americans, tried to "play the game." One case is that of the writer and journalist Vicente Sotto (1878-1950). Vicente and brother Filemon, sons of a Tagalog migrant from Manila, published and edited the pioneering Cebuano newspapers, *La Justicia, El Nacional, El Imparcial, El Pueblo,* and *Ang Suga.* In the afternoon of 2 September 1899, while working on his newspaper *El Nacional* at the Hospital Printing Office, Vicente Sotto was arrested by two American soldiers for alleged complicity with the insurgents. The charge was that his newspaper had expressed approval of the murder of two American soldiers before the outbreak of open hostilities in July 1899. Found in his possession were insurgent press reports —"Ecos de Cebu," dated 2 September 1899, written by "Dayag" and "Cronica de la campaña" by "Samban"—which Sotto said were given him by someone he did not know. The Americans, nonetheless, accused him of being part of the insurgent propaganda network.[42] Sotto was hauled to prison in Fort San Pedro.

On 14 September 1899, and then on September 20, Vicente Sotto wrote from his Fort San Pedro cell to the American military governor (in Spanish, pencil-written on scraps of paper) pleading for his release as he was "seriously ill."[43] He declared: "I have never taken any part in the insurrection. I have never been an insurgent.... I am a peaceful citizen, a lover of order and obedient to the established authority." He eschewed any sympathy for the insurgents, "those warlike rebels who, under the cloak of desiring independence, devote themselves to sacking and robbing the towns." He ended his plea: "I believe I am on the brink of the grave and before I die I want the fact of my innocence to shine forth." In still another letter, he denied that he was the director of *El Nacional*, said that Miguel Logarta and Florentino Rallos can attest to his innocence, pledged his loyalty to the U.S., and offered his services to the American governor.[44]

Sotto was released after two-and-a-half months in prison. He took his oath of allegiance to the U.S. on 4 November 1899 and again on 23 March 1901.[45] Sotto, however, continued to cause U.S. authorities some trouble with his writings. He purchased his own printing press in 1900 and launched the newspapers *El Pueblo* and *Ang Suga*.

Vicente Sotto walked the thin line between resistance and collaboration, calling for Philippine independence but "under U.S. protection" and invoking the ideals of the American political tradition.[46] He and his brother Filemon, however, were never trusted by the Americans who saw them as troublemakers of anti-American bent. An American officer, in 1902, referred to Vicente as "very anti-American" and a "public agitator" whose *El Pueblo* should be suppressed.[47] An intelligence report of March 1902 called the Sotto brothers "the two best insurgents in this section of the country, likewise the smoothest," because of the ideas carried in their papers.[48]

Sotto remained active in politics. He was elected Cebu councilor in 1902 and then Cebu mayor in 1907, a year after he passed the bar, but was unable to assume the position as he fled to Hong Kong. It appears that in Vicente Sotto's case, anti-Americanism was partly based on principle and partly on political and personal circumstance. A freethinker, Sotto was militantly critical of the friars and sympathetic to Gregorio Aglipay's Philippine Independent Church. He was an exile in Macao and Hong Kong from 1908 to 1914 to escape imprisonment for the alleged abduction (*rapto*) of a minor in 1906. In Hong Kong, he became involved in anti-American agitation as editor of *The Philippine Republic* and associate of Artemio Ricarte in the Hong Kong-based Revolutionary Council of the Philippines. The U.S. government tried to have him extradited three times but failed since the British authorities considered him a political refugee.

Many in the business community of the city, however, considered themselves apolitical and their primary concern was for stability and normalcy in business operations. It is said that even prior to the U.S. arrival in Cebu there were Cebuanos who already sent appeals to the American commanding general in Iloilo for the U.S. to assume control as Cebuanos "could not maintain a successful, independent government."[49] Wealthy businessmen, therefore, quickly accommodated themselves to U.S. rule. An insurgent manifesto said that big Cebuano businessmen, *"interesados de dollares,"* were turning traitors to the motherland.[50]

Illustrative of the case of many of the local businessmen was that of Nicasio Chiong-Veloso (1842–1903), a prosperous and propertied Chinese merchant. He did business with the Americans (among others, a house of his was leased to American officers) and adopted a low profile in politics. He declared on 27 July 1901, in a letter to the American commander in Cebu:

> I have never been engaged in any rebellion or insurrection
> against the authority of the United States nor am I now so
> engaged but on the contrary have always given such aid and
> encouragement to the United States authority in these
> Islands as lay in my power, well knowing that my personal
> and property interests would be better preserved and pro-
> tected under that government than any other.[51]

Chiong-Veloso expressed the sentiments of many of the city's merchants and property owners. Such sentiments facilitated the relative normalization of business conditions within the city. On 29 June 1899, the leading merchants of Cebu asked American authorities to have the Port of Cebu opened. Closure of the port, due to the hostilities, had harmed business and interrupted the flow of supplies to and from neighboring provinces. Signatories to this petition, addressed to Governor Hamer, were Mariano Veloso, John Sidebottom, Joaquin Castro, Tomas Osmeña, Juan Veloso, Ceferino Rodriguez, and representatives of the major commercial houses in the city.[52] By late 1899, the Port of Cebu had been reopened and by mid-1900, the U.S. Customs House in the city was clearing from 4 to 17 vessels simultaneously, loading or discharging such goods as hemp, sugar, copra, rice, and flour.[53]

Even then, hostilities continued well into 1901. Fighting intruded right into the city itself. On 24 February 1901, a band of around 15 to 20 guerrillas entered the city from the north and, according to the American report, fired two volleys down one of the principal streets, killing four and wounding eight residents, two of them policemen.[54] Lyman J. Carlock, who arrived in Cebu on 2 July 1901 to assume the post of judge of the court of first instance of the Cebu-Bohol district, said that conditions were bad in his early days in Cebu. "The insurgents under Del Rosario and Luga were firing on the town every few nights. I became somewhat accustomed to trying cases by day and listening by night to the rather menacing and sleep-disturbing song of Mauser bullets, flying over the roof of our house....The majority of the people were in sympathy with the insurrection."[55]

The last Spanish bishop of Cebu, Martin Garcia Alcocer, who played a key role in the transfer of power from the Spaniards to the republican forces in Cebu in 1898 –*Cebuano Studies Center*

Leon Kilat (Pantaleon Villegas), the legendary Negrense who helped lead the anti-Spanish revolution in Cebu –*Cebuano Studies Center*

The Seminario-Colegio de San Carlos on Martires St., the leading educational institution in Cebu –*Cebuano Studies Center*

Spanish troops resting in the wake of the initial suppression of the April 1898 uprising in Cebu –*Cebuano Studies Center*

The arrival in Cebu of the U.S. gunboat *Petrel* on 21 February 1899, which signaled the start of American occupation –*Cebuano Studies Center*

Warwick Barracks, the main U.S. camp in Cebu, 1899 –*Michael G. Price Collection*

An American encampment, possibly in Pardo, south of Cebu City, 1899 –*Michael G. Price Collection*

American troops disembarking in Cebu, 1900 –*Michael G. Price Collection*

Unloading supplies at the Cebu pier, near Fort San Pedro (right) and the U.S. Army-Navy Club (left), 1900 –*Michael G. Price Collection*

An American firing squad in Cebu –*Michael G. Price Collection*

Photo Supply Co. Manila, P. I.

Cebuano republican soldiers in the anti-American war –*Cebuano Studies Center*

The Government House (Casa Gobierno), facing Plaza Independencia, 1900 –*Cebuano Studies Center*

Julio Llorente, the Madrid-educated lawyer who served as governor under the Americans–*Cebuano Studies Center*

Luis Flores, the first Filipino governor of Cebu, 1899–*Cebuano Studies Center*

Juan Climaco (left), the "brains" of the republican war in Cebu—*Cebuano Studies Center*

Arcadio Maxilom (extreme left), the "supreme chief" in the anti-American resistance—*Cebuano Studies Center*

Republican leaders Mateo Luga (seated), Pantaleon del Rosario (right), and Gavino Sepulveda (left), ca. 1901 —*Cebuano Studies Center*

Vicente Sotto (seated left) with Artemio Ricarte (center) and other leaders of the Philippine revolutionary council in Hong Kong, 1911 —*Cebuano Studies Center*

Troadio Galicano, one of the chiefs of the republican resistance —*Cebuano Studies Center*

Sergio Osmeña in 1907 —*Cebuano Studies Center*

10

Infrastructure of Consent

A MERICAN PACIFICATION of the island of Cebu took other forms. A policy of attraction was joined to the policy of armed suppression to convince Filipinos that their aspirations could be realized within the framework of American sovereignty.

At the outset, the Americans allowed the existing provincial and municipal governments to function under American military supervision. For a complex of reasons, U.S. officials recognized that Filipinos had to handle local administration. "Filipino rule" impressed the natives with American "benevolence" and disinterestedness; the Americans worked out of a political tradition of representative government; and the Americans simply did not have their own personnel to handle civil administration on the local level.

The state of war, however, rendered the loyalties of local officials suspect. With the escalation of hostilities and the difficulty of closely supervising local officials, the Americans moved to abolish the municipal councils or juntas. General E. S. Otis himself commented:

> This junta proved to be nothing more or less than an insurgent body which failed to give any protection whatever to friendly disposed inhabitants.... It therefore became an absolute necessity to overthrow this so-called civil government and any future government of a civil character must await a manifested, more pacific disposition on the part of many of the influential natives.

In August 1899 General Otis, as military governor of the Philippines, issued General Order No. 43 that established a uniform procedure of municipal organization for areas under the army's control. Each town was to be governed by a municipal council, consisting of a president and representatives ("headmen") from each barrio. Headmen were chosen by the residents of their barrios and the town president was elected by a voice vote of the residents of the town. The American commanding officer in the area, however, had to approve the election of president and the municipal ordinances.

General Order No. 43 was replaced by General Order No. 40, issued by General Otis on 29 March 1900. Less democratic in procedure, the new order strengthened the powers of the American commanding officer in the supervision of municipal governments. It preserved elite dominance by limiting the electorate to males, 23 years old and over, who had any of the following qualifications: (1) previous service as capitan municipal, gobernadorcillo (the title given before 1890 to the mayor), teniente (a title held by several high-ranking town officials during the Spanish period), or cabeza de barangay; (2) annual payment of 30 pesos in taxes; or (3) ability to speak, read, and write in English or Spanish.

Under General Order No. 40, the military commander of an area calls for an election. The election announcement is posted in the tribunal and published or announced to the community by a crier. To be elected by secret ballot are the mayor (alcalde), vice mayor (municipal lieutenant), and councilors (the number depending on the town's population). A panel is formed to administer the oath of qualified electors. Judges as well as tellers of election are chosen. Results are then forwarded to the military governor of the province for approval.[1]

Under General Order No. 40, nine Cebu towns were organized. These were:

Town	Population	Date of Election (1900)
Bogo	18,000	31 July
Medellin	5,830	2 August
Dumanjug	10,000	2 August
Cebu	10,875	16 August
Naga	12,000	16 August
Balamban	10,005	1 September
Alegria	7,695	1 September
San Sebastian	3,069	1 September
San Remigio	4,890	14 September

General Order No. 40 formalized early efforts of the American military authorities to reorganize towns in occupied territory in the Philippines. The order preserved the Spanish system of town government, but the Americans assumed the powers of veto and supervision.[2]

At the provincial level, the Americans also combined the principles of Cebuano participation and American control. On 2 April 1900, upon his assumption of command of the subdistrict of Cebu, Colonel E. J. McClernand recommended that the provincial officials, after taking the oath of allegiance to the U.S., be allowed to continue in office until firmer arrangements were made by the Philippine Commission.[3] The senior American military officer, however, was the person who exercised effective power.

As part of limited self-rule, the Americans also appointed Cebuanos to positions in the judiciary. These included Mariano Cui and Gavino Sepulveda (as court of first instance judge and fiscal, respectively, of Bohol, on 18 October 1900), Agapito Hilario and Juan Villarosa (as justice of the peace and supplementary justice of the peace, respectively, of the municipality of Cebu, on 10 December 1900), Ceferino Abadia (as justice of the peace of San Nicolas, on 8 January 1901), Segundo Singson (as fiscal of Leyte, on 21 June 1901), and Mariano Albao Cuenco (as clerk of court of Cebu, on 27 June 1901).[4]

The Maxilom government recognized how American efforts at reorganizing the towns threatened to dissipate mass support for the resistance. The Cebuano government responded with its own clandestine propaganda campaign urging noncooperation. An undated Maxilom circular, probably circulated around the time of the visit of the Schurman Commission to the Visayas in the middle of 1899, offered instructions to counter the Americans' civil pacification drive. It warned Cebuanos that an American commission, accompanied by the "traitors" Llorente, Rallos, and Segundo Singson ("who have sold their souls to the enemy"), will try to impose its own government in Cebu. The people were urged to signify that they oppose the establishment of a provisional government. If the Americans insist on their plans, Cebuanos should resign their posts in the municipal government and ask the local principales to refuse posts offered to them. If pressed, they should flee from their towns. If they are asked for their representatives, they should, as a last recourse, sign a petition signifying the following as their representatives: Miguel Logarta, Marcial Velez, and Vicente Sotto. The circular warned that if the Americanistas Llorente, Rallos, and Singson become the Cebuano representatives, this would be a blow to the cause of the resistance.[5]

When the U.S.-supervised reorganization of local governments proceeded in earnest under General Order No. 40 in 1900, protests were registered by various Cebu towns in an orchestrated effort by the Maxilom government. A draft of the protest was circulated to the towns by Maxilom's men.[6] Letters were also sent to the town presidentes explaining to them the American designs in establishing municipal governments and urging them to have residents manifest their opposition to the plans of the *imperialistas*.[7] In the period March to October 1900, 28 towns formally protested the establishment of the new municipal governments and the requirement to have the people take the oath of allegiance to the United States. These towns were Danao, Pilar, Tudela, San Francisco, Carmen, Balamban, Alcantara, Ronda, Aloguinsan, Catmon, Barili, Sogod, Badian, Moalboal, Santa Rosa, Borbon, Mandaue, Liloan, Tabogon, Tuburan, Madridejos, Talisay, Pardo, Minglanilla, San Nicolas, San Fernando, Asturias, and Ginatilan. The resolutions of protest were signed by presidentes, members of the local council, barrio headmen, and prominent citizens.

The resolutions manifested the desire of the towns for the political and territorial independence of the country and the suspension of hostilities; opposed the taking of the oath of allegiance and the American move to establish new municipal governments; and called for the creation of a civil government exclusively managed by Filipinos. The resolutions were skillfully worded. For instance, the municipal resolution of Carmen, drawn up in a popular assembly on 5 March 1900 and signed by 55 persons led by the *presidente*, invoked American ideals by declaring that the Filipino people were "desirous of having the principles of the (U.S.) Declaration of Independence applied to the Filipinos and of having the Constitution become the regulator of justice," and that, in seeking self-determination, they were only following "in the footsteps of the Americans."[8]

An interesting case is that of Danao. On 29 July 1900, at the Danao town hall, councilmen and citizens—there were 35 signatories—gathered to discuss the American plan to set up new municipal governments and have the people take the oath of allegiance. They agreed to manifest that (1) their cooperation with the U.S. was exacted under duress and "against our will," (2) their oath of allegiance to "the Filipino republican constitution" was spontaneous and reflected their true sentiments, and they cannot, therefore, take a different oath "as if it was an article of merchandise easy to exchange," (3) "that in our hearts we recognize only the Filipino constitution and the Filipino authorities elected by the people" and thus they recognize the authority of "Arcadio Maxilom as commander-in-chief and Juan Climaco as second-in-command," (4) they oppose all violence and bloodshed, and (5) their relations to Americans are one of "passive resistance" and they will "continue to recognize the national Filipino government at heart."

Apparently, all this was not mere rhetoric. Two months later, on 25 September 1900, eight members of the popular junta of Danao filed a formal protest saying that they were coerced into taking the oath of allegiance to the United States. For refusing to take the oath, the Danao officials wrote, they were thrown into prison and "obliged to work in an objectionable and mortifying way" from 9 August to 25 September. Foreswearing the oath they were forced into taking, they were compelled to leave the town to avoid reprisals by soldiers under "a despotic American captain stationed in that town." The letter of protest also said that their presidente, Victorino Buot, and the local delegate of justice, Felix Batucan, were taken as prisoners to the provincial capital for refusing to sign the oath of allegiance.[9]

Cebuano opposition to the U.S.-supervised reorganization of local governments was also raised in a formal petition addressed to the U.S. Congress. This petition— jointly issued by Climaco and Maxilom on 2 October 1900 and subscribed to by "over two thousand Cebuanos"—eloquently affirmed Cebuano aspirations for nationhood. The petition set forth a history of the Cebuano revolutionary struggle and argued that Cebuanos would have no part in U.S. plans to reorganize the government.[10]

Few towns were organized under General Order No. 40 because of the unsettled conditions. There was a lack of enthusiasm for government positions in many places. There were cases of members of the local junta going into hiding to avoid serving under the Americans. The American commander in northern Cebu reported: "I am confirmed in the opinion that the attitude of the leading people in this end of the Island is one of waiting and expectancy."[11] He said there was some anxiety over the type of local government the Americans would introduce. He noted that there was "some little suppressed rivalry for the different offices," but local leaders were not keen about General Order No. 40, preferring a more permanent government to one that was "provisional."

Several towns encountered difficulties in holding elections. In Tabogon, an election scheduled on 1 October 1900 could not be held as the electors failed to appear. Reports had it that insurgents in Tabogon threatened people against participating in the U.S.-sponsored elections. In Bogo, officials elected on 31 July were sworn in only on 15 September, while in San Remigio, officials elected on 14 September could not be sworn in until 11 December.

The reorganization of the towns was slowed down by the lack of American personnel (U.S. troops were stretched out thinly across the whole island), Cebuano suspicions about American designs, and the unsettled conditions due to continuing guerrilla actions carried out by the Maxilom government.

At about this time, too, municipal police forces were reorganized by the Americans. The police reorganization was decreed by General Order No. 87 of the military governor of the Philippines (18 June 1900), later supplemented by Act No. 58 of the Philippine Commission (20 December 1900) and then by the Municipal Code of 31 January 1901. As of 9 June 1902, there were 1,017 policemen in the province (ranging from 7 in Alcantara to 160 in Cebu).[12] Local policemen were inadequately armed. Only the police in Cebu, Carcar, Sibonga, Argao, and Dumanjug had some rifles and revolvers. The rest were only armed with bolos and knives (*armas blancas*). While there was a great deal of hesitation on the part of the U.S. military to arm the local police, the local police, in the main, actively aided the Americans by acting as guides, informers, and auxiliaries in military operations.

On 31 January 1901, General Order No. 40 was superseded by the new Municipal Code, passed as Act No. 82 by the Philippine Commission. Designed "to secure the confidence and affection of the Filipinos," this advanced local autonomy and the rule of localities by Filipinos.[13] It retained the suffrage requirements in General Order No. 40. The only amendment was to the effect that males over 23 years old who owned real property valued at 500 pesos or more were also entitled to vote. In Cebu province, a municipal organization committee was formed with an American officer, Capt. William P. Evans of the Nineteenth U.S. Infantry, as chairman.[14]

On 13 April 1901, under the Municipal Code, six more towns were organized with the election of a president, vice president, and a council:

Town	Population
Argao	35,000
Sibonga	30,000
Carcar	20,000
Minglanilla	4,500
Barili	21,640
Dalaguete	10,230

Six days after the passage of the Municipal Code, the Philippine Commission also enacted Act No. 83 (6 February 1901), otherwise known as the Provincial Government Code, which provided for the establishment of provincial governments, with the provincial governor elected biennially by the municipal councilors of the province. The governor administered the province together with the supervisor and the treasurer, both appointed by the Philippine Commission. The three constituted the provincial board.

On 9 February 1901, Gen. Arthur McArthur asked the commanding general of the Visayan Military Department to report which provinces in his command were ready for the establishment of civil government. All provinces, except Bohol, Leyte, and Cebu, were suited for such establishment.

The establishment of civil government in the Province of Cebu came only with the visit to Cebu City of the Second Philippine Commission, also known as the Taft Commission, on 17–18 April 1901. William Howard Taft, chairman of the commission, came with Commissioners Dean C. Worcester, Henry C. Ide, and Bernard Moses. Also in the visiting party were Cayetano Arellano, chief justice of the Supreme Court, and T. H. Pardo de Tavera, president of the pro-American Federal Party, and American as well as Filipino news correspondents. The purposes of the Cebu visit were (1) to ascertain the peace-and-order conditions in the province and find out if it was appropriate to establish civil government in Cebu, and if so, (2) to pass a special act applying the Provincial Government Code to Cebu and, after having passed the act, (3) to appoint the new officials of the province.

The U.S. transport *Sumner*, bearing the Taft party, landed shortly after 9:00 A.M. on 17 April. The Cebuano elite went all out to impress the visiting dignitaries. At the shipside welcome, Cebu officials came in European suits and black patent leathers, some of the women in full evening dress with white gloves. The welcoming crowd included two squads of the local police and two brass bands. American gunboats fired their 17-gun salutes as the Taft party disembarked. The city was spruced up for the visit and big arches decorated the principal streets. In the course of their stay in Cebu, the visitors were treated royally: whenever the commission members stepped out into the streets, "they were preceded and followed by a squad of native police, with an ever-present band in attendance." They were treated to sumptuous banquets, one of which was a marathon dinner at Club Filipino (also called Club Popular) on Colon Street, complete with a printed menu that listed 34 dishes obviously intended to impress the visitors with the local elite's knowledge of cosmopolitan cuisine. The fare covered everything from roast turkey, veal cutlets, and boiled ham in jelly to apple pie, peach pie, and various other kinds of pies, cakes,

and puddings. It was a feast that must have been excessive even for the
guest of honor himself, the corpulent former judge who, years later, would
be president of the United States (1909–1913). A commission staffer remarked: "The banquet was one of the most pretentious affairs we have
been up against."[15]

The main event of the visit was a meeting at Teatro Junquera that
started at 10:00 A.M., 17 April, and continued the following day.[16] Less
than one-half of the towns (23 out of 58) were represented at the assembly.
Chairmen of the town delegations were Florentino Rallos (Cebu), Luciano
Bacayo (San Nicolas), Florencio Noel and Adriano Enriquez (Carcar), An-
tonio Ruiz (Sibonga), Alejandro Ruiz (Argao), Ruperto Buenconsejo
(Dalaguete), Pacifico Albarracin (Ronda), Juan Lozada (Dumanjug),
Hilarion Alquizola (Barili), Nicolas Rafols (Toledo), Sixto Milan (Balamban),
Fausto Tabotabo (Tuburan), Fortunato Villaceran (Bantayan), Victorino de
la Viña (Bogo), Hugo Torres (Pilar), Elias Espina (Mandaue), Pedro de
Gracia and Filomeno Fadullon (Naga), Eugenio Fernandez and Emilio
Deiparine (Talisay), Felipe Sotto (Poro), Julian Castro (Medellin), Juan
Garcia (Moalboal), Crisanto Cuison (Alegria), and Vicente Palacio (Daan
Bantayan).

Taft bluntly asked the assembled Cebuanos whether they would allow themselves to be intimidated by some 200 riflemen waging a guerrilla
war in the countryside. He declared that the Americans could, if they
wished, "put a force of men on the island and sweep it from end to end,"
but he would prefer that the Cebuanos themselves settle the affair. If the
people are desirous of peace, he said, they must organize to get it as the
people in the other provinces had already done. Only when they show
themselves capable of doing this will civil government be established. Taft
lectured: "We believe in speaking plainly and showing what our attitude is
and what we believe your attitude should be." He went on: "We want to
give you the benefits of civil government; to give you such individual rights
as are enjoyed by every citizen of the United States, but within the sound
of arms the law is silent and individual rights will not be observed."

After Taft issued his challenge, the delegates proceeded to express
their views. Many delegates declared that civil government should be established and municipal governments strengthened. Adriano Enriquez of
Carcar went on to say, "his people would assist the Americans in hunting
down these men who are still out." Alejandro Ruiz of Argao said that the
establishment of civil government would convince the insurgents that they
are in error. These people can be persuaded to surrender, he said, and if
not, a large military force should be deployed in Cebu to sweep it clean of

insurgents from end to end. Ruiz declared that the people of Carcar, Sibonga, Argao, and Dalaguete have already taken the oath of allegiance and are in accord with the Americans.

Florentino Rallos also endorsed the establishment of civil government and batted for more revenues for local governments and the improvement of the Cebu harbor. Luciano Bacayo, presidente of San Nicolas, endorsed civil government but said that the people of San Nicolas were doing their duty in maintaining peace and order and that the town could defend itself against the *insurrectos*. San Nicolas, he said, would prefer to call in the U.S. Army only when its help is needed. The other delegates expressed similar views, calling for civil government as a way of pacifying the island. Like Enriquez, Ruiz, and Rallos, other delegates raised another major concern of the officials: that the revenue-generating powers of town governments be strengthened and that more public works be carried out.

In the afternoon of 18 April, with the public hearing concluded, Taft presented the decision of the commission. The commission passed Act No. 116 extending the provisions of the Provincial Government Code to the island of Cebu, with a special provision incorporating San Nicolas into the municipality of Cebu. The act also provided that the town presidents convene a meeting on the third Monday of January, July, and October of each year for the purpose of recommending to the provincial board improvements in their respective towns.

After this, the commission announced appointments for the Cebu provincial government. The new provincial leadership was made up of two American officers and three familiar faces:

PROVINCIAL OFFICIALS, 1901

Governor	Julio Llorente
Secretary	Leoncio Alburo
Treasurer	Lt. Fred S. Young
Supervisor	Maj. James F. Case
Fiscal	Miguel Logarta[17]

Chief Justice Cayetano Arellano administered the oath of office after which speeches were delivered by Arellano, T. H. Pardo de Tavera, and Governor Llorente. Llorente, at this time already a leading member of the Federal Party, was particularly pleased at his having been reinstalled to the governorship he relinquished a year earlier because of the war.

In the wake of the establishment of civil government, work proceeded on the organization of the 42 towns that were not organized under General Order No. 40 and the Municipal Code.[18] These 42 towns were:

Town	Population	Date of Election (1901)
Talisay	12,250	5 May
Santander	3,285	8 May
Talamban	3,000	9 May
Toledo	7,000	11 May
Mandaue	8,060	11 May
Samboan	4,070	11 May
Danao	5,625	13 May
Oslob	5,555	18 May
Bantayan	10,210	13 June
SantaFe	2,250	14 June
Boljoon	4,100	28 June
Ginatilan	6,195	29 June
Alcoy	5,330	24 June
NuevaCaceres	2,560	29 June
Malabuyoc	7,450	30 June
Moalboal	7,650	30 June
Ronda	6,445	1 July
Alcantara	3,660	2 July
Pinamungajan	5,005	3 July
Badian	9,025	4 July
Aloguinsan	5,500	4 July
Asturias	6,855	6 July
Tuburan	10,665	8 July
DaanBantayan	7,500	10 July
Borbon	3,425	11 July
ElPardo	5,000	6 August
SantaRosa	2,400	6 August
Liloan	8,500	8 August
Compostela	3,500	9 August
Opon	6,676	17 August
Cordoba	4,000	17 August
SanFernando	9,170	26 August
Consolacion	4,000	29 August

From May to August, the shift from military to civil government was vigorously pushed in Cebu. Governor Llorente went around the island on board the *Philadelphia*, visiting towns and organizing the *comites* and juntas in the places where the people had "recognized American sovereignty." Llorente, however, reported that in one case, Catmon, the town could not be organized immediately as "the inhabitants were nowhere to be found."[19]

Due to unsettled conditions in northern Cebu, it was not until January 1902 that the towns of Tabogon, Sogod, Catmon, Carmen, Poro, Tudela, Pilar, and San Francisco were organized. The organization of Madridejos was delayed as the residents had expressed the desire to be annexed to Bantayan due to the poverty of their town. The towns in Camotes Island were organized late due to difficulties of transportation.

The policy of organizing local governments and placing them in the hands of Filipinos had a profound effect on the course of the war. Giving the elite a share in government—the American "policy of attraction"— was a keystone in the pacification of the islands. The Americans recognized that local autonomy had a particular political significance because Spanish centralism had deprived Filipinos of political participation in the past. As the earlier Schurman Commission put it:

> the general substitution throughout the archipelago of civil
> for military government (though, of course, with the reten-
> tion of a strong military arm) *would do more than any other*
> *single occurrence to reconcile the Filipinos to American sovereignty*,
> which would then stand revealed, not merely as irresistible
> power, but as an instrument for the preservation and develop-
> ment of the rights and liberties of the Filipinos and the
> promotion of their happiness and prosperity.[20]

With the unfolding of the policy of "Filipinization," Filipino ilustrados saw that they could maintain *their* power under the Americans. An important groundwork was thus established for the suppression of armed Cebuano resistance.

The Americans were careful to hold the reins. All municipal officials were Filipinos. Yet, in the provincial board, only the governor (since the fiscal and secretary were not considered members of the board) was a Filipino. Until 1906, the two other members of the board, the treasurer and the supervisor, were appointed by the central government and were usually Americans. The provincial government did not enjoy much autonomy and the governor exercised limited powers. The treasurer controlled provincial and municipal funds while the supervisor handled contracts, provincial property, and public works. Provincial governments were supervised by the Executive Bureau in Manila, which was under the office of the governor-general and was headed by an American. Though Filipinos enjoyed a wider range of participation under the Americans than under Spanish rule, the U.S. maintained effective power.

The Maxilom government tried to counter the American policy of attraction by sending out circulars and manifestoes. On 24 March 1901, Juan Climaco issued an open letter, *al pueblo Cebuano*, saying that the campaign of the Partido Federal and the organization of local governments were part of an American "drama" (comedia), a trick to divide-and-rule and create an illusion that the resistance was over and that the people supported American rule.[21] On 16 April 1901, the insurgent government appointed Pantaleon del Rosario and Gervasio Padilla as special commissioners to travel to the towns and engage in propaganda and political work to counter American blandishments.[22]

As the reorganization of the towns went on, insurgent hostilities remained. There were continued reports on the movement of insurgents in the hinterlands. The Americans themselves pressed on with their military campaign. Between 28 February and 2 March 1901, a group of 50 American soldiers of the Fifth and Nineteenth Infantries, with 21 Filipino scouts, under the command of Lieutenant F. G. Lawton, left Cebu for an expedition to the hinterlands of Danao and Catmon.[23] The column arrived in Mt. Capayas in the afternoon of 1 March, after following trails marked with bamboo traps and pitfalls. Here, they were ambushed by insurgents armed with two smoothbore cannons and about six rifles. The insurgents, however, quickly withdrew after burning their "camp" of around three large houses. The Americans themselves proceeded to burn the other houses in the area. No casualties were reported on either side, however.

Occasional encounters took place even in the outskirts of the city. On 14 July 1901, the president of Cebu reported that close to midnight of 13 July, insurgents killed a Cebu policeman and injured another in Pagina.[24] The presidente asked U.S. military authorities to issue guns to the local police as they were vulnerable to attack. On 14 July 1901, soldiers of the Nineteenth U.S. Infantry, scouting the outskirts of the city, ran into an insurgent band and captured 15 insurgents. On 27 July, a combined force of the Nineteenth U.S. Infantry and the Philippine Scouts struck a band of some 60 insurgents in Labangon, San Nicolas, killed 7 and captured 13. Three on the American side were wounded.[25] On 25 July, around midnight, insurgents with about 50 rifles and 2 small cannons, staged an attack inside Cebu City but were driven off. There were no casualties.[26] Judge Carlock recorded this nocturnal attack in his diary, saying that, from where he resided on Colon Street, he could hear "over a hundred shots not far from our house."[27]

It was clear, however, that the tide had begun to turn against the insurgents. Of the "policy of attraction," Gen. James F. Smith said in 1907:

> The policy, new as it was, "did things" . . . and not withstanding the prophesies to the contrary it charmed the rifle out of the hands of the insurgent and made the one-time rebel chief the pacific president of the municipality or the staid governor of a province. *It brought peace to the islands*, constituted out of those lately in arms against the sovereign power a constabulary force for the maintenance of public order and made feasible the establishment of a civil government while every barrio and municipality was still smoking hot with insurrection and rebellion. In a word, *the policy of attraction*, the policy of giving the Filipino people as large a measure of local self-government as they might be capable of exercising and enjoying, proved successful and accomplished all and more than *was expected of it*.[28]

11

Decade of Death

I
T WAS not—as some American soldiers called it—"a splendid, little war." It is estimated that in the course of the Filipino-American War, from 1899 to 1902, a quarter of a million lives was lost in the whole country. A total of 2,811 armed engagements has been recorded for the entire war. Direct casualties were some 25,000 Filipinos and around 5,000 Americans, a ratio of 5 to 1. Indirect casualties have been estimated at 200,000 Filipinos.

In the case of Cebu province, it is difficult to get at precise casualty figures, particularly for the Cebuano side of the war, owing to gaps in the records and the nature of the documents that have survived. U.S. reports are more reliable for American rather than Filipino casualties and insurgent circulars often underplayed Cebuano deaths and inflated enemy losses for propaganda purposes. I estimate direct war casualties in Cebu province, from 1899 to 1906, at 1,000 Cebuanos and less than 100 Americans.[1]

The war in the Philippines involved a great number of combatants. From an initial expeditionary force of 12,000 American land troops in July 1898, the U.S. occupation force expanded to 60,000 by the end of 1899 and then 75,000 by late 1900. It took over 125,000 American troops to suppress Filipino resistance to U.S. rule. We do not have complete records to show how many American soldiers were in Cebu throughout the war years. The average U.S. troop strength in Cebu province in 1900 was around 1,500 officers and men at any given point of time during the year. A third of this was stationed in Cebu City while the rest were posted in the various towns of the province, with San Nicolas, Naga, Dumanjug, Balamban, Mandaue, Danao, and Bogo as major stations.[2]

War was just one of the specters that stalked the Cebu countryside at the turn of the century. The Filipino-American War was fought in a time of exceptional crisis in the Philippines. The nineteenth century opened up the Cebu countryside to exogenous influences through the medium of expanding trade and population movement, resulting not only in prosperity for those sectors of society plugged into the market economy but also in ecological and economic imbalances that occasioned poverty and death. The movement of goods and persons, impelled by economic changes, occasioned the spread of communicable diseases. The intrusion of urban entrepreneurs and merchants into towns and villages resulted in new forms of exploitation and dispossession. The conversion of large tracts of land from the cultivation of food crops to cash crops (sugar, tobacco, and hemp) created strains in rural subsistence systems. In the nineteenth century, rugged Cebu was already a food-deficit area. Shortfalls in the supply of rice and corn had to be filled with grain importations from neighboring provinces and from as far away as Hong Kong and Saigon. Disruptions in agricultural production and transportation owing to the war were also aggravated by hoarding and accumulation in urban centers.

At the turn of the century, Cebu had a largely agricultural population living off an overworked, badly eroded, and highly segmented land. As early as the midnineteenth century, the forest area of the island had already been reduced to about 6 percent of the total land area.[3] Even at this time, Cebu was already the most densely populated island of the Philippines.

The nineteenth century—particularly 1883 and 1889—saw "crises of mortality" in Cebu province.[4] As one of the most exposed areas in the country, being an open port, Cebu was affected by the Philippine-wide cholera epidemics that raged in the colony at various times throughout the nineteenth century. Cebu was one of the affected areas in the cholera epidemic of 1888-1889 that claimed close to 100,000 lives in 20 provinces in the Philippines. Climatic conditions, the susceptibility of an impoverished rural population, and urban crowding, created fertile ground for disease and death.

The state of insurrection in Cebu from 1898 to 1906 sharply aggravated the situation. The revolution in 1898 left Cebu in dire straits. The Spanish bombardment of the city razed Lutao (the present Carbon market area) and a section of San Nicolas. Stocks of rice, flour, and other essential commodities were lost as fire destroyed shops and warehouses on Calle de la Escolta (M. C. Briones). The subsequent blockade of Manila, in the course of the Spanish-American War, disrupted shipping and the flow of goods. Responding to the crisis, the Catholic Church in Cebu had to undertake relief measures, petitioning for donations as well as procuring rice, flour, cloth, and other goods from neighboring provinces as well as from Hong Kong. From April to June 1898, the Catholic Church imported goods valued at 150,000 pesos, and distributed rice and corn to city residents.[5] The war between Cebuanos and Spaniards was brief but brutal. It is estimated that around 1,000 Cebuanos died in the anti-Spanish Revolution of 1898.

The war against the U.S. compounded the crisis. It unsettled the population, led to the abandonment and destruction of farms and properties, and occasioned food shortages and famine. Economic activities were disrupted by military blockades, confiscations, curfews, and restrictions on travel. The protracted, provincewide character of the Cebuano-American War made it more calamitous than the anti-Spanish hostilities. The U.S. campaign of suppression led to the burning in late 1901 of the poblaciones of Pardo, Mandaue, Catmon, and Tabogon, and the districts of Mabolo, Basak, and Labangon. In 1900, the Americans also burned the town of Sogod. As the fighting waxed and waned, towns were periodically deserted by their residents.

The period of U.S. occupation was marked by epidemics and other aberrations. A cholera epidemic devastated Cebu from 1902 to 1904. This began when the first case was reported in July 1902 (ascribed in one source to a disease-carrying traveler from Leyte and, in another, to a Japanese servant newly arrived from Manila). In the space of a few days, cholera spread from the city to nearly all the towns in the province. At first, cases numbered from 10 to 15 a day, until August when it increased to 30 to 43, with a rate of mortality approaching 50 percent. The height of the epidemic ran from July to mid-October 1902 during which, in Cebu City alone, there were 1,300 cases and 700 deaths. The epidemic waned and then waxed strong once more in 1903, in 1904, and again in 1905. From July 1902 to March 1904, there were 14,210 cases and 9,983 deaths in Cebu (in a total provincial population of 667,057), the second highest among provinces after Iloilo. The ratio of cases to the population ranged to as high as 1 to 46.[6]

Other diseases—malaria, smallpox, beriberi, tuberculosis, and leprosy—were prevalent and exacted a mortal toll on the population in the first years of the century. In 1902, there were 20,920 deaths in Cebu province, or a death rate of 32 per 1,000 population. Cholera and malaria accounted for 12,820 deaths. Mortality was highest in the capital of Cebu where the death rate was 100.2.[7] From 20 July 1903 to 31 May 1904, there were 19,923 deaths in Cebu province, making for a monthly average of 1,992 deaths and a ratio of 30 per 1,000 population. The greatest mortality was exacted by cholera (5,942 deaths) and smallpox (2,351). Leprosy was also a bane as public health authorities estimated the total number of lepers in the province in 1903 at 1,011.

American and Cebuano authorities adopted various measures to check the spread of the cholera epidemic. A detention camp to isolate afflicted persons—called Cholera Camp—was established in the suburb of Mabolo. Teams of *sanitarios* (sanitary inspectors) and policemen were fielded to search out and report cases, and houses where such cases were found were either disinfected (by gangs of sanitary workers using such disinfectants as lime or carbolic acid mixed with water) or burned. To quickly dispose of infected bodies, the dead were cremated by the authorities, often against the violent objections of relatives.

Plagues of locusts and rinderpest recurred from 1903 to 1906 and did extensive damage to cattle and crops. In 1903, the provincial governor reported that rinderpest destroyed "nearly all the cattle and carabao in this district."[8] In the rinderpest epidemic in 1904-1905, Cebu province lost 3,090 carabaos, 667 cattle, and 94 horses.[9] Medical inspector Dr. Arlington Pond reported that from January to August 1904 alone, rinderpest killed nearly 2,000 animals in just four towns north of Cebu City.[10]

A writer observed: "The problem of the shortage of the carabao was in great measure the root of the serious guerrilla warfare which took command of the islands for more than a decade."[11] The loss of essential work animals contributed to the further stagnation of provincial farms. In 1901, the carabao population in the Philippines was down to one-tenth of the normal number and the cost of a carabao shot up from 20 pesos to more than 200 pesos.

Droughts and typhoons also wreaked havoc on the provincial food supply. Droughts in 1902-1905 upset the agricultural cycle. In the first half of 1903, Cebu experienced one of the longest droughts in its history, destroying the year's corn crop.[12] In 1904, two crops of corn failed due to excessive rains in June and July 1904, followed by a prolonged drought from October 1904 to April 1905.

As though these calamities were not enough, a series of fires also struck Cebu City during this period. On 11 March 1905, for instance, fire razed the business district of the city, resulting in losses amounting to 1.7 million pesos.

Death and famine stalked the land. Many plantations and farms were abandoned or neglected because of the revolution and the war against the

Americans. An official report states that sugar production dropped from a high of 300,000 piculs before the revolution to 15,000 piculs in 1904. The output of other agricultural products, such as tobacco, decreased by half.[13]

Turn-of-the-century reports depicted the effects of social dislocation. In late 1899, there were reports of people in Naga eating only once a day, of children dying of starvation in Minglanilla.[14] The flow of food supply was disrupted because of the hostilities and the blockade enforced by U.S. naval gunboats to cut off traffic to hostile territories. The insurgents themselves curtailed the movement of goods to towns friendly to the Americans. We have glimpses of the straitened situation of the towns from documents that have survived. On 17 November 1899, Presidente Alejandro Ruiz of Argao wrote to the captain of the port of Sibonga, Lt. William T. Merry, for permission to send out the lorcha *Angeles*, owned by the Compania General de Tabacos (of which Ruiz was local agent), to get supplies since the people of Argao were suffering from hunger due to the blockade.[15] Again, on 1 August 1901, Presidente Ruiz sent an urgent message to the military governor of Cebu, saying that the situation in Argao was "deteriorating by the day," this time because the town was blockaded by insurgents under Gaudencio Saniel, who were collecting the grains and other food supplies in the surrounding countryside. Ruiz asked for additional American troops to be stationed in his town and that arms be supplied to the local police so they can go after the insurgents.[16] Other towns were in the same straits as Argao. On 28 June 1900, Presidente Ruperto Buenconsejo and the council of Dalaguete also sent to the capital a petition, raising the problem of hunger in the poblacion because of the American blockade and seeking permission to have townspeople go out in boats to procure rice from other towns.[17] In the face of the acute food shortage in the towns, the U.S. Army, in mid-1899, distributed rice to the affected areas. However, the Army decided not to send relief to unfriendly areas because of fear that the rice would be diverted for use by the insurgents. Relief measures adopted by the authorities proved woefully inadequate to the situation.

In his report on the situation of the province, dated 1 January 1902, Governor Llorente said: "The actual or present condition of the pueblos of this province could not well be worse than it is. The roads, streets, squares, wharves and bridges are in bad condition; and the people have suffered from every kind of calamity, from war, rinderpest, smallpox, and locust plague."[18]

In 1903, Governor Climaco reported that people were "obliged, in order not to die of hunger, to wander about the forests and mountains in search of roots with which to feed their families. . . they cannot find work with landed proprietors... or emigrate to other points as it would be necessary for them to have a little money to leave with their family or for travel expenses if they take their family with them." The governor said: "It is impossible to get at the number of persons suffering hunger, but it is estimated that two-thirds of the inhabitants of the towns of this province live only on bananas, tubercles, buri meal, and shellfish in small quantities."[19]

Beggars were seen roaming the towns, schoolteachers were approached by people begging for work, brigands carried off food supplies, residents tore apart furniture or houses to sell in the towns as firewood, and deaths were reported from the eating of tubers that are poisonous when not well cooked.

The provincial government had to initiate public works to generate emergency employment at 20 centavos daily wage (half the normal wage), payable either in cash or rice. About 1,000 to 1,500 men were employed in the construction of the Cebu-Toledo road at a rate of 25 centavos a day. In 1902-1903, conditions were so bad for Cebuanos that paying taxes, according to the Cebu governor, had been "extortion and anguish equivalent to the taking of bread from the mouths of their children, who perhaps are lying in a critical condition with the mortal or icy breath of famine upon them."[20] On 13 September 1905, the Philippine Commission ordered the remission of the land tax for the year 1905 due to an "unprecedented drought" in Cebu province which had resulted in crop failure and "great hardship" to the inhabitants of the province.[21]

Social instability marked the first decade of the century. People felt menaced not only by famine and by death but also by strange, impersonal laws. When the local board of health undertook stern measures in 1902 to keep the cholera epidemic in check, there was a public outcry—even a public meeting of protest at Teatro Junquera—against the quarantine of infected homes and the forcible removal of the sick.[22] There were cases of people not reporting afflicted family members for fear that their loved ones would be carted away from their homes. When the Bureau of Health sent out inoculators as a measure against rinderpest, word spread in the villages that the Americans were sending out men to kill off the cattle.

Poverty and disease left the population enervated and with few resources to wage a long and active resistance against the Americans. The burning of houses and crops by the Americans drove an already weakened population to the ground. Indeed, the turn of the century was a time of death in Cebu. I estimate that, between 1898 and 1906, war and disease killed close to 100,000 Cebuanos—in a provincial population of around 600,000.

There were times when the city looked like some medieval city under siege: open wagons carried the dead to Carreta for burial, the night sky glowed as the infected houses burned, American soldiers patrolled the streets, and in many houses sounds of lamentations were raised. Under these conditions, an "end-of-the-world" feeling permeated popular consciousness and gave rise to social banditry and millenialism. In the backwoods of the island, prophets and strange men moved through the villages foretelling the coming cataclysm. At no other time in local history was the situation as desperate and death-haunted for Cebuanos.

12

Surrender of the Generals

WHEN THE Taft Commission established civil government in Cebu on 18 April 1901, there was the sense that the war was winding down. The insurgents were engaged in last-gasp efforts to sustain the resistance. Elsewhere in the country the situation was as bad. Emilio Aguinaldo, the head of the Philippine Republic, fell to American hands in the remote town of Palanan in northeast Luzon on 23 March 1901.

On 1 April, a week after Aguinaldo's capture, Juan Climaco issued a circular asking the Cebuanos not to be discouraged. The loss of a leader is a great loss, the well-worded circular said. However, "The moral strength or essence of the revolution rests on its ideals and conviction; likewise, its material strength or essence consists in cohesion and in the quantity of elements physical and moral for war." The Climaco pronouncement ended with the words of hope: *El Rey muerto, Rey puesto.*[1]

On 24 June 1901, Maxilom issued a proclamation recognizing Gen. Miguel Malvar as the successor of Aguinaldo. The proclamation declared that Malvar's succession has united again the revolution's "severed organisms, which have become loosened from the center of gravitation by the natural accidents of the war."[2] While eloquent, the declarations of the Maxilom government were borne of bravado rather than strength. In the early months of 1901, Maxilom's army had dwindled to less than 300 men. Continued Cebuano resistance was a reaction to American military intransigence rather than action based on any real hope of victory.

Early in the war, there was the sense among combatants and non-combatants that the Cebuanos could not win the war in purely military terms. Among many Cebuanos there was a desire for peace and a speedy termination of hostilities. On 28 July 1900, three prominent Cebuanos— Miguel Logarta, Gabino Sepulveda, and Pedro Rodriguez— wrote to the American military governor of Cebu proposing the formation in the city of a peace commission (*junta de la paz*) patterned after that "begun by prominent Filipinos in Manila" for the purpose of "pacifying" the province.[3] They wrote: "The said Junta de la Paz will devote itself to whatever work, material or moral, that will assist directly or indirectly in preparing the most honorable peace for this country." The commission proposed its agenda: first, to conduct periodic meetings to hear "the opinions of all and everyone of the most distinguished Filipinos of this province, and especially the local chiefs of the towns of the same," to ascertain "the legitimate aspirations of the natives"; and second, to contact the most important leaders of the resistance and discuss with them the possible grounds for a peaceful settlement. The signatories asked for authority from the military governor for them to undertake the work and convene the first meeting of the proposed commission (set to be held at a house on Calle Vasco de Gama [Sanciangco] in the city on 28 July 1900). Involved in these moves were other prominent city residents, including British consul John Sidebottom.

The Americans offered amnesty to insurgents sometime in the middle of 1900. Those who turned themselves in were required to take the oath of allegiance to the United States. The offer of amnesty included a payment of 30 pesos for each serviceable rifle turned in and free transportation to bring the surrenderee to his home if he is a resident of another province or lived distant from the place of surrender. Nothing, however, came out of these early efforts at bringing about a negotiated settlement since—in the case of the petition of the peace commission—the American governor would not accept any proposition except unconditional surrender.[4]

In April and June 1901, the hard-pressed insurgent leadership initiated moves for a negotiated settlement to the war.[5] On 15 April 1901, on the eve of the visit of the Taft Commission, Maxilom sent a letter to the American military governor expressing the desire for peace "compatible with our ideals and the dignity of citizens desirous of the liberty of their country." Maxilom offered to send a commission to negotiate a peace settlement and, in expression of good faith, outlined proposals for the organization of local government that the insurgent leadership hoped to present to the Taft Commission. The letter indicated a softening of the stand of the Maxilom government since it no longer raised the issue of independence. Instead, it focused on procedures in the organization of provincial and municipal governments in Cebu.[6]

Faced with the hard-line American position, however, Maxilom and his men had little choice but to continue fighting. Continued Cebuano resistance led the Americans to revise their policy on the extension of civil government to Cebu. On 17 July 1901, the Philippine Commission passed Act No. 173 returning Cebu to military control.[7] Officials appointed by the commission remained in office unless otherwise removed or replaced by the military governor. The writ of habeas corpus was suspended. Though civil courts continued to function, military courts were created and the military governor determined which court had jurisdiction over certain cases.

With the return of Cebu to military rule on 17 July 1901, American troops took to the field in earnest. Many of the American sorties at this time were plain killing expeditions. During a four-month period, from July to October 1901, when the insurgent surrenders took place, there were no less than 23 recorded encounters in various parts of the province, resulting in more than 100 Cebuanos killed and around 50 captured.[8] No American was reported killed. The encounters indicated it was clearly an unequal war. On 1 August 1901, soldiers of the Nineteenth U.S. Infantry, aided by the Argao police, attacked a group of men at a public dance in a barrio near Argao. The revelers were suspected to be insurgents and the Americans proceeded to kill 20. One American soldier and an Argao policeman were wounded. On 2 October 1901, men of the Nineteenth U.S. Infantry drove a band of "bolomen" into a cave near Dumanjug and killed 11 men. The only injuries sustained by the Americans were from stones hurled at them by the Cebuanos trapped in the cave. In some of the encounters, prisoners were killed as they reportedly "tried to escape."

On 15 September 1901, Gen. Robert P. Hughes was moved from Samar to Cebu to take charge of operations on the island. Hughes took personal command of Cebu from Lt. Col. James Miller. Two companies of Panay Scouts were also stationed in Cebu to assist in the pacification campaign. Hughes's policy was to open the door for insurgents to come but at the same time to maintain "a hot fighting in the field." His plan was to station troops in the towns fringing the island, and with the aid of the town police to whom arms would be supplied, would cut off sources of munitions for the insurgents. From the coast, the Americans would then run a line of independent mobile commands into the interior of the island to root out the insurgents.

Barely a week after Hughes's arrival, things were already "hot in the field." Judge Carlock wrote in his diary on 21 September 1901: "Gen. Hughes has begun very active campaign. Today, Basac, Labangon, and El Pardo are burning. While riding in San Nicolas we saw the roads lined with fugitives carrying many of their personal effects."[9] Subsequently, Mabolo and Mandaue were also burned in the course of the anti-insurgency campaign.

Hardline action by the Americans is illustrated in the anti-insurgency campaign in the Mandaue area. Mandaue had been a volatile area. On 7 September 1900, for instance, there was an insurgent raid on the poblacion that left five civilian residents with gunshot wounds.[10] An American soldier wrote: "Mandaue was one of the hot beds of the insurrection and... in no other place on the Island of Cebu were the people so unfriendly and treacherous and. . . they were constantly lending assistance to the insurgents in every way possible."[11]

A case that caused a great deal of concern among Cebuanos was the killing of the presidentes of Mandaue, Consolacion, Opon, and Cordoba. The mayors were Benito Ceniza, Cayetano Sosing, Vicente Baring, and Melecio Suson, respectively.[12] The killings took place in two separate but suspiciously similar occurrences. On 28-29 September 1901, the presidentes of Mandaue and Consolacion were arrested on charges of aiding the insurgents by men of a mobile command of the Nineteenth U.S. Infantry under First Lt. George I. Feeter. This was an independent command of 60 men of the Nineteenth Infantry and a company of Panay Scouts based in Parel Valley and operating in the country north and east of Cebu City. Sometime in September 1901, a captured prisoner of war, a *consejale* of Talamban, had told the Americans there was a "revolutionary committee" operating in the central zone of Cebu. The prisoner claimed that the presidentes of the central zone were actively supporting the committee by collecting funds and supplies for the insurgents.

With this information, Feeter proceeded to crack down on the "sympathetic" towns. On 23 September 1901, American soldiers and native scouts under Feeter burned houses in Mandaue. On 28 and 29 September, the presidentes of Mandaue and Consolacion were taken into custody. In the evening of 29 September, the two presidentes were taken out from their cell, under guard, to fetch water and corn for the horses of the Americans. They were gunned down "in consequence of their attempt to escape from the guard." An investigation into the killing was ordered by General Hughes after Fr. Emiliano Mercado, the Mandaue parish priest, reported the matter to higher U.S. military authorities.

In the morning of 6 October 1901, the presidentes of Opon and Cordoba, together with the Opon sergeant of police, were also arrested by Feeter's men for "aiding the insurrection." That same night, after undergoing interrogation by Feeter, the two presidentes were gunned down when they reportedly tried to flee from the Mandaue convent where the Americans and the prisoners were quartered. There was a public outcry against the execution of the four mayors. There were, however, no witnesses other than the soldiers who fired the shots and the American investigation of the case was closed with the conclusion that the killings were justified.[13]

The provincial government under Llorente played an active role in bringing the war to an end. The Llorente government believed that Cebuanos were inclined toward U.S. rule, were tired of the war, and needed American protection. Working in consultation with U.S. military authorities, Llorente openly worked to hasten the "pacification" of the province. The Americans demonstrated both their power and resolve to run resisters to the ground. Llorente shed off his hesitancy of the early days and acted resolutely in behalf of the Americans.

On 10 August 1901, Llorente issued a circular to the towns, urging them "most emphatically to prevent, by every means in your power, the inhabitants in your pueblo from assisting, with money or with kind, the insurgents in the field, for if your pueblo renders any assistance to the insurgent cause, it will be razed to the ground, and its authorities will be made prisoners."[14] Upon Hughes's arrival in Cebu in September, Llorente instructed the town governments to cooperate in the anti-insurgency campaign by sending information and providing assistance to the U.S. military.

On 23 September 1901, he again sent instructions to the town officials to gather their residents and have them choose between war and peace. He said that if they choose peace, they should render aid to the American troops in suppressing the insurgents. On 24 September, he sent another message, saying that "Pardo and Mandaue, and the district Mabolo, have been entirely destroyed" and that towns should consider themselves duly warned of the consequences of aiding the insurgents.

Because of these moves, town meetings were held in all towns, "except in the deserted pueblos of Tabogon, Sogod, Catmon, and in the recently destroyed villages of Mandaue and Mabolo." Llorente reported that the towns, seeing the large units of American troops, learning that some of the towns had been burned, and knowing that the insurgents could not defend them, hastened to join the American side.

Filipino losses in the field and the lack of unity in the resistance eroded the will to war. The time had come for a concerted civil-military effort to bring the insurgent leaders in. Llorente organized a peace commission composed of Valeriano Climaco, Tomas Osmeña, Miguel Logarta, Arsenio Climaco (who had already returned to the "fold of the law"), and Pedro Rodriguez. On the grounds of age and sickness, Valeriano Climaco and Tomas Osmeña asked to be excused from serving. In creating the commission, Llorente worked in close consultation with General Hughes and Judge Carlock.[15]

On 25 September 1901, the Department of the Visayas issued a circular designating a "neutral zone" for the meeting of "the committee of Señores of Cebu" and the "leaders of the *banditti* on this island." It was decreed that no American troops will enter the "neutral zone" and troops already in it will engage only in defensive action. The zone covered the area between Sogod and Liloan, extending two miles inward from the coast. Another circular also suspended for 10 days the destruction of the "property of the enemy," with the exception of war materials. A subsequent circular extended the effectivity of the neutral zone until midnight of 10 October.[16]

The peace commission embarked for Carmen on 26 September and then Danao where the commissioners set up shop. The commission stayed in the field for days conducting talks with insurgent leaders.

Juan Climaco, the "brains" of the resistance, surrendered in Carmen on 26 September 1901. As early as December 1900, Climaco and other leaders were hoping for a political settlement to what they saw was an unequal war. On 22 December 1900, "from the field," he wrote to a friend that he was a "partisan for peace" but that the Americans had put an obstacle to "peace with honor and dignity" because of their mailed-fist tactics of burning villages and devastating the countryside. At this time, Climaco was already an ailing man (*gipasahan sa gutum*, according to an account).[17] In early February 1901, his nephew and aide, Arsenio Climaco, himself reported to be ailing, surrendered to the Americans. The surrender was arranged through the intercession of Arsenio's aging father, Valeriano Climaco, and local partisans of the Federal Party. Arsenio was set free after taking the oath of allegiance and played an important role in negotiations for terminating the war.[18]

As early as April 1901, Juan Climaco was already in the process of effecting his surrender and was working with Segundo Singson (judge of the court of first instance) to get Maxilom to capitulate. In a letter "from the field" addressed to the military governor of Cebu, dated 27 April 1901, Climaco acknowledges a letter the governor had sent him on 16 April.[19] The letter indicates that arrangements were being worked out with Climaco acting as intermediary in negotiations for safe-conduct and amnesty. Undoubtedly, the establishment of civil government in Cebu at this time, with an almost entirely Filipino leadership, must have attracted Climaco.

The actual surrender of Climaco was occasioned by the government's drive for the towns to deny support for the insurgents. A "peace commissioner" of the provincial government had gone to the town of Carmen for an anti-insurgency town meeting, to convince the inhabitants to return to their homes and organize into a municipality. At this time, Climaco was sick and living in an outlying district of the town. Hearing of the result of the meeting, unable to move from place to place because of ill health, and fearful for his personal safety, Climaco decided to surrender.[20]

By October 1901, the Americans had broken the back of the anti-American resistance. On 4 October, 12 bolomen under insurgent chief Silvestre Cañete surrendered in Talisay. Between 8 and 20 October, 136 bolomen surrendered in Dumanjug.[21]

The appeal of the peace commission and the pressures of the American military campaign set the ground for the surrender of the entire insurgent leadership. Hard-pressed by the scorched-earth tactics of General Hughes, Maxilom called a meeting of his officers in the mountains of Natim-awan, Carmen, on 8 October. In this meeting, an insurgent commission—composed of Pantaleon del Rosario, Andres Jayme, and Melquiades Lasala—was formed to arrange the terms of surrender with General Hughes.[22]

On 9 October, Del Rosario, Jayme, and Lasala, accompanied by peace commission members Miguel Logarta, Pedro Rodriguez, and Arsenio Climaco, presented themselves to the American detachment in Danao. They were promptly picked up by the American launch *Troy* for the trip to the capital, arriving in Cebu City at around 4:30 P.M. to the rousing welcome of thousands of Cebuanos. The talks between Hughes and the insurgent delegates took place in the morning of 10 October at the offices of General Hughes on Magallanes Street. Also involved in the discussions were Governor Llorente and Judge Carlock. The insurgents asked for (1) pardon for military offenses, leaving each person to answer for common crimes; (2) restoration of the insurgents' civil and political rights; (3) the prerogative to appoint a committee to handle and dispose of property in insurgent possession; (4) license for the insurgent leaders to retain their sidearms; and (5) employment of insurgent soldiers in the Philippine Constabulary. General Hughes gave his word that surrenderees would not be deprived of their civil and political rights, specifically the eligibility to hold public office. (Subsequently, on 1 February 1902, the Philippine Commission passed Act No. 343 amending Act No. 78, which barred insurgents from public office.) As a result of these talks, an Acta de la Paz was signed by Hughes and Del Rosario.[23] On 12 October, orders for a ceasefire were issued by U.S. military authorities.

In the days that followed, resistance leaders Del Rosario, Lasala. Mateo Luga, Angel Libre, and Saturnino Echavez came in from the hills and were warmly received by city residents. With the end of the war, the city was in a festive mood. On 12 October, for instance, Pedro Royo tendered a big dinner for the insurrectos at his house on Calle Alfonso XIII (now D. Jakosalem). Among the guests were Judge Carlock, the Spanish consul, and various government officials.[24]

On 18 October 1901, in Barili, the insurgent leaders operating in the south and west coast of the province—Pantaleon del Rosario, Nicolas Godines, Troadio Galicano, Saturnino Echavez, and Francisco Rodriguez—met and formally accepted the propositions for peace laid down by General Hughes.[25] Other leaders also met in other places and accepted the terms of surrender.

In the days that followed, the formal surrender of the insurgent generals and their men took place. The prominent surrenderees are listed in the table following.

All in all, the Americans collected 132 rifles, 11 shotguns, 2 revolvers, and 5 cannons. This represented virtually the entire insurgent arsenal at the close of the war. There is no full record of the total number of men who surrendered in October. Available data, including the surrenders in Talisay and Dumanjug earlier in the month, indicate that around 700 men participated in the formal surrenders in October.[27]

Arcadio Maxilom, the head of the insurgent government, surrendered to Lt. John L. Bond of the Nineteenth U.S. Infantry in Tuburan in the afternoon of 27 October 1901.[28] He surrendered with 78 of his men and turned over 29 rifles, 4 cannons, 1 pistol, and about 40 bolos. Present at the surrender was Don Pedro Rodriguez of the peace commission who acted as intermediary in the surrender.

After his surrender, Maxilom was brought to the city where he called on friends and officials. Carlock wrote down his impression of the man when the head of the insurgent government paid him a visit at his home on 29 October: "Found him ignorant, fanatical, courteous, and bespangled with gold decorations on his flashy uniform."[29]

Subsequently, Maxilom was used by the Americans to convince other Visayan insurgent leaders, such as Dionisio Sigobela (Papa Isio) and Rufo Oyos of Negros, to surrender. In a letter to Papa Isio on 17 January 1902, Maxilom urged the Negrense leader to surrender, saying he would help arrange the terms of surrender. He said it was an act of patriotism to surrender as lives would be saved and a war so unequal ended. To surrender, Maxilom said, was to accede to "the wishes of heaven." In a postscript, he told Papa Isio that the Americans would pay 30 pesos for each rifle and 20 pesos for each revolver turned in.[30]

Others who participated in the surrenders in October-November 1901 were Lorenzo Eje, Alejo Miñoza, Gaudencio Saniel, Felix Aliño, and Potenciano Aliño. In early November 1901, four chiefs of bolomen also

LIST OF MEN AND ARMS SURRENDERED, 1901

Name	Place and Date	Men	Arms
Enrique Lorega	Guadalupe, 22 October	16	8 Remingtons, 1 Winchester rifle
Justo Cabajar	Guadalupe, 25 October	35	1 Krag, 1 Mauser, 2 Colt, 2 Remington rifles
Troadio Galicano	Barili, 26 October	115	1 Springfield, 1 Colt, 1 Murata, 7 Remington rifles
Mateo Luga	Guadalupe, 27 October	38	3 Krag, 2 Murata, 1 Colt, 10 Remington rifles, 4 shotguns, 1 brass cannon
Nicolas Godines	Dumanjug, 27 October	258	2 Krag, 1 Winchester 24 Remington rifles, 2 rifles of unknown make
Angel Libre	Dumanjug, 21 October		1 Springfield, 27 Colt, 2 Winchester, 3 Remington rifles, 1 rifle of unknown make
Arcadio Maxilom	Tuburan, 27 October	78	16 Remington, 2 Colt, 1 Mauser, 3 Springfield, 7 rifles of undetermined make, 4 shotguns, 4 cannons, 1 revolver
Saturnino Echavez	Dumanjug, 29 October		1 Winchester rifle
Francisco Rodriguez	Toledo, 31 October		1 Winchester carbine
Melquiades Lasala	Danao, 3 December		2 Krag, 7 Mauser, 3 Murata, 6 Remington rifles, 3 Remington carbines, 1 sporting rifle, 3 shotguns, 1 revolver[26]

surrendered in Bogo through the mediation efforts of Pedro Rodriguez, completing the pacification of the northern end of the island.[31] On 4 November 1901, the elderly Jacinto Pacaña and his son, Felipe, also surrendered in Consolacion. Jacinto was captured by the Americans on 23 November 1899 but apparently returned to the field to rejoin the struggle. He took his oath of allegiance to the U.S. on 9 November 1901. The Pacañas, among the original members of the Katipunan, were in the field for three years and seven months.

With the formal surrender of Lasala's men in Danao on 3 December 1901, nearly all the important insurgent leaders were accounted for. Throughout the war, the insurgent leadership had been decimated. Leoncio Alfon was captured west of Danao on 15 January 1900, imprisoned in Fort San Pedro, and convicted of the murder of a woman committed in the early days of the war. In one of the important losses of the war, Emilio Verdeflor, one of the leading generals of the republic, was killed at Gapur mountain on 7 December 1900 by soldiers of the Forty-fourth U.S.V. Infantry under the command of Major H. B. McCoy. Gervasio Padilla was captured in San Nicolas on 30 June 1900. He received harsh treatment. He was sent to Manila and imprisoned at Fort Santiago and would have been deported to Guam were it not for the suspension of deportations after Aguinaldo's capture.[32] Severino Enriquez and three of his men were captured by the Sibonga police on 11 April 1901 in the mountains back of Simala.[33] Enriquez took his oath of allegiance to the United States on 25 May 1901. The maverick Francisco Llamas, operating independently of Maxilom, surrendered in Talisay in 1901 and died in the same year of causes unknown to us.

There were exceptions. Marcial Velez and Andres Jayme stayed in the field after the October surrenders and subsequently moved to Leyte to help insurgents under Florentino Peñaranda until the fall of Vicente Lukban. Jayme surrendered to U.S. authorities in Maasin, Leyte, on 27 June 1902. Velez fled to Misamis and was captured sometime in July 1902.[34] The Aliño brothers, who had their own feud with the Maxilom government, did not reconcile themselves to the fact of surrender. Hilario Aliño refused to surrender and fled to Negros and was never heard from. On 22 October 1901, it was reported that the brothers Fermin, Potenciano, and Sulpicio had gone back to the hills with 30 men. Though they again surrendered to the Americans on 6 November, they continued to cause the authorities some trouble. Potenciano was jailed for *bandolerismo* in 1903 but was acquitted after a trial that same year. Sulpicio was also jailed on the same charges in 1903, convicted by the lower court, and released by the Supreme Court in 1905. Both Potenciano and Sulpicio (their brothers

Felix and Fermin had died in 1902) remained unorthodox in their politics in the years that followed: Potenciano as writer, associate of Vicente Sotto, and supporter of the Aglipayan Church, and Sulpicio as a Protestant involved in feuds with the Catholic authorities.[35]

With the surrender of the insurgent leaders, the war in Cebu was declared formally at an end. The provincial government reported that "peace and tranquillity have been completely restored throughout this island." The war was winding down all over the country. The "Philippine insurrection" was officially declared at an end by President Roosevelt. For many Filipino leaders, the sphere of action had clearly shifted from the field of war to the realm of politics.

On 17 December 1901, Governor Taft declared that "there was no military reason why civil government should not be reestablished in Cebu." On 20 December, the Philippine Commission passed Act No. 322 restoring civil government in the province of Cebu effective 1 January 1902. The gradual withdrawal of American troops also began. The following subposts were abandoned by the Americans on the dates indicated: Carmen, 5 January 1902; Talisay, 8 January 1902; Carcar, 11 January 1902; Sibonga, 17 January 1902; Toledo, 17 January 1902; Dalaguete, 18 January 1902; and Barili, 28 January 1902.[36]

On 3–5 February 1902, the first election for the governorship of Cebu was held in the city. For the occasion the vice presidents and councilmen of the towns were transported by steamer to Cebu. Election proceedings were held in the main assembly room of the Provincial Building on Calle Martires and participated in by 425 (out of a possible 570) delegates. The election process took all of three days since the officers of the election— presiding officer, secretary, and four tellers—had to be elected by secret ballot by the delegates.

There were two candidates: Julio Llorente, who had the support of the Americans, and Juan Climaco, candidate of the "nationalists." Climaco won handily with 249 votes against Llorente's 122. (It was found out that 35 delegates could not write but questions of eligibility were waived.) The election concluded with a round of speeches.[37]

Climaco was sworn in as governor on 3 March 1902. An American source claimed that Climaco won because insurgent elements actively backed him, "accompanied by secret threats by ex-insurgent officers toward delegates of unprotected towns."[38] A truer explanation for Climaco's victory, however, lies in a complex of factors: nationalist sentiments and the closer personal and social ties that Climaco— landowner, former town presidente, and member of a large and well-connected family— had with the municipal leaders who constituted the electorate.

Despite American reservations, Climaco provided no cause for concern among Americans. In his inaugural speech, Climaco affirmed the spirit of the new order: Filipino leaders were closing ranks, turning away from the adversarial politics of the war to a "partnership for progress" with America. Climaco called for work in the business of government, particularly in such areas as peace and order, public works, mass education, and the promotion of agriculture and industry. Of American rule, Climaco said: "We must engrave in our hearts that confidence and faith in the promises of the American nation to lead us to the goal of our liberties for they are sacred promises formulated by the conscience of its own people and before all civilized nations."

In the swell of American developmentalism, the Climaco government, and the provincial administrations that followed, was highlighted by the American promotion of popular education, public health, fiscal and bureaucratic reform, and public works—the improvement of the Cebu harbor and port facilities, the establishment of the Cebu railroad in 1906–1908, and the construction of roads, the most important of which was the intercoastal Carcar-Barili Road.

In a move to streamline public administration, the Philippine Commission, on 23 October 1902, passed Act No. 952, which reduced the number of municipalities in Cebu from 57 to 41. Twelve towns—Cebu, Mandaue, Liloan, Catmon, Dalaguete, Opon, Oslob, Samboan, Moalboal, Dumanjug, Bantayan, and Tudela—incorporated the territories of other municipalities, while 29 towns retained their existing jurisdictions.

After the insurgent surrenders, Cebuano leaders settled down to the business of governing local affairs under the new American order. From January 1903 to June 1904, the Cebu provincial board held 214 sessions and acted upon 1,082 matters. Over much of the same period, municipal councils in the province adopted 206 resolutions.[39] The city of Cebu itself (a municipality at this time) passed a total of 104 ordinances between 1899 and 1910. A review of these ordinances indicates preoccupation with the problems of sanitation and public safety, taxes and fiscal matters, and the control of such practices as gambling, vagrancy, prostitution, and the traffic in opium.[40]

Internal government reform was pursued through the purge of undesirable public officials. The purge highlighted not only American interest in an efficient civil service but also Cebuano predilection for litigation and politics. In 1902, during the Climaco administration, five municipal mayors were suspended from office due to charges filed against them.[41] Other officials, like municipal treasurers, were also involved in suspension proceedings during the year.

Cebu mayor Florentino Rallos was suspended twice. The first suspension stemmed from a melee at Teatro Junquera on 27 February 1902 during a theatrical performance.[42] It started when Vicente Sotto and the Spaniard Fidel Moas nearly came to blows after an argument. They were about to be brought to the municipio when local Spanish consul Guillermo Leyra and some Spaniards intervened. The consul allegedly assaulted the police to prevent them from taking Moas. Presidente Rallos appeared and quieted the crowd and ordered Moas and everyone else creating trouble to be taken to the municipal hall. This developed into a confrontation between Rallos and the Filipinos against Leyra and the Spaniards. Some American soldiers and other foreigners, many of whom were under the influence of liquor, took the side of the Spaniards. A commotion ensued with people brandishing sticks, cudgels, and a few revolvers. In the melee, Leyra fell wounded. Llorente, the governor at the time, stepped in and suspended Rallos on the spot. The incident was subsequently protested by the Spanish consul in Manila and the Spanish legation in Washington. Rallos was reinstated by Governor-General Taft on 9 October 1902 upon the recommendation of the provincial board.

On 10 August 1903, Rallos was again suspended. (Municipal vice president Filemon Sotto, who succeeded Rallos, was himself suspended from office for disobedience on 23 December 1903.) The suspension came in the wake of charges of falsification of documents and other irregularities.[43] It was charged that Rallos had Chinese businessmen arrested for opium-smoking for the purpose of getting them to pay fines to fatten municipal coffers, and that he failed to pay license fees for the cockpit he operated in the city.

American-style elections raised levels of personal and factional rivalries. Cebuanos took to elections with a great deal of zest. However, electoral activity focused on a parochial range of issues and had something of an intraclub quality as it mainly involved members of the local elite. In fact, the first elections were a contest of social and civic clubs rather than political parties. At this time, the Partido Federal had virtually disappeared from Cebu. What emerged instead was a whole range of sociorecreational clubs, each with obvious political and nationalistic overtones.[44] They were typically dominated by young ilustrados, many of whom had been uninvolved in either the revolution against Spain or the war against the United States.

This can be seen in the case of the elections in the capital municipality of Cebu. On 13 November 1903, in preparation for the general municipal elections of 1 December 1903, members of Club Gente Nueva, Kagauasan, and Mabini gathered to select their candidates and draw up a campaign platform.[45] They drafted a set of candidates led by Florentino Rallos, for president, and Filemon Sotto, for vice president. They also approved a platform that carried—together with *democracia* or "obedience to the will of the people"—the following planks: a water system for the city, campaign against gambling and vagrancy, children's education, a municipal cemetery and a good hospital, roads and bridges, and a larger and better-equipped police.

The other clubs in the city—like Club Popular (the leading club, founded in 1899) and Circulo Cebuano—contested the elections with their own candidates. Elected officials of the capital municipality of Cebu were Luciano Bacayo as president and Raimundo Enriquez as vice president. The elected councilors were Vicente Sotto, Pantaleon del Rosario, Troadio Galicano, Dionisio Jakosalem, Arsenio Climaco, Andres Roa, Mamerto Escaño, John M. Switzer, Manuel Roa, Esteban Manuel, Jose Rocha, Jose Vaño, Laureano Abella, Leoncio Tabasa, Andres Abellana, Cresencio Velez, Celedonio Mina, and Pastor Corro.[46]

Elections were warmly contested. Of the municipal elections in the whole province of Cebu, 35 were approved and six disapproved on grounds of irregularities. With undisguised condescension, a high-ranking American officer observed in 1902: "The prominent insurrecto leaders in Cebu are now occupying important provincial positions and they have not yet been altogether reconstructed. They are fast coming around, however, and with a vigorous hand to aid them I think the question in that province will soon be settled."[47]

In the poblaciones—particularly in the capital and among the "better-educated" segment of the population—there was acceptance of U.S. rule and the terms under which personal, local, and national aspirations had to be pursued. Preoccupation with the "new politics" was to characterize Cebuano public life in the years that followed. Judge Lyman Carlock said in late 1902: "The fact that Cebu is so tranquil within such a short time after the termination of the war is something remarkable. Everywhere the people are returning to their farms."[48]

Everything was not quiet in the land.

13

Face to Face

U NDER CONDITIONS of war, Filipinos and Americans carried largely distorted notions of each other, their perceptions shaped by their own cultures and the realities of conflict. In a translation of their experience with American blacks and Indians, many Americans carried with them the racist conceptions of the time and believed, with Theodore Roosevelt, that they were the civilized race come to one of "the earth's dark places." Many American soldiers saw Cebuanos as *niggers* and *Indians* and the war as "the subjugating and civilizing of an inferior people." Letters American soldiers sent home commonly depicted a shadowy, indistinct image of the natives in the towns or "in the bush." There was little personal contact and, for many soldiers, the stay in the Philippines was a temporary tour of duty in hostile territory and there was little occasion or interest to get to know either the place or its people.

Through adversarial lens, Cebuanos were described as "morose, idle and treacherous." It is easy to understand such judgments. In the state of war, the natives adopted the age-old "weapons of the weak": They avoided contact with the enemy, looked either impassive or outwardly friendly, engaged in petty sabotage (including laziness), and lied or feigned ignorance when questioned on the whereabouts of insurgents.[1]

In the guerrilla war of 1900–1902, the evasiveness and tenacity of the insurgents frustrated the Americans. An American soldier who fought in Cebu and Bohol in 1901 wrote: "We can burn them out and kill them one by one and thus quiet them down for a time, but the spirit of combativeness, born in their savage breasts, will never consent to remain quiet, and it is my belief that we can expect permanent peace only when the last Filipino plants his little brown feet on the golden shore."[2]

In 1903, American troops were to be found all over Cebu City and its environs. The main concentrations were in Fort San Pedro (referred to by the Americans as "the military reservation") and Plaza Washington (now Freedom Park). Fort San Pedro housed storerooms and the offices of commissary and the quartermaster. At Plaza Washington, the army had their headquarters, infantry barracks, and parade grounds. Later called Warwick (after a U.S. officer killed in Panay), the main structures were built of American lumber. Americans also occupied a portion of the nearby Recollect convent and grounds. On the road to Mandaue, American soldiers were stationed in a two-acre camp called Cholera Camp as well as in a small section of the Carreta cemetery. In the inner city, soldiers of the Twenty-ninth U.S. Infantry occupied a building in Parian. The Americans also maintained a building on corner Alfonso XIII (D. Jakosalem) and Calle Teatro (Colon) as an army hospital; another building on Calle Colon as a telegraph office and quarters of the Signal Corps; and the upper story of a building on Calle Infanta (Magallanes) as dental surgeon's office and operating room.[3]

Within Cebu City, high-ranking American officers socialized with "the better elements of the city" and attended parties and dinners in the wealthiest homes. The ordinary American soldiers had their own respite from the drudgery of camp life and the dangers of "insurgent-hunting" in the hills. In late 1899, American soldiers were already organizing variety shows featuring vaudeville acts and boxing exhibitions at places like Teatro Junquera and Club Popular.[4] In addition, soldiers indulged in ballgames in Plaza Washington. At the turn of the century, bars and restaurants mushroomed overnight, sporting such names as American Exchange, S. Francisco de California, and American Sport. English-language notices in *La Justicia* advertised "houses to let" and carriages and riding horses for hire.

Prostitution and liaisons between Americans and local women caused American authorities to worry about the high incidence of venereal diseases. With the large concentration of American troops in the city, there were, in the early years of the century, American and Japanese prostitutes, as well as camp-followers of other nationalities, maintained by local and foreign entrepreneurs (notably, recently discharged American soldiers). Some Japanese prostitution houses were to be found on Calle Pelaez, close to the quarters of U.S. officers. A medical check-up conducted in February 1903 showed 41 cases of venereal disease in the American detachment stationed in Cebu City.[5]

Health was not the only concern. Racist notions led American authorities to discourage or prohibit interracial marriage involving American soldiers and Cebuano women. American officials worried that the influence of "the tropics" and loneliness made their American boys susceptible to the attractions of women of undesirable blood and character.

In the towns, the Americans must have made quite an impression since rural Cebuanos had never seen foreigners in such large numbers. In mid-1902, for instance, there were three officers and more than 100 American soldiers stationed in Argao, an important military post in the province at the height of the war. (At this time, as base of field operations in southeastern Cebu, Argao also maintained subposts in Sibonga and Oslob.) In the Argao poblacion, the Americans leased six of the more substantial houses of the town (two-story structures of wood, with nipa roofing) for use as officers' and enlisted men's quarters, post hospital, quartermaster's storehouse, commissary, and guardhouse. Argao was considered a "friendly" town. An American officer remarked of relations with the townspeople thus: "These relations have been very amicable. . . the people think nothing of the soldiers except for what money they bring amongst them.... The people are docile and peaceful and apparently contented."[6] The Americans purchased food supplies locally—like rice, chickens, and vegetables. They were not, however, without commissary stocks brought in from the United States, from American beef and canned food to Castle Bros. coffee, raspberry and strawberry preserves, Ivory soap, and shaving sticks. While there were restrictions in the contact between soldiers and Filipino civilians, there were many occasions for interaction. Americans were invited into homes for the parties of which Filipinos were extremely fond; they patronized the local *tiendas* for liquor and native wine; and officers stayed in close contact with local officials, giving advice on matters like roads, taxes, and public sanitation. There was, of course, also the business of war: They conducted patrols in the neighboring countryside, collecting intelligence information, and arresting "suspicious-looking" persons (such as strangers or persons carrying the native pinuti).

Within Cebu City, there were strains in Filipino-American relations. Most of the recorded complaints against individual American soldiers were relatively minor in nature.[7] The most common were drunkenness and disorderly behavior, such that, in August 1899, the military commander in Cebu City ordered the closing of saloons and native liquor shacks at 10:00 P.M. and, in February 1900, prohibited (also on sanitary grounds) the sale of local liquor to soldiers. There were also complaints from citizens about fast and reckless driving of carriages by Americans on Cebu streets.

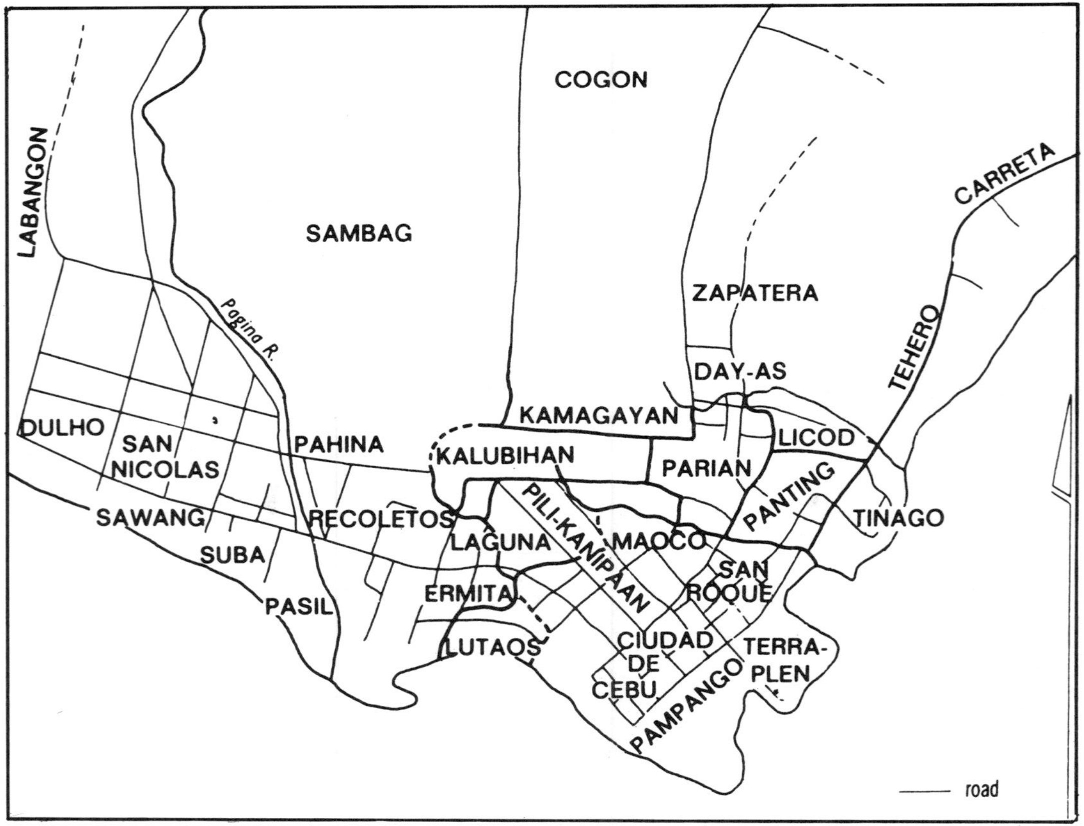

Districts of Cebu City, circa 1900

LABANGON

SAMBAG

COGON

ZAPATERA

CARRETA

TEHERO

DAY-AS

LICOD

PANTING

TINAGO

KAMAGAYAN

PARIAN

SAN
ROQUE

CIUDAD
TERRA-
DE
PLEN
CEBU

PAMPANGO

KALUBIHAN

PILI-KANIPAAN

MAOCO

LAGUNA

ERMITA

LUTAOS

Pagina R.

PAHINA

RECOLETOS

SUBA

PASIL

DULHO

SAN
NICOLAS

SAWANG

——— road

More serious were assaults on persons, illegal searches, and confiscation or damage to private property. There were cases of soldiers arbitrarily confiscating or appropriating rice, coconuts, and corn, or shooting pigs and chickens for food or sport. In search operations, American soldiers burned houses on mere suspicion that these were "insurgent lairs and storehouses." In response to such abuses, the military authorities in Cebu issued orders on 2 October 1899 prohibiting the burning of houses or other properties and the seizure of property except under great emergency, in which case receipts for confiscated property were to be duly given.[8]

On 6 February 1900, for instance, American soldiers on a scouting mission in Guadalupe came upon what they suspected to be "insurgent" houses. Finding only women, they proceeded to destroy stocks of rice and corn, "some gunpowder and ammunition," and confiscated six carabaos before returning to their camp in San Nicolas. On 16 January 1901, a force of 25 men under Lt. Leon Roach of the Nineteenth U.S. Infantry also searched and burned houses in the Talamban area while out on a reconnaissance sortie in the Lahug (Hoag) Valley.[9]

On 26 June 1901, Alfred E. Williams, a local sugar planter, filed a complaint with the U.S. military, saying that on 21–22 June 1901, American soldiers entered the Canlumampao Sugar Estate outside Toledo.[10] The soldiers gunned down two Cebuanos, set carabaos loose, appropriated poultry for food, damaged canefields, and maltreated estate workers. As a result, Williams reported, the workers fled and abandoned the estate.

Three cases of military atrocities acquired some prominence as a result of articles published in *El Pueblo* (29 June and 2 November 1902) and *Ang Suga* (30 June 1902), which called for the establishment of a military court in Cebu to investigate American abuses.[11]Consequently, the U.S. military reinvestigated three cases involving people of some prominence: the killing of the four Cebu presidentes, the use of the "water cure" on Cebuano prisoners, and the rape of two women and maltreatment of the priest and some citizens in Bogo.[12]

In one of these cases, two well-known citizens of Cebu City, Diego Cabrera and Filomeno Veloso, were arrested in the night of 24 August 1900 by American soldiers under Capt. Samuel C. Samuels, quartermaster of the Forty-fourth U.S.V. Infantry in Cebu. Veloso was the chief of police of Cebu while Cabrera was his immediate predecessor in this post. The affair started when Veloso was arrested by an American night patrol for carrying a revolver. (The American soldiers reportedly did not know that he was the police chief.) Veloso was brought before Captain Samuels in the U.S. barracks and was physically manhandled and given the "water cure." A revolver was forcibly thrust into his mouth, knocking out his teeth, and a lot of water poured down his throat so that the water flowed out of his nose.

That same night, around 10 American soldiers forced their way into the house of Diego Cabrera on Calle Gravina (now Lapulapu) on the basis of the information that Veloso's gun used to belong to Cabrera, the former chief of police. The soldiers threatened the occupants and searched the premises. (Some valuables were later reported lost.) Cabrera, who was ill at the time, was forced to go with the soldiers dressed in nothing but his drawers and undershirt. Also taken to the barracks was Cabrera's houseguest (who happened to be the provincial treasurer of Bohol) and a cousin. Cabrera was subjected to "water treatment" until he fell unconscious. The prisoners were released only the following morning when the misunderstanding was finally cleared up and Samuels, reportedly intoxicated at the time of the arrests, was reprimanded and confined to quarters.

The Maravilla case was much more serious.[13] The case stemmed from an insurgent attack in the night of 12 February 1901 on the American detachment in Maravilla (now a barrio of Tabuelan), an American military substation of San Remigio. It was a well-planned attack. Telephone wires connecting Maravilla to San Remigio and Bogo were cut before the assault. The attacking party, a large group of insurgent riflemen and bolomen under Recaredo Gonzales (chief of the First Fraccion), came at about 11:00 P.M. (Recaredo was the nephew of Florencio Gonzales, prominent Katipunan organizer of Cebu, who was executed by the Spaniards in April 1898 together with Recaredo's father, Fortunato.)

The American reports on the attack vary, with estimates of the size of the enemy ranging from 260 to 800, with from 60 to 100 armed with rifles. The detachment of 20 American soldiers was caught by surprise, as everything had been quiet in the area prior to the attack. As the residents of Maravilla had shown themselves friendly to the Americans, the soldiers were complacent. The night was warm, the soldiers retired early to sleep, and only one sentry was posted. Firing from the attackers came from the surrounding hills and the Americans found themselves hemmed in from three sides since Maravilla is situated in a cove with a range of hills touching the sea on either side.

After fighting for two hours, with their ammunition nearly spent, the Americans, shoeless and clad only in undershirts, hastily retreated to the sea, took a banca, and headed for Balamban. On the American side, three were killed (including two native helpers) and three were wounded. (A later American report exaggeratedly claimed that 80 insurgents were killed.)

Since the residents gave neither warning nor assistance, the Americans concluded there was complicity on the part of the town. The Americans arrested two prominent Bogo citizens, the brothers Magdaleno and Ceferino Ruedas, together with their wives (who, it was later charged, were made to do laundry duty for the soldiers and treated as common servants). The teniente alcalde of Bogo, Leoncio Mansueto (a cousin of insurgent leader Melquiades Lasala) was also arrested together with three other persons, including a tailor accused of supplying the insurgents with clothing. The parish convent of Bogo was searched and yielded, according to the American report, an insurgent's uniform and a Filipino flag.

There were allegations of the "water cure" being applied to the prisoners although a subsequent American investigation of the case absolved the U.S. officers and men involved. The leading military officer in Bogo, Captain A. S. Rowan, had been involved in a worse atrocity while stationed in the province of Bohol. An American corporal was assassinated by a Boholano whose girlfriend had been raped by the corporal. The Boholano was caught and killed, and Rowan also ordered the burning not only of the village of the Boholano but also that of the girl who was raped.[14]

Another case in Cebu was that of Fr. Emiliano Mercado (b. 1865), parish priest of Mandaue, who was tortured sometime in late 1901 by Lt. Geo. F. Feeter of the Seventeenth Infantry, the same officer responsible for the death of the four municipal presidents. Feeter tied Father Mercado's hands behind the back with a rope, one end of which was thrown over the beam of a fanlight, and in this manner strung the priest up to force him to give information. The maltreatment of Father Mercado was occasioned by nothing more than the discovery by the Americans of a store of rice in the convent basement. Feeter accused Father Mercado of supplying food to the insurgents despite the priest's explanation that he had received the rice from the vicar-general in Cebu for feeding the poor in his parish.[15]

The agitation of local newspapers and the involvement of prominent persons focused a lot of interest on these cases. Many other cases went unnoticed. Numerous American field reports suggest many cases of Filipinos killed or imprisoned on mere suspicion of being insurgents: carrying a bolo, refusing to act as a guide, transporting rice to the mountains, or "acting like a spy." On the other hand, the American strategy of denying the enemy shelter and supplies led to the loss or damage of houses, crops, and essential work animals, and aggravated the economic crisis of the time. The U.S. military campaign left behind a wide swath of destruction, most visibly indicated in the burning of the towns of Pardo, Mandaue, Catmon, Sogod, and Tabogon, and such districts of the city as Mabolo, Basak, and Labangon. U.S. military records do not reflect the actual cost of this campaign of large-scale destruction.

Still, there were Americans who believed that they did not carry out the war as harshly as they should have. Charles Crane, an officer assigned to Cebu in 1901, thought Cebuanos "the meanest in the islands excepting the inhabitants of Samar." Upon his return to Cebu in 1910, he found Cebuanos "still just as mean, and in need of good killing." He recalled how he had advised General Hughes not to listen to the insurgents who came in to negotiate surrender in October 1901, "telling the General that we had not then whipped those people sufficiently to make them willing to behave themselves as American subjects." He believed that "nothing but more defeating and killing of their leaders would have properly pacified Cebu."[16] The same view was expressed in 1901 by Maj. Henry T. Allen (who later became chief of the Philippine Constabulary), who said that if the men behind Cebu City's newspapers and "about twenty important men (mostly from the City of Cebu) were jugged like ordinary *tao*s we would make a good step towards complete pacification there." He observed: "From what I have heard the Cebu people do not admit that they have been *licked* and the city of Cebu contains a lot of young natives with swelled heads."[17]

A vain and pompous officer, Colonel Crane judged Cebuanos untrustworthy. When he was stationed in the city in 1910 after the hostilities, he limited his contact with local residents, hired only Chinese as household help, and spent much of his time, alone or with fellow Americans, on such pastimes as horseback-riding and snipe-hunting in the city's outskirts. When he was reassigned to Cebu in 1912, he was unhappy about the attitude he found among Cebuanos and constantly complained about incidents of stoning of American soldiers and harassment of Americans by the local police. In a letter to Provincial Fiscal Andres Borromeo on 10 May 1912, Crane said:

> We Americans do not expect the natives of these islands to
> love us yet. It is still too early for that. But we have hope, by
> perseverance in our efforts to improve the condition of the
> entire Archipelago, first to outlive the absence of good will on
> the part of the native and finally to win evidence of a friendly
> disposition towards us from the great body of the Filipino
> people.[18]

He complained that the people of the city of Cebu—"more so than Filipinos elsewhere"—have shown "decidedly an unfriendly feeling toward us." Even outside the city, this was so. Crane mused that no longer did the children hail Americans as they did in the past with the friendly greeting of "Hello, boy."

Many American officers had an arrogant and patronizing attitude toward the Filipinos. In a U.S. Senate investigation in 1902 into possible U.S. military atrocities, the commanding officer of the Visayas, General R. P. Hughes, made light of the burning of Filipino houses by saying that these structures, after all, cost only between $1.50 and $4.00 and took only a few days to construct. He justified injuries done to women and children in these burnings by saying that this was an effective way of punishing the men. Hughes (described by an American scholar as "a soldier of marginal understanding and limited ability") had a cavalier attitude not only towards Filipino life and property but also towards Filipino intellectual capacity. As provost marshall of Manila, he headed the American panel in negotiations with Filipino leaders in January 1899 before the outbreak of hostilities. In a subsequent testimony to a U.S. Senate committee, he said that Filipinos thought independence was "something to eat" and that all Filipinos really wanted was "to go to cockfights, gamble, and whet up their bolos."[19]

However, other Americans made a genuine effort at sympathetically understanding the society and, for this reason, gained the confidence and respect of Cebuanos. One such man was Judge Lyman J. Carlock, a young lawyer from Illinois, who came to Cebu on 2 July 1901 to assume the post of judge of the court of first instance. A respected official, his sudden death from cholera at the age of 35 on 19 April 1903 was mourned by city residents.

A few Americans crossed the line towards advocacy of Filipino causes. We know of two cases of American defections to insurgent ranks. In October 1900, a Private James Cupples of the Nineteenth U.S. Infantry was arrested for desertion "with intent to join the forces of the enemy."[20] A more dramatic case was that of Pvt. Frederick M. Baker of the U.S.S. *Charleston* who deserted on 30 June 1899, before the outbreak of hostilities. He went to Compostela, placing himself under insurgent leader Apolinario Diel, then found his way to Bogo where he acted as a captain of a Cebuano guerrilla band, headed by Melquiades Lasala, which was under the patronage of Don Pedro Rodriguez. Baker won some local fame for his daring as a guerrilla. With Mateo Luga, he led a raid in the vicinity of Calle Manso (now Bonifacio Street), close to the heart of the city, in the night of 22 April 1900. He spoke Spanish, learned Cebuano, and had a fiancée in Bogo. After a battle in Guadalupe in which he participated, the Americans were said to have recovered clothes in which were found "very poetic" letters he had penned for the woman in Bogo.[21] Baker surrendered to the U.S. Army on 4 May 1900.[22]

Fed by ignorance, the spirit of resistance, as well as the anti-American propaganda of the Spaniards in the days of the Spanish-American War, Cebuanos also demonized the *Yankis*. The "hillfolk" were said to have believed that Americans are "black and eat children and live on babies."[23] In the cholera epidemic of 1902, there were rumors that deaths were caused by the poisoning of drinking water by Americans and other foreigners. A *pasquin* on the wall of a house on Calle Infanta called for death to American *inspectores* and poisoners.[24] There was reported resistance to the census among the folk in the belief that this was for the purpose of imposing more taxes, and people in the countryside were suspicious that the traveling vaccinators of the Bureau of Health were agents out to kill the people's cattle.

There were those who looked up to Americans as carriers of an advanced culture and saw mirrored in America their aspirations for progress. This, in many ways, engendered myopia about native realities. In the middle of the brutal American pacification campaign under General Hughes, Escolastico Duterte wrote an open letter to his fellow Cebuanos on 30 September 1901 in which he saluted the American flag, endorsed the pacification campaign, and lamented the death of American soldiers so "we can live in peace." He attacked the "Cebuano nationalists" for acts of rapine and praised American conduct in the war, saying that all these proved "Americans know how to govern whereas Filipinos do not." He declared: "Long live the brave army of the United States."[25]

Among city residents, resistance to U.S. rule was muted and, at times, seemed mere dalliance with the limits of censorship. *El Nuevo Dia*, the newspaper of the prominent young triumvirate of Rafael Palma, Jaime C. de Veyra, and Sergio Osmeña, adopted a largely moderate, conciliatory position. Some of its items were censored by the Americans (prior censorship of newspaper articles was in force) and, once, left with no fillers for rejected articles at presstime, the editors decided to just invert the print molds of the censored items. The paper thus appeared with dark spaces (where the censored items would have been) when it hit the streets. The editors liked the effect and decided to follow the same procedure as a subtle form of protest whenever items were rejected by the American censor. The American censor at the time, Frank McIntyre (secretary to the Cebu military governor, who later became chief of the Bureau of Insular Affairs in Washington, D.C.), saw what the editors were up to and meted *El Nuevo Dia* a two-week suspension.

Vicente Sotto's newspapers—*La Justicia, El Nacional, Ang Suga, El Pueblo*—gave the American censors more cause for worry. Sotto found himself in frequent trouble: charged with sedition, accused of being a revolutionary agent, was jailed, and his newspapers suspended. In 1900, he was charged with sedition and levied a fine for the short story, "Ang Gugma sa Yutang Natawhan," which approvingly depicted the assassination of an American collaborator.[26] In 1903, he was again hailed to court for sedition for an editorial he wrote condemning the maltreatment of political prisoners in Fort San Pedro. (There was basis for the complaint. In October 1903, two pulahanes jailed in the fort died of beriberi because prisoners had to sleep on the cold ground. Earlier, in May and June 1901, it was also reported that 26 prisoners died of beriberi inside the fort.)[27]

Sotto also taunted the censors with his work in the theater. Two plays of his, *Ang Paghigugma sa Yutang Nataohan* (1902), considered the first modern, realist play in Cebuano, and *Elena* (1902), avoided confronting U.S. rule directly by dealing with the anti-Spanish revolution. By raising the themes of foreign rule and native patriotism, however, the plays invited viewers to reflect on current conditions. When *Elena* was staged in Teatro Junquera (on Colon Street) in May 1902, the American inspector of the local constabulary objected to the display of the Philippine flag.[28] These productions, however, did not attain the level of notoriety that the "seditious zarzuelas" had in Manila and environs, in part because of a largely conservative Cebuano audience. It is to be noted that in Manila Tagalog playwrights, like Aurelio Tolentino and Juan Matapang Cruz, played largely to working-class audiences. In Cebu, the working class was smaller, less organized, although Vicente Sotto tried to mobilize worker support. As head of Club Kagawasan, Sotto organized *zapateros*, escribientes, and other workers into mutual protection guilds. He conscripted workers in his paper and printing press as cast and personnel for his stage productions.

With centuries of experience with Spanish rulers, Cebuanos had a store of knowledge for coping with the Americans. On the other hand, U.S. initiatives in public welfare broke down barriers of hostility and mistrust. This is evident particularly in the area of public education. The war disrupted the operation of schools and, for a time, the U.S. Army had control over the educational system. Prior to the arrival of the first professional American teachers in late 1901, some American soldiers did work in Cebu as English teachers. Civilian control of public education was returned when the Bureau of Public Instruction was established on 21 January 1901. By 1903, there were around 24 American teachers in Cebu province.

The "Americanization" of local society had begun. In 1903, Cebu City had a registered population of 18,330 (while adjoining San Nicolas had 12,749). The main commercial district covered several blocks and was alive with commerce. Chinese shops, European bazaars, Filipino eateries, and other commercial establishments were concentrated on Calle Magallanes and its tributary streets. The Americans occupied some of the best houses in the city for many of the best residences (some 30 of the around 180 permanent structures in 1902) were leased by Americans as offices or living quarters for officers.

Cebu City was the nerve center of American military operations on the island and a naval base for the American gunboats plying the Visayan waters. Early in 1902, a military telephone line connected Cebu to Talisay in the south and Danao in the north. Telegraph wire connected the city to all garrisoned towns as far south as Oslob and, by branch line via Sibonga, to Dumanjug and Balamban on the west coast.

From 1899 to 1902, with hostilities still in progress, Americans patrolled the city streets. At night, these streets were dark, as there was no electric service in the city. In other respects, life went on normally. There were entertainments like barrio or district fiestas, the regular *serenata* of the Banda Municipal at Plaza Maria Cristina, and occasional performances of visiting troupes (such as the Circo Filipino at Teatro Junquera in April 1900). Four newspapers—*El Nuevo Dia, El Pueblo, Ang Kaluasan,* and *Ang Suga*—competed for readers. Off-duty American soldiers hung out in the city's saloons, restaurants, or hotels (Hotel Recoleto, operated by Rudolph Klapperhalz, or Hotel New Century, owned by Isidoro Aldanese). The favorite meeting place for Cebuano politicians and pundits of the time was Club Popular but, by 1900, the Americans had established their own club, the large nipa-and-wood country-style structure by the sea (near Fort San Pedro) called Army and Navy Club (later, United Service Club).

American culture was beginning to make inroads into Cebuano society. English reading matter was available at Libreria de Moas on Colon Street and makeshift *cinematografos* showed reels of foreign films. English lessons were being given at Club Popular in 1899 under Eugenio Cordero, a government interpreter, and by Josephine Bracken-Abad (Rizal's widow who had married a Cebuano) at her residence on Calle Magallanes near Plaza Rizal.[29] In schoolrooms, children could be heard singing "patriotic songs of America" in the English language.

14

The Underside of the War

WAR HAS a way of turning the world "upside down." Unhinging social relations, putting them under stress, war reveals society's underside where contend dark human tendencies and bright visions of new social possibilities. This fact stands revealed in the action of the "folk" in times of exceptional stress. Such times have been witnessed by Cebuanos at various points in local history. It was at the turn of the century, however, that rural ferment was most pronounced. The stress of rapid social change combined with the experience of plague, revolution, and war gave many Cebuanos the sense that the foundations of their familiar world were shaking under their feet.

At the beginning of the Cebuano insurrection against Spain, only a small percentage of the provincial population had received a modern education. Cebuanos practiced a Catholicism permeated with animism and elements of an older religion. Through the nineteenth century, economic changes had led to the peasantization of Cebu, infusing rural dwellers with some understanding of a larger economic and political world but, at the same time, transforming them into dependents as urban entrepreneurs acquired large tracts of ancestral land for the cultivation of cash crops for an expanding world market. The contracosta and northern part of the province, particularly the stretch from Barili to the north and around the island to Borbon—a primary source of insurgents and social bandits—was opened to sugar cultivation and commercial exploitation as early as the 1870s.

Given this situation, the revolution against Spain could not but be many sided for while there was a widely shared animosity against Spanish rule there was also ground for class-based resentment against the native elite. When authority broke down in many places in 1898, peasants rushed in not only to strike against Spanish rule but also against native overlords. What the revolution unleashed was not a single, cohesive nationalist movement but a Hydra-headed resistance expressive of a mix of religious, social, and political motives. At certain points, various motives came to be subsumed in the imperatives of opposing Spanish power and, later, U.S. occupation; yet, the complexion of mass resistance was highly diverse and problematic.

To what extent, for instance, was the Katipunan society in Cebu organized around modern libertarian ideas? While libertad (*kagawasan*) and the more political notion of independencia were the main organizing ideas of the resistance, people did not have the same understanding of what these concepts meant.[1]

The fact that the revolution was heavily permeated with religious (both Catholic and animist) ideas indicates that folk moral notions were intertwined with ideas of a modern political and civil order. It is intriguing to consider that the Katipunan in Cebu was organized by men associated with the Bonifacio rather than the Aguinaldo faction of the revolutionary society. The Bonifacistas gravitated around the peasant and proletarian elements of the revolution and were more strongly oriented towards folk ideas than the more gentrified Aguinaldo faction. The initial links of the Cebu revolutionaries in 1897–1898 were with such Manila-based Bonifacistas as Gil Domingo and Hermogenes Plata.[2] The first carriers of Katipunan ideas in Cebu were seamen, artisans, and socially marginal personalities.

Katipunan activities in Cebu were strongly infused with religious symbolism, animated by a belief in initiatory rites and amulets, and led by men believed to be invested with supernatural powers. The Katipunan uprising in Cebu was originally scheduled to take place on a Good Friday (8 April 1898), a true "time between times," the Day of the Lord's Death, when the world was charged with cosmic possibilities. On the eve of Holy Week, the Katipunan leaders went on a pilgrimage to Opon, across the channel from Cebu, to pray before the black-faced Virgin of the Rule (Nuestra Señora de la Regla), an object of popular veneration in the Visayas. This movement of pilgrims caught the attention of the authorities and was one of the factors that led to the Spanish discovery of the plot of a Holy Week rising, the early arrest of some of the plotters, and the decision of the Katipunan to advance the uprising to 3 April.

In the initial flush of victory on 3 April, the revolutionaries shouted the victory cry of "Viva Santo Niño!" and had a mass celebrated in thanksgiving.[3] Animist elements flowed freely into Catholic observance. Amulets and *oraciones* were ubiquitous in the revolution and were not just tools for mass mobilization but were emblematic of the revolution's ideological underpinnings. Their importance is repeatedly stressed in the popular accounts of the revolution.[4]

Katipunan members in Cebu carried symbolic names: Pantaleon Villegas was Kilat; Luis Flores, Unos; Eugenio Gines, Lindol; and Alejo Miñoza, Suot. They underwent an initiation ceremony similar to the rites of the Tagalog Katipunan. The initiate was blindfolded and then asked a series of questions to test his commitment to the cause. After the initiate had passed the test, his blindfold was removed—in the transition from the "darkness" of ignorance and oppression to the "light" of knowledge and freedom—and the new Katipunan member was given amulets for protection. Extant descriptions of such ceremonies are sketchy: There are references to tests of courage and to Leon Kilat, the legendary Katipunan leader, shooting at the initiate with a pistol to show that the initiate's amulet had made him invulnerable.[5]

There were several kinds of amulets. One was a triangular piece of paper, with Latin words, placed on the forehead, the brim of the hat or, (in the case of women) on the breast. Another was a circular piece of paper, like the Host and thus called Hostia Redentora, also with Latin inscriptions, which was placed in the mouth at the time of battle. A third kind was the *hanig*, a piece of cloth that was to be worn like a vest or chasuble. On it were Latin words and drawings of God the Father, the Apostles, and angels in martial poses. A variant was a piece of cloth, with similar writings and drawings, worn around the stomach or around the forehead like a scarf.[6] With such amulets, the wearers were to become invulnerable to bullets and would experience neither hunger nor thirst during battle.

Together with these amulets, there were ritual proscriptions to ensure the efficacy of the amulets. Women should let their hair hang loose during battle. Money and metal objects should not be carried in the pockets during combat. Oraciones (prayers) were to be recited or chanted as talisman against death and danger.

Pantaleon Villegas (Leon Kilat), the military leader of the Katipunan, is a figure associated with these amulets and prayers. His central position in the revolution underscores the importance of the mystic aspects of the struggle. A native of Bacong in Negros Oriental, Villegas (1873–1898) came to Cebu sometime in the early 1890s and was variously employed as baker's apprentice, druggist's assistant, messenger, and horse jockey.[7] Fulfilling the life-pattern of a *picaro*, he was said to have joined a Tagalog circus troupe that had stopped in Cebu and was, it turned out, owned by a member of the Katipunan. The young Villegas was brought to Manila where he joined the revolutionary society, learned the "occult science" (*ciencia oculta*), and participated in the Tagalog hostilities of 1896. Other accounts claim that he was already a participant in folk revivalist movements while a young man in Negros. His name is mentioned in association with the revivalist movement of Ponciano Elopre (Buhawi) in Negros; and to him was attributed such powers as disappearing at will, swallowing swords, and flying on a magic handkerchief.[8]

Villegas was sent by the Katipunan to Cebu in March 1898 to help organize the Cebuano insurrection. A popular account describes the anticipation that awaited his arrival in terms suggestive of a Second Coming.[9] This was very much a part of the ideological climate of the time: there was the folk belief, for instance, that Jose Rizal did not die in Bagumbayan but was alive and would appear to herald his people's redemption.

The revolution stirred the consciousness of the masses. Accounts of the early phase of armed resistance in such places as Carcar, Toledo, and Tuburan indicate how quickly the rural dwellers were stirred into action. Peasants, *gente plebeya*, hillfolk, bukidnon, mountain people: they formed the bulk of those who actively resisted the Spaniards and then the Americans. They were led by folk personalities, to whom was attributed *kalake* (extraordinary powers), and who, at certain points, worked at cross-purposes with the ilustrado leaders of the resistance. The folk attributed supernatural powers to such insurgent chiefs as Francisco Llamas, Hilario Aliño, and Martin Cabuenas.

The guerrilla war waged by scattered bands in the Cebu countryside may have had roots going even deeper in time to older socioreligious revolts against the Spanish order, the flight of *montescas* and *remontados* (discontented hamlet dwellers who fled to the hills either to escape the authorities or the constraints of town life), and the social tensions that existed between lowlanders and mountain folk, between peasants and lords.

There is the case of Claudio Bakus (called Claudio Bukidnon), the "fierce and brave" fighter who operated in the Toledo-Balamban area in the anti-Spanish uprising. At the head of "hundreds of rebels," he and his men occupied the outbuildings and warehouses of the Canlumampao Sugar Estate near Toledo on 19 April 1898. The rebels did not harm the American estate owners, Alfred E. Williams and his mother. Claudio was believed to be invulnerable and his powers were attributed to a red flag he carried. In late April, however, a Spanish force engaged the rebels in battle, killing some 40 men and scattering the rest. The Williamses were arrested by the Spaniards for giving aid to the insurgents and brought to Cebu where they were released only after the intercession of the British-American consul John Sidebottom.[10]

Another folk leader was known only as Bando. He led "people from the mountains" in the Asturias-Balamban area. He operated independently of the insurgent Flores government. He had an *anting-anting*, was a skilled swordsman, and "could leap from hill to hill." He continued to operate independently in the early part of 1899 when the republican government was already in control of Cebu. Sometime in 1899, he was killed in an encounter with the troops of Gen. Emilio Verdeflor in the hinterland of Balamban.[11]

In short, the anti-Spanish revolution was not a single, uniform movement of men sharing the same political ideas and visions of society. The widespread use of amulets and oraciones and the presence of such folk-figures as Leon Kilat, Rafael Tabal, Bukidnon, and Bando attest to a strong folk religious element in the resistance. The revolution and the subsequent overthrow of the Spanish government turned society "upside-down" and created a vacuum into which rushed forces other than those represented by the ilustrado leadership of the revolution.

Religious certitudes were also shaken by the war. Anti-friar sentiment spawned a rebel Catholic Church in the Philippine Independent Church led by Bishop Gregorio Aglipay. Aglipayanism was publicly launched in Cebu with a rally at Plaza Rizal on 12 July 1903, attended by Aglipay himself. The introduction of Protestantism and the resurgence of millenarianism also sharpened religious conflicts. From 1900 onwards, Vicente Sotto's *El Pueblo* (1900–1904) and *Ang Suga* (1901–1912) and the Catholic *Ang Camatuoran* (1902–1911) aired debates on religious questions as the hegemony of the Catholic Church came to be challenged by competing beliefs.

The Catholic Church was on the defensive as there was a great deal of antifriar sentiment in the city. On 13 September 1901, for instance, the Cebu provincial board passed a resolution requesting the expulsion of the friars from the Philippines.[12] On 22 March 1902, on the occasion of the visit to Cebu of Governor-General Luke Wright, around 500 people, led by Vicente and Filemon Sotto and Alfredo Mercado, participated in an antifriar rally at Teatro Junquera. In the street march that followed the rally, the demonstrators shouted in front of the Recollect convent: *"Papahawa-on ang mga fraile—Mabuhi ang America!"* The demonstrators then proceeded to Carlock's house in San Nicolas (where Wright was billeted) where they formally presented to the governor-general their demands for the expulsion of the friars.[13] There was also agitation for the sequestration of the Augustinian estates of Banilad, Talisay, and Minglanilla.

While most actions were directed against the friars, many high-ranking members of the secular clergy felt called upon to defend the church and the orders.

The revolutionary takeover in 1898–1899 unhinged the social order. Both on the eve of the Spanish withdrawal and that of the American landing, there was fear among propertied city residents that the "hill-men" would come down and sack the city.[14] Within the ranks of the revolutionaries, tensions surfaced in the conflict between the *taga-patag* (lowlanders) and *taga-bukid* (mountain dwellers) over such issues as the insurgent occupation of the city, leadership in the new government, the treatment of collaborators, and the surrender of the city to the Americans.

We have indications of the disturbed situation from the report of a person who identifies himself as a "commissioner of Cebu" and "assistant delegate to Sr. Julio Llorente."[15] In his report to Aguinaldo on 19 February 1899, he said that in his trip to the northern towns (to prepare them for local elections scheduled for 19 February under the provisions of the Superior Decree of 18 June 1898), he found some of the towns in disarray because of the activities of the "fringe elements" of the revolution. He found the district of Talamban demoralized by the fear of "the mountain tribes" of Sudlon who attacked and maltreated Talamban residents. As a result, many people had fled from their homes. He said that similar anxieties ruled in other places over the arbitrary acts of "so-called Captains, Majors, Colonels, Generals, and Captains-General" who have confiscated horses and carabaos. In Bantayan island, the commissioner reported, a self-styled "expeditionary commander" had installed himself as local chief and was forcing people to support him and his band of 50 men.

Other reports provide us with glimpses of a "war within a war" in the resistance against the Spaniards and the Americans. At the time when the Americans were still confined to Cebu City, Fausto Tabotabo, a big landowner in Tuburan, wrote to the editor of *La Justicia* on 24 June 1899 that there was anarchy in the towns because of the "impotence of constituted authorities." He complained of the agitation of the mountain people and the problem of robberies, burnings, rustling, and sequestrations.[16]

It is clear that there were tensions left unhealed by the establishment of the republic in Cebu. This is not surprising. In many Cebu towns in the nineteenth century, the visible elite was Filipino (mostly Chinese mestizo) and usually the only Spaniard to be found in the town was the parish priest. Outside of the friar estates of Cebu, Mandaue, and Talisay, the big landowners were Filipino, many of whom moved into the countryside only in the nineteenth century, impelled by the economic opportunities made available by commercial, export-oriented agriculture. Equipped with capital, entrepreneurial skills, and knowledge of wider economic and bureaucratic systems, they dispossessed rural cultivators in the course of acquiring large tracts of land. The dispossession of rural dwellers created a reservoir of nascent class antagonism. It is clear that the revolution was fueled not just by aspirations for national independence but by visions of social egalitarianism.

The revolution, however, left unchanged much of the local-level power structure. The same local overlords (caciques) remained as the leadership of the revolution came to be controlled by Cebuano ilustrados. Continuities of leadership in the towns through the three changes of government in this period (Spanish, republican, and American) show that the provincial and municipal power structures remained relatively intact. In the towns where the revolutionary transition created political tensions (as in Tuburan), the problem was often more of an intrafamilial or intraelite competition rather than a class takeover.

This pattern of elite rule was not a local phenomenon but was true elsewhere in the country. That the elite had the right to rule was a given in the established politics of the time. The Aguinaldo government, in the decree of 18 June 1898, provided that municipal officials will be elected by those who—in addition to being at least 21 years old and "friendly to Philippine independence"—are "distinguished for high character, social position and honorable condition."[17] The gap between the political aims of the elite and the social aspirations of the poor and dispossessed created the potential for internecine conflict within the anti-American resistance.

Diverse currents of resistance coursed through the Cebu countryside as the war against the Americans was fought. Certain individuals and groups operated independently of the Maxilom-Climaco command. On 7 January 1901, in response to complaints about the activities of irregular armed groups, Troadio Galicano (commander of the area between Carcar and Dalaguete) had to issue a warning against these groups and an appeal for information so their leaders could be arrested.[18] In a decree of 5 March 1901, Maxilom declared that "those who shall organize armed groups or forces within Philippine camps without proper authority from me, shall be considered as bandits." The republican army shall be "obliged to scatter them by persuasion or force if necessary and to proceed to the capture of the ringleaders or instigators."[19]

On 27 May 1901, Pantaleon del Rosario sent instructions to Mateo Luga and Damaso Tablada (first and second in command of the fourth fraccion in the central zone) on the problem of spies in the mountains.[20] He cited the case of "bandit Adoy Tabal" who had joined the enemy and "abused the indulgence of the revolution." Anatalio (Adoy) and Quintin

Tabal were renegade insurgent chiefs who broke away from Maxilom's government and staged a guerrilla war against both the Americans and the republic. Del Rosario ordered that all persons caught within the jurisdiction of the towns of "San Mateo" and "Santo Rosario" without a personal cedula or pass issued by the insurgent authorities should be considered traitors and spies of the enemy and dealt with accordingly. This measure was aimed at controlling the presence in the mountains of elements hostile to the republic.

In the murky conditions of the countryside roamed social bandits and independent bands of rebels against whom the army of the republic had to wage a war even as the war against the Americans was fought.

15

Rise of the Pulahanes

T HE WAR did not end with Arcadio Maxilom's surrender on 27 October 1901. A state of civil agitation remained as scattered groups of rebels continued to wage irregular, guerrilla resistance until 1906.

Gov. Juan Climaco reported that there were people who, either out of self-interest or out of their "heated imaginations," did not reconcile themselves to peace. "They imagined hundreds of guns hidden in the bowels of the Cebuano mountains although the quondam revolutionary forces had scarcely 200 in all." Because of this "aberration," Climaco reported that the situation of Cebu was like that of "a house built on the top of a volcano" due to the mood of anxiety, resentment, and fear.[1]

After the surrender of the insurgent generals in October 1901, groups of social bandits and quasi-revolutionary elements stayed out in the field. These groups came to be given the generic name pulahanes, irregular, half-organized groups of mixed political, religious, and criminal persuasions which flourished in Cebu (and elsewhere in the country) in the early years of the century. In Cebu, Leyte, and Samar, their name came from the strips of red (*pula*) cloth that decorated their clothes. Philippine Constabulary analysts pointed to the hybrid character of these groups by classifying "outlaws" of the period into three categories: *ladrones, ladrones politicos,* and *ladrones fanaticos.*[2]

A millenarian theme informs many of these groups. Their members are usually *diwatahan* (animists), use anting-anting, and are recorded to have observed esoteric rituals. Their mixed character is indicated in the varying descriptions of these groups: They are referred to as brigands, "ig-

norant and excitable" people receptive to self-proclaimed messiahs, mountain folk in traditional enmity with town residents, and anarchists who have
not been effectively brought under the influence of the law.

In Cebu, the pulahan movement was at its peak in 1902–1905. In
1903, the Philippine Constabulary reported 10 engagements, 291 "outlaws" killed, and 157 captured. The PC also captured 3 carbines, 1 rifle, 3
shotguns, 11 revolvers, 308 bolos, 1 cannon, and 25 spears.[3] In the same
year, 72 cases of bandolerismo, and 13 for sedition were filed before the
Cebu court of first instance. Eight more cases of bandolerismo and one for
rebellion were added in the first half of 1904.[4] In the year ending 30 June
1905, the military reported 31 engagements, 126 "outlaws" killed, 7
wounded, and 136 captured. Over the same period, 120 men were imprisoned for bandolerismo. Of these, 64 were sent to the Bilibid Prison in
Manila. In all these engagements, Philippine Constabulary casualties were
disproportionately light: two men were killed in 1904 and one in 1905.[5]

Pulahan activities ranged from Bogo and San Remigio in the north to
Sibonga and Barili in the south, with much of the action taking place in the
central zone (in the mountains bounded by Tuburan, Balamban, Toledo,
and Pinamungahan, on the west coast, and Danao, Cebu City, and Naga,
on the east).

It is not known when the pulahan movement began. Pulahan is a
convenient term for what is, in fact, a diverse range of groups that operated
independently of each other (and at times coalesced), following different
charismatic leaders. It probably traces its origins to the Spanish period in
the remontados, followers of folk religion, and social bandits who inhabited the fringes of the more organized lowland communities. These elements were imperfectly integrated into the ilustrado-led revolution against
Spain and the subsequent war against the Americans. When the prominent insurgent leaders surrendered in 1901, many of these elements remained in the hills, bearers of a long tradition of social instability and armed
struggle. Out of these elements and a rural populace unhinged by rapid
social and political change sprung the various bands of social rebels, variously referred to as brigands, tulisanes, cattle thieves, religious fanatics,
criminals, and patriots.

Several early twentieth-century sources ascribed the rise of the
pulahanes to military abuses, particularly by the Philippine Constabulary
(PC).[6] The PC was organized on 18 August 1901 by virtue of Act No. 175.
The country was divided into several districts with Cebu as part of the
Third District. In 1905, the constabulary in Cebu province consisted of 8
officers and 199 men stationed in Cebu, Balamban, Toledo, Tuburan, and Camp
Walker. In addition, some 300 Philippine Scouts were stationed in Cebu.

In his annual report of 1902, Governor Climaco cited military abuses as a major reason for social instability during the year.[7] He reported 15 cases, between 14 March and 27 October 1902, of abuses against civilians, such as illegal detention, arbitrary confiscation of property, indiscriminate raids on private homes, theft, assaults, and murder. Some of the cases involved harassment of local officials. Involved were American soldiers, Filipino scouts, and members of the Philippine Constabulary.

Climaco presented a catalogue of cases in his report. On 11 May 1902, the Tabogon president reported that one Mariano Abayon was arbitrarily arrested by a PC officer and then killed for "attempting to escape." The Tabogon president and justice of the peace also accused the officer of usurping civil functions and acting as a local "dictator," forcing many residents to leave town. The night of 4 June 1902, a 20-year-old resident of Talisay, Matias Baguio, was accosted on the beach by a group of eight constabulary soldiers led by an American officer. They called him an insurgent for not complying with an order requiring citizens to carry a light when they are out at night. Despite the young man's denials, the soldiers insisted he was an insurgent and ordered him to run. When he did, they gunned him down. On 23 June 1902, a grasscutter (*mangongompay*) working in the field near the Carcar-Barili Road was gunned down by an American officer on horseback. The officer later claimed the man was about to assassinate him as "he was carrying a bolo."[8]

Some of the insurgent leaders found themselves persecuted after their surrender. In the first days of April 1902, former insurgent general Nicolas Godines (who took his oath of allegiance to the U.S. on 27 October 1901) was arrested in Cebu City and then taken by steam launch to Dumanjug. He was arrested on suspicion that he had stashed away in Moalboal weapons he should have surrendered. Godines was kept handcuffed during the entire boat trip and then forced to mount a horse for the trip from Dumanjug to Moalboal still handcuffed. No weapons were found. Pantaleon del Rosario, deputy to Governor Climaco, revealed that he was asked by the American senior inspector of the constabulary to testify against Godines but refused. Godines stayed in jail until September 1902 when he was set free by Judge Carlock under President Roosevelt's general amnesty proclamation.[9]

Harshly persecuted was the Maxilom family.[10] On 18 March 1902, Arcadio Maxilom was arrested by Lieutenant. J. F. McCarthy of the detachment in Tuburan on grounds that Maxilom had kept some guns hidden. Seven Krags, 1 Winchester, 1 Mauser, and 700 rounds of ammunition had been found in the Tuburan mountains and there were reports that Maxilom had a cache of 40 more rifles.[11] Intelligence reports as early as 30

October 1901 claimed that Maxilom had from 100 to 300 rifles before his surrender and that those not turned in had been buried somewhere near a large house Maxilom used as a refuge 15 or 20 miles east of Tuburan.

Maxilom's brother, Nemesio, was also placed under arrest. On 25 March, Arcadio and Nemesio were taken under heavy guard on board the steam launch *Philadelphia* for the transfer from Tuburan to Cebu. While on board, the despondent Nemesio lost control of his wits and ran amok after wresting a bayonet from one of the soldiers. He was gunned down and killed. Earlier, on 23 March, another brother of Maxilom, Samuel, was arrested after his arrival in Tuburan from Bantayan in his trading boat. While a prisoner of the constabulary, he was killed inside the jail. Five other Maxilom relatives and friends were also arrested.

Arcadio Maxilom was brought to Cebu and confined at the constabulary barracks. Subsequently, it was reported that the Americans recovered 7 cannons and 2 cans of gunpowder in Montealegre and Capayas in Tuburan. In June and July, Maxilom's case was tried in Barili since the Barili court had jurisdiction over Tuburan. In his trial, Maxilom said he was framed by the American officer stationed in Tuburan since he had refused to accede to the American's request for him to secure some pearls and intercede for the American with a pretty Filipina teacher in Tuburan.

Maxilom was formally charged for violation of his oath of allegiance and convicted on the basis of the testimonies of his servants and former insurgent chief Ramon Allego to the effect that Maxilom had stashed away guns and ammunition in the mountains. Maxilom was meted a 10-year prison term and a 4,000-peso fine on 16 July 1902. Dionisio Novicio, a Maxilom relative and former insurgent chief, was handed a seven-year sentence. The case was appealed to the Supreme Court but Maxilom stayed in the provincial jail from March to sometime in 1903 when he was granted pardon.

Governor Climaco believed Maxilom was unjustly persecuted by the constabulary through the machinations of some local families who wanted to retain the cacique status they lost in the revolution.[12] Judge Lyman Carlock, the CFI judge in Cebu at the time, believed that Maxilom had hidden the guns for "personal purposes," to protect himself against enemies in Tuburan in case he failed to get a government position. The guns had nothing to do with any plot to resume the resistance. Carlock added that Maxilom did not enjoy the support of people in his town. "Maxilom had no influence then, nor has he any influence now."[13]

Military abuses and harassments by persons in authority were just part of a larger picture. The years of war had left an agitated countryside that bred recalcitrant rebels, social bandits, and folk prophets with visions of the advent of a new millenium. After the insurgent surrenders of 1901, the resistance did not come to an end; its complexion merely changed.

Early in 1902, there were already newspaper reports of tulisan activities under Adoy (Anatalio Tabal) in the mountains of Kantipla (between Cebu and Balamban) and Oslob.[14] On 12 May 1902, *Ang Suga* also reported that tulisanes threatened to enter Danao but were repulsed by the police. Upon the request of the town president, PC soldiers were dispatched to Danao.[15] On 15 May 1902, authorities in Catmon arrested 19 men on the ground that they had formed a "fraudulent" association. The prisoners said that their only aspiration was to pray to God that they might not be contaminated by the cholera epidemic then raging in Cebu. They said that two men from Danao gave them, in exchange for alms, pieces of paper with the sign of the cross. These pieces were supposed to be a talisman against disease. The authorities, however, claimed that these were "registration certificates" of the "pulahan society."

One of the most sensational cases of the time was the murder of four American teachers who were recent arrivals in Cebu. The four Americans— Clyde O. Tranes, Ernest Hager, Louis A. Thomas, and John Wells—disappeared while on a hiking trip to the hills of Guadalupe in the outskirts of the city on 10 June 1902. Constabulary and civil officials mounted an intense search that lasted for days. It was Mateo Luga, former insurgent leader who had become a Philippine Constabulary inspector, who, acting on a tip, led a raid on 26 June on the house of "bandit" leader Damaso Tablada in the Guadalupe mountains. In the shootout, Tablada was killed while his companions escaped. In the house were found several personal articles that belonged to the missing American teachers. A search was conducted in the days that followed, netting arrests, until the graves of the Americans were found. The bodies were exhumed and brought back to Cebu on 9 July 1903.[16]

Tablada was no common bandit; he used to be a lieutenant of guerrillas under Luga himself. He had surrendered to the Americans, taken the oath of allegiance, and then retired to Mandaue. He was jailed after a fight with a neighbor and later escaped to the hills to live the life of an outlaw.[17]

There were seven or eight known leaders of dissident groups in the island. One was Policarpo de la Peña, a native of Carcar operating in the mountains of Carcar and Aloguinsan, whose followers, called *capioanes*, wore red strips of cloth on their shoulders. Another was Anastacio de la Cruz of Pinamungahan whose men wore red strips of cloth across their bodies and were called pulahanes.[18] Both capioanes and pulahanes believed in amulets and oraciones. Another leader, mentioned as an associate of De la Cruz, was Eugenio Alcachufas, said to be a lieutenant of the famous folk leader of Negros, Papa Isio. Alcachufas operated in both Cebu and Negros until his surrender to the government in 1911.

More prominent were the groups of Roberto Caballero and Petronilo Esnardo, men who were already operating as rural chiefs at the fringes of the ilustrado revolution as early as 1899–1900. The group of Caballero (who was also known as Mintong and Leon Bato) was active until its suppression in the latter part of 1903.

The Caballero group—described in official reports as a "religious and fanatic aggregation"—first came to public notice in 1902 and operated in the mountains of northern Cebu (bounded by Tuburan, Asturias, Borbon, and Sogod, and as far south as Carmen and Danao). Caballero claimed to be "one sent by God and a supernatural being able to perform all sorts of miracles."[19] Authorities regarded him as a charlatan and reported that he did good business with rural dwellers in the sale of stamped images to which were attributed extraordinary virtues. These were sold by "vagabonds" who peddled them from town to town. "The stamps when first placed on sale were much larger than the present ones .... The latter are of two kinds, printed in blue and black ink. The first are known by the name *ituman* and the second by that of pulahan."[20] Reports said that, during the revolution, Caballero was hunted by the republican forces for similar misdeeds in the exploitation of the country people. He had to take refuge in Negros where he remained until shortly after "pacification" when he returned to his old stumping ground to begin anew his work of "fanaticizing" the people. He reportedly sold stamped images together with other amulets against the plague. In the mountains of Tuburan, he presided over a community made up of people who had left their homes to gather around the "prophet" in the hope that they would be saved from the coming deluge.[21]

Associated with the Caballero group was a group under Petronilo (Pitong) Esnardo that operated in the mountains of Bogo and Tabogon. It is said that Esnardo, a farmer-guerrilla with friendly relations with Maxilom, acknowledged Caballero's leadership. After the insurgent surrenders, certain persons sought to implicate Esnardo in crimes imputed to Maxilom. Governor Climaco claimed that Esnardo was only driven to outlawry by persecution carried out by Maxilom's enemies who sought to maintain their caciquism in Tuburan.

There is already a reference to Pitong as leader of a large band in Malagasi, in northern Cebu, as of 15 December 1900 when men of the Nineteenth U.S. Infantry raided his lair, killed two men, captured three, and destroyed his camp. The American report refers to Esnardo both as ladrone and as insurgent.[22]

Several depredations were attributed to the Caballero group. In the night of 8 June 1901, a group of men under Caballero descended from the mountains of Banban (in Asturias) and entered the barrio of Colonia in Tuburan and boloed to death the barrio lieutenant, his wife and son, and one resident.[23] They also wounded several others before going back to the hills. On 6 September 1902, a band of some 50 men entered Granada in Asturias, surrounded the house of a policeman named Andres Masayon in an aborted attempt to abduct him. On 29 September and 2 October, the president of Tuburan, Bonifacio Alburo, sent messages to the capital saying that Caballero's men were gathering in the Capayas and Pandong mountains and making preparations to descend on Tuburan. The president also reported that residents in the barrios of Carmelo and Antolayan in Tuburan were made to pay a tax of one *real* each and duped into paying money in exchange for protection against disease.

The best known of the pulahan leaders were the Tabal brothers.[24] A family with a remarkable history of resistance, the Tabals were prosperous landowners in Sudlon where they cultivated corn and tobacco long before the anti-Spanish revolution, and had a network of kinsmen, followers, and allies. The rugged highland of Sudlon was a natural stronghold, endowed with food supplies and accessible from the plains only by mountain trails. It was to this redoubt that the Katipuneros withdrew after Leon Kilat's assassination in April 1898. Around 13 April 1898, Luis Flores, the Aliño brothers, the Pacañas, Alejo Miñoza, Eugenio Gines, and Elpidio Rama gathered in Sudlon (another account cites the place called Tabla, below Sudlon and Bitlang) to reorganize and discuss the conduct of the anti-Spanish resistance. They were later joined by other leaders of the revolution, such as Francisco Llamas, Enrique Lorega, Nicolas Godines, Emilio Verdeflor, Lorenzo Eje, and Saturnino Echavez. It was at this time that the Tabals assumed a prominent role in the revolution since they did not only bring their followers into the ranks of the revolution, they were the "chiefs" of Sudlon and the insurgents drew their food and supplies from the Tabals' land.

The leading Tabals were the brothers Rafael (1866–1898), Anatalio (1868–c1935), Quintin (1878–1921), and Serafin (d. 1899). In addition there must have been other Tabal family members and relatives involved in the resistance. Rafael Tabal was named jefe of the Sudlon revolutionary zone, with the rank of teniente general, while his brothers became officers of the revolution.

Rafael Tabal (known as Teniente Pael) was a legendary fighter reputedly endowed with supernatural powers (kalake)—such as extraordinary strength and the ability to "leap over mountains"—but he died in a bloody battle against Spanish cazadores in Pardo on 28 September 1898.[25] An account says that the Tabals became disenchanted with the Katipunan leadership as they blamed the death of Rafael on the city people whose intrusion into Sudlon had destroyed the "power" (*virtud*) of Rafael's amulet (anting-anting). It is possible that there were other sources of tension, one being that the Tabals blamed the Katipunan leaders for not coming to Rafael's aid in the battle of Pardo. Though the leadership succeeded in mollifying the Tabals, later events suggest that the relationship between the Tabals and the taga-patag (lowlanders) had become strained.

When the revolutionaries occupied Cebu City in December 1898, Quintin Tabal was one of the revolution's "generals" who marched triumphantly into the city. On the eve of the American landing in February 1899, Quintin Tabal is cited as one of the most vocal in arguing for putting up a stand to prevent the American landing even if this meant burning the city. Another account says that the Tabals had become disenchanted at this time because they were not given positions in the newly established Cebuano government on the grounds that they were uneducated.[26]

When the revolutionaries again set up headquarters in Sudlon after the U.S. occupation of the towns, the Tabals were still with the army of the republic. As late as August 1899, the Tabals were still with the Maxilom forces and Anatalio Tabal had the designation of "general de Sudlon" while Quintin Tabal had the rank of teniente general.[27] At this time, however, there were already suspicions that the Tabals had switched loyalties to the Americans.[28]

The break between the Tabals and the ilustrado revolutionaries eventually became irreparable. Towards the end of 1899, Quintin and Serafin, with a group of followers, "invaded" the headquarters of Maxilom in Sudlon, a wooden house that belonged to Rafael Tabal. The Tabals dared Maxilom's men to a fight, calling them "usurpers," but the challenge was allowed to pass and the Tabals withdrew. Subsequently, Troadio Galicano was sent to talk to the Tabals but the brothers refused to listen. An exchange of gunfire between the Tabals and Galicano's men ensued, killing Serafin and some of his men. While Quintin and the others managed to escape, Anatalio (Adoy) was arrested and kept a prisoner in Tabla (Sudlon) for a few days before he was released.

After the fall of Sudlon, Maxilom and Climaco transferred their headquarters to Capayas at the boundary of Catmon and Tuburan. It was at this

point that the Tabals reportedly formed their own "revolutionary government" with Adoy as head. Some revolutionaries disgruntled with the
Maxilom leadership also affiliated themselves with the Tabal "government," including two "generals" (unnamed but said to be townsmen with
some education) who acted as gobernador militar and head of the *estado
mayor* in the rebel government.[29] The identity of these "generals" (who
surrendered to the Americans in 1901 together with Maxilom and the other
leaders) cannot be determined, although two possibilities are Francisco
Llamas and Potenciano Aliño, insurgent generals branded as renegades by
the Maxilom government. Their exact relationship to the activities of the
Tabal group is problematic and they may have filled largely symbolic roles.

The Tabals operated as a group separate from the Maxilom government. On 23 January 1900, Maxilom issued orders for Anatalio Tabal and
his group to be captured or shot on sight.[30] There is a report that when the
American troops took Sudlon in January 1900, they were "guided by Adoy,
the brother of Quintin."[31] Condemned and hunted as *revoltosos*, traitors
and spies, the Tabals led a wandering life in the mountains until the surrender of the insurgent generals in 1901.

After the insurgent surrenders, the Tabals, according to Adoy, went
back to farming, Quintin in Sayaw and Adoy in Panas, in the Talamban
area.[32] Their wartime enemies, however, continued to hound them and,
fearing for their lives, they took up arms once more. With six rifles (and
later two more), the brothers resumed their rebel activities. Another account states that even after the insurgent surrenders the Tabals continued
with their "secret government" and sold their own cedulas.[33] By February
1902, there were already newspaper reports of Adoy's "bandit" activities
in the mountains of Cebu.[34] These activities continued in the next three
years. Ang *Camatuoran*, for instance, reported in its issue of 14 January
1903 that three men captured by Mateo Luga had been sentenced for collecting cedulas for "bandit" leader Quintin Tabal.[35]

In his annual report of 1902, Governor Climaco described the Tabals
as brigands:

> In the mountains of the central part of this island a
> small band of confirmed cattle thieves led by the Tabal
> brothers and composed of the dregs of the country folk are
> the constant nightmare of small farmers and stockmen. They
> have about five guns but, it is thought, no ammunition.
>
> It is not regularly organized, with members living in
> dispersed places, only meeting in small numbers when called

upon by their leaders. Their operations are restricted to the central portion of the province as they are unacquainted with the lay of the ground to the north and south of them.[36]

There is then a tangled background to the resistance of the Tabals. Undoubtedly, they are not mere brigands and cattle thieves. In his report of 1904, Governor Climaco refers to the Tabal group once more as "cattle thieves," yet qualifies by saying that "the certificates of membership sold by them denote political ideas against the constituted government."[37] In 1908, Gov. Dionisio Jakosalem called the Tabals "revolutionaries who were afterwards called bandits."[38]

However, the Tabals and the pulahanes were not part of a more organized political movement. In a 1906 interview, Adoy Tabal said that they had no links to Macario Sakay of Luzon.[39] The American authorities themselves saw no direct connection between the pulahanes of Cebu and those of the Leyte-Samar area.[40] The Tabals also rejected, after their 1906 surrender, the label pulahanes, saying they were not diwatahan and did not possess anting-anting. Quintin could read and write while Adoy could read but not write. Adoy said that their followers were "all those who had been unjustly accused, hounded, maltreated, persecuted, and dispossessed."[41]

In the war against the Americans, therefore, the Tabals operated as an independent, irregular band engaged in a running feud with the army of the republic, particularly with the men of Mateo Luga who operated in the mountainous central zone, the Tabals' stumping ground. American military reports in 1900 referred to the Tabals as "friendly natives" and recorded instances of the internecine Luga-Tabal "war." In the night of 9 March 1900, for instance, a group of 70 men "dressed as American soldiers" burned Talamban in the attempt to capture the Tabals. A report identified the attackers as insurgents under Lorenzo Eje (and possibly Mateo Luga).[42] An American officer reported on 15 December 1900: "There is a fierce hatred between Luga and Tabal and each seems to have made some weak attempts at fortifying himself against the other. Last month, in a fight, Tabal lost two men and had four wounded."[43] Then, sometime in December 1900, in the Sudlon area, Luga was reported to have shot two men he claimed were followers of Tabal.

Mateo Luga was an Ilokano (a native of Tumauini, Isabela) who fought with the Katipunan in various engagements in Rizal province and was, according to Luga's own account in 1924, imprisoned in Manila's Fort Santiago in 1896 at the time when Rizal was a prisoner there.[44] In his 1924 account, Luga said that Aguinaldo and Luna sent him to Cebu in April 1899. He arrived in Cebu as a *marinero* of the boat *Butuan* and quickly linked up with Climaco and the insurgent leaders. When the war with the Americans broke out, Luga claimed, the island of Cebu was divided into three zones by the insurgents, with the north under Maxilom, the south under Troadio Galicano, and the central part of the island under Luga. Luga earned a reputation during the war as a fierce fighter, and variously called Alimokon, Agta, and Tagolilong because of his daring and elusive ways. One story is that he once entered the city carrying weapons concealed in a coffin for a quick raid to free his wife and child whom the Americans had imprisoned in order to force him to surrender. After his surrender in Carcar on 27 October 1901, Luga joined the Philippine Constabulary and played a leading role in hunting down outlaws and insurgents. In the constabulary, Luga continued the campaign against the Tabals that he carried out while still an insurgent officer.

Chronicler Victor Hurley described Luga's service in the constabulary thus: "No member of the corps wore the uniform of the jungle police with greater distinction than this swart, fearless Filipino."[45] Luga, Hurley said, won over insurgents, brought back Filipino deserters from the U.S. Army, and earned the admiration of Americans. Luga resigned from the PC with the rank of captain around 1914. He then joined the Philippine Refining Company, an American firm, and moved out of Cebu to take up residence in Manila.

Between 1902 and 1906, the Tabals and other groups waged an irregular war against the Filipino-American authorities.[46] In 1904, the U.S. military estimated the strength of the pulahanes and other "malcontents" at from 500 to 1,000 men. The rebel arsenal was estimated at 12 guns, a few revolvers, 2 brass cannons, spears, and bolos. Their stumping ground encompassed an area about 35 miles long by 18 miles.[47]

In the year 1903, large bands entered the insufficiently protected towns of Tuburan, Aloguinsan, and Borbon. Barrios entered included Lambusan, Luyang, and Victoria (San Remigio), Punay (Aloguinsan), Cabcaban (Barili), Monte (Danao), and sitios in the vicinity of Toledo. In early 1904, pulahan bands entered Cogon (Cebu), Tangob (Pinamungahan), and Casili (Consolacion). In the above actions, some houses were burned, seven residents (including two barrio lieutenants) killed, and some residents kidnaped. On the other hand, four attackers were killed.

A report says that in the pulahan attack on Tuburan in 1903, many of them wore white suits (*americanang maputi*) with red cloths as bands and ribbons. Their "generals" wore red ribbons and sashes as well as pieces of paper on which oraciones were written, hanging from their necks or pinned to their breasts.[48]

It cannot be accurately ascertained whether the Tabals were involved in these actions as several independent groups of varying persuasions operated during this time. After their surrender, the Tabals declared that they did not participate in the many raids and encounters imputed to them and that they had not killed anyone. Adoy disclaimed any participation in the raids on Consolacion and Pinamungahan and said that their names were just used. Since these statements, however, were made in a newspaper interview shortly after their surrender, the disclaimers must be taken critically.

A 1904 U.S. military report says that Quintin and Adoy were "robbing and burning along the west coast of this island."[49] These actions, the report says, were in retaliation for recent activity of the Philippine Constabulary in driving the Tabal band of some 250 men from their stronghold in the Sudlon mountain range.

The first major action attributed to the Tabals took place dawn of 18 July 1904 when Pinamungahan was attacked by a group of men said to be led by Quintin Tabal and one Pedro Lipao. The men entered the town from three points and then emplaced two small cannons on one of the walls of the church then under construction. The attackers also had five rifles. The town was caught by surprise and could not offer a resistance, as only the town president and treasurer had revolvers. The police had none. After the residents fled, the rebels sacked the town, burning the municipal building, the president's house, and other houses. It was later reported that many of the attackers were inhabitants of the town's outlying barrios.

Tuburan and the west coast were in a state of turbulence. On 4 May 1904, the provincial governor arrived at Tuburan on board a government launch but could not land, as the town was occupied by the rebels. A force of 80 PC soldiers in three columns was dispatched to Tuburan but the outlaws withdrew before the troops arrived.

On 13 May 1904, Second Lt. Ward V. Walker led a PC force to track down pulahanes in the Aloguinsan area. The force was ambushed by a large group of pulahanes. Walker and six of his men were killed before the remaining members of the force could withdraw in the direction of Barili. The PC also lost seven Springfield carbines in the ambush. Two days later, reinforcements under Capt. Robert Page, sent out to track the rebels, encountered a large group of pulahanes. In the ensuing battle, the PC killed 30, wounded many, and recaptured three Springfield carbines. On 18 May, the body of Lieutenant Walker was recovered from a deep canyon and brought back to Barili.

On 22 May 1904, a PC force of 23 soldiers, assisted by about 80 volunteers, commanded by Lt. Richard Poggi and Mateo Luga, surrounded pulahanes holed up in a high, rocky retreat in Guimpilican in Aloguinsan.

The soldiers scaled bamboo ladders and engaged the pulahanes in a fierce, close-quarter engagement. They killed "more than 100" and captured 30 to 40 men. (Another source says 50 men were killed and 40 to 50 captured.) So fierce was the battle that a local account recorded that dead bodies littered the field "like corn grains thrown to the ground."[50]

A local account says that the pulahanes who engaged the PC in Aloguinsan was a joint force of the capioanes of Policarpo de la Peña and the pulahanes of Anastacio de la Cruz of Pinamungahan. In the encounter of 22 May, De la Peña was killed but Anastacio de la Cruz and Eugenio Alcachufas, another pulahan leader, escaped.

After the 22 May battle, the PC enforced "judgment by the sword" (juez de cuchillo) in the area, shooting men on sight. "The killing was so terrible that the place was almost abandoned." Barili presidente Clodoaldo Rocamora had to intervene with the military authorities to prevent further bloodshed.[51]

In Aloguinsan, a report was received that the pulahanes under Carlos Gerardino planned to capture the constabulary headquarters in the city after which they would set up an independent "republic" with Gerardino as president. The report added that the pulahanes, to stir rural dwellers into joining the movement, had spread the rumor that the Americans would withdraw from Cebu. Word about this "plot" reached American authorities. Immediately, Major A. J. Robertson, senior PC inspector in Cebu, commissioned Lieutenant J. T. Reyburn to proceed to Aloguinsan to arrest the ringleaders. Entering the outlaws' hideout, Reyburn, armed only with a revolver (so the American report goes), caught Gerardino and his men totally unaware and arrested them.

The pulahan movement simmered through the years 1902 to 1905. In April 1903, pulahanes based in the hills of Olango in Aloguinsan sent messages to Barili and Carcar saying that they will attack these towns, boasting that they will finish Barili by breakfast and Carcar by dinner.

On 21 August 1904, close to midnight, a group of men, led by Juan Aliño, a resident of the town, entered Talisay. A fight ensued between the band and the police. One attacker was killed and two were injured before they fled. A policeman was injured. Arrests of suspected accomplices took place the following day.

On 30 August 1904, the presidente of Danao reported that bandits in the hills of Sacsac tried to collect thirty pesos from the barrio lieutenant of Cahumayhumayan. A force was sent out after the bandits. Still in Danao, on 9 October 1904, three persons were kidnaped in Barrio Mantigan (Mantija). They were able to escape on 23 October when the band of abductors was pursued by the constabulary.

On 4 September 1904, at 5:00 A.M., some "200 bandits" entered Asturias armed with eight rifles and two cannons. The residents and local police put up a fight but ran out of ammunition and fled. The bandits then sacked the place, looting the municipal treasury and private houses. The municipal building and 35 houses were burned. In this raid, two attackers were killed. Three policemen were killed and six wounded. The attackers were said to be residents of Asturias and Balamban.[52]

On 28 November 1904, a group of three policemen and two volunteers from Mandaue were set upon by bolomen in Barrio Lanipga (Lanibga). A policeman was killed.

On 7 May 1905, around a hundred bandits, "including women and children," entered the district of Consolacion, in the town of Mandaue, between 4:00 and 5:00 A.M. They were said to be led by Quintin Tabal. In the face of the raid, residents and the unarmed police fled. Five inhabitants were wounded and one woman murdered. In the one hour the raiders stayed in the town, they ransacked houses, stores, and set fire to the old municipal building, the schoolhouse, and five dwellings. The following day, a pursuing constabulary force caught up with part of the group, killed some and captured the others. An investigation into the raid implicated a barrio lieutenant and several inhabitants who, it was claimed, wanted to exact revenge on some persons in the town.

On 18 July 1905, a band of "outlaws" entered Minglanilla early in the morning, raided the local treasury, burned the municipal building and part of the town, cut telephone and telegraph wires, and killed 18 residents.[53]

From 1903 to 1906, bandolerismo was a major problem of the American military authorities and the provincial government. In the campaign against the pulahanes, the authorities were handicapped by the small, inadequately equipped municipal police force. Early in 1904, Cebu province had a total municipal force of only 632 men in 41 towns. The police was poorly armed, mostly with Remingtons of "so inferior a class that they have resulted in accidents to the men handling them, the barrels being very liable to explode."[54]

In the middle of 1903, in the face of rising pulahan activity, a volunteer force was organized by Capt. Robert H. Page, the senior inspector of the constabulary. Organized under Act No. 1309 of the Philippine Commission, the volunteer force was a citizen army under the municipal president, with the municipal councilor heading a "company" and the barrio lieutenant heading a "section" (representing a barrio). Volunteers acted as *vigilantes* and had a system of patrols and alarms. Those enlisted had to serve on pain of a fine or imprisonment or both. The volunteer units were disbanded in the beginning of 1904 although some municipalities retained them.

In the anti-pulahan campaign carried out by the PC and the municipal police, there were, as of 30 June 1904, 12 skirmishes of some importance, resulting in the capture of prisoners and the killing of eight "bandits." Twenty-five rebels were captured in several municipalities, including a chieftain called Bito who was captured with his men in the hills of Naga by a PC force under Captain H. P. Neville and Lt. Mateo Luga. Several leaders—including "Gen." Martin Cabuenas (a former insurgent officer)—surrendered together with their men. Between July 1904 and June 1905, municipal policemen and volunteers captured 22 suspected bandits in San Fernando, Balamban, Talisay, Ronda, Toledo, and Liloan. This did not include arrests made by the PC itself.

By early 1905, however, the pulahan movement was still far from being suppressed. The movement was many headed, rearing in many places, and it gathered in its wake many rural dwellers. A local account describes a march of pulahanes in 1905, said to be led by the Tabals, passing through Toledo towards the mountains of Aloguinsan. The pulahanes were so numerous that "though they started to pass through Toledo at the break of day the tailend [of the march] did not finish moving through the town until it struck seven o'clock that night."[55] Though the pulahanes were reported to have massed in formations of 100 or 200 men, the average band, however, consisted of some 10 or 20 men. The standard pulahan method of operation was to gather in groups, descend to the plains to raid the towns, and then withdraw to the mountains where they dispersed and hid deep in the interior of the mountainous district. A military report of the period states: "One of the greatest difficulties to be overcome in the pacification of this section is the cohesion and bond of sympathy that exists between all the mountain people, whether pulahanes or farmers."[56]

In the countryside, the pulahanes were in their element. They moved in small groups, were familiar with the terrain, and blended easily with the rural population.

16

The Leveling of the Mountains

T HE SUPPRESSION of the pulahanes required new measures. The authorities knew that purely military action would not bring an end to pulahan activities. In mid-1905, Gov. Juan Climaco—who was on his second term after defeating Alejandro Ruiz in the gubernatorial election of 4 February 1904—called for additional civilian support in the campaign against brigandage. He called on the town mayors (1) to organize a secret service in their towns, (2) conduct periodic searches by police and volunteers, and (3) impose sanctions on barrio lieutenants who give shelter and aid to brigands and rebels.

The most important measure undertaken was the reconcentration program in the central mountain district of Cebu. On 1 June 1903, the Philippine Commission had passed Act No. 781, otherwise known as the Reconcentration Act, to counter insurgency and brigandage in various parts of the country. In 1905, the government decided to implement a reconcentration program in Cebu, one of the few areas in the country where the Americans carried out a forced relocation of the population in an attempt to deprive rebels of mass support.

The "reduction" of the population was also aided by American efforts in infrastructure building. Roads and bridges brought the hinterland closer into the orbit of the centers of state power. In 1904, work was underway in the construction of the first intercoastal road, joining Talisay and Toledo. By 1908, a 60-mile railroad running through the provincial capital connected Danao in the north and Argao in the south. By 1908, Cebu had a total of 639.2 kilometers of roads all over the island.[1] The old frontier areas began to disappear with the incursion of plainsmen and agents of the state into the island's interior.

Under the reconcentration program an estimated 35,000 inhabitants in the critical zone were to be gathered in designated barrios.[2] The government either created artificial barrios or designated existing communities as places for reconcentration. Of the existing barrios designated as points of reconcentration, 10 were in Danao (with a combined population of 3,557), 10 in Balamban (population 11,238), 13 in Toledo (9,452), and 6 in Pinamungahan (3,655). Eighteen mostly new barrios (with a projected population of 7,000) were programmed within the jurisdiction of Cebu, Mandaue, and Liloan.

At the center of this zone, located about 3,100 feet above sea level, a constabulary detachment called Camp Walker (named after the American lieutenant killed in Aloguinsan) was established. Reached by a trail from Talamban, Camp Walker was situated 12 miles northwest of Cebu at a point called Canlumagong in the mountain range between Sudlon and Adlaon in Talamban. It had a view extending as far as Mactan Island and it commanded the hinterlands of Cebu, Balamban, Mandaue, Asturias, and Liloan. Camp Walker was the pivot for a zone where 18 artificially created, stockade-surrounded barrios, with an estimated population of 7,000, were laid out within a fixed radius from the military post. The majority of the residents of this zone, living in the mountains of Panas, Mayog, and upland villages in the Talamban area, were regarded to be sympathetic to the brigands.

In support of the reconcentration program, the municipal presidents were given instructions to give aid in the establishment of Camp Walker by organizing labor for constructing a shelter for the soldiers. The provincial governor issued guidelines to local officials governing the control of the mountain population. The barrios included in the reconcentration were to have a teniente appointed by the municipal council. The teniente's duties included drawing up a list of all barrio residents, indicating duration of their residence; keeping a daily record of outsiders remaining in the barrio overnight; and keeping track of absentee residents, date of absence, and date of return to the barrio. Absentees for a number of days beyond the period granted them were to be reported to the municipal president, who would in turn refer this to the constabulary detachment officer. Lists of residents were supplied to the constabulary.

The "reconcentrated" villages also had to organize a volunteer force of from 40 to 50 men, armed with spears and bolos, to assist the PC as lookouts, auxiliaries, and cargadores. They were supported with funds from the provincial government.[3]

Additional detachments were established in the interior: one between San Fernando and Pinamungahan, another (called Camp Barry) in the mountains eight miles west of Danao. On 1 July 1905, the governor also recommended another detachment to be set up between Cebu and Balamban or Toledo.

In his report of 19 July 1905, Col. Wallace C. Taylor, commanding officer of the Third District of the constabulary, acknowledged that reconcentration curtailed individual rights but argued that such rights were not universal. He argued that for such "inferior" subjects as American Indians and Filipinos, such rights could be suspended or withheld. He wrote:

> It will plainly be a restriction of the liberty of the individual
> to prohibit him from building his abode outside prescribed
> limits; but it should be recognized that men so low in the
> depths of ignorance, being, as they are, a constant menace to
> society, are not fit to enjoy the same liberty as those of the
> same blood who are under the influence of civilization.[4]

The reconcentration program proved effective in containing the pulahan movement in Cebu. By extending state surveillance to the remote villages, the freedom of action of rural dwellers was curtailed. By stationing armed detachments in the highlands, the government demonstrated its capability to react promptly to rebel activities in the hills. The government restricted the rebels' movements and disrupted their ties with the mountain population. The leveling of the mountains had begun.

Governor Climaco reported that as of 1 July 1905, only the Tabal brothers, with some 10 men armed with 5 or 6 revolvers, remained active. When Sergio Osmeña assumed the governorship on 5 March 1906, he took up peace and order as the first priority of his administration. Osmeña resolved to track down the outlaws "until the last man is placed within the reach of the law."

Osmeña's resolve hardened when, on 7 March, just two days after his assumption of office, some 40 pulahanes attacked a detachment of scouts under an American officer in Mt. Biga in Toledo. An American private was killed and two Filipino scouts were wounded.[5]

Governor Osmeña stressed that the pulahan was not just a military problem but a political one. He knew that the support of the people was needed since the government was not dealing with an organized army but bands of disaffected individuals that found refuge in the barrios.

Osmeña later wrote: "I concerted a plan with the constabulary involving active and popular cooperation on the part of all elements."[6]

Osmeña methodically embarked on a campaign to "attract" the rebels. He traveled on horseback for some 150 miles around the province in the company of the provincial board to conduct official business in the field and gather information, particularly on the peace-and-order situation.

The governor then gathered municipal presidents, councilors, barrio lieutenants, and other prominent leaders to a one-day convention in Balamban, with the constabulary supplying the steamer *Ranger* for transport and Osmeña himself paying for the other expenses. The choice of Balamban as convention site was symbolic as it was within the troubled zone of pulahan activity. The Balamban convention, a large, unprecedented gathering attended by top PC officers in the province, presented resolutions calling for the following initiatives:

1. Reorganization and expansion of the police so that the police forces of the towns can be welded together as homogeneous tactical units under the direct command of the provincial governor and with the same equipment, uniforms, armaments, and supplies;
2. Reorganization of the town volunteers as an auxiliary force of the police; and
3. Organization of committees on public order to attract the rebels to return to the fold of the law. These committees are to be composed of prominent citizens of the town.

The resolutions were enthusiastically approved and some property owners even offered to contribute to the support of the police units. The antipulahan campaign was to be two-pronged: (1) the municipal police force and local volunteers would protect the towns while (2) the regulars—constabulary soldiers and scouts—would be deployed for field operations. In field operations, the policy was not to use volunteers and paid secret service men as they were often the cause of abuses that had undesirable political results. Premium was placed on winning the people's sympathy and trust. The local peace committees were to launch a propaganda campaign to convince the rebels to come in and surrender.

In addition, a reward of 3,000 pesos was placed on the head of Quintin Tabal. Each rebel, who was not a leader, would be assisted in securing a full pardon and would receive 200 pesos from Osmeña for each rifle surrendered. Relatives of "bandits" already in the Bilibid Prison were told that if they aided the government "their relatives would probably be pardoned."

After the Balamban convention, Osmeña organized a similar convention in the east coast. The government was particularly interested in bringing in Quintin and Anatalio Tabal and their men, as they appeared to be the best armed and best organized of the pulahan groups. The Tabals' long association with the revolution also made them the most visible symbols of continuing resistance to the authorities.

Initial surrenders took place in Pinamungahan. Then, through such emissaries as Cebu councilor Laureano Abella and Guadalupe barrio lieutenant Joaquin Labra, word was relayed to Governor Osmeña that Quintin Tabal wanted to meet with the governor. Osmeña sent back word suggesting a meeting in Buhisan for Quintin and one companion to confer with Osmeña and Major H. P. Neville, the senior PC officer in Cebu. No arms were to be carried to the meeting.[7]

At the time of the scheduled meeting, however, Osmeña was in bed nursing a fever while Major Neville was in Leyte on constabulary business. It was later learned that Quintin and nine of his men had encamped near Buhisan for four days waiting for the conference to take place. Subsequently, Osmeña sent out word for Quintin to come and see him in the city, with assurances of safe conduct.

On 24 June 1906, Quintin Tabal made a surprise appearance in Osmeña's house at around 10:00 P.M. Osmeña, who was running a temperature of 39.5°C at the time, received him. Except for San Nicolas presidente Luciano Bacayo, Councilor Laureano Abella, and a few people in the household, no one else was present.

Quintin impressed Osmeña as a reserved but self-assured young man. Soft-spoken and deliberate, Quintin told Osmeña that his forebears were not brigands. His family owned farmlands in Sudlon and was more than relatively well-to-do before the revolution against Spain. When the insurrection was headquartered in Sudlon, the insurgents drew their supplies from the Tabal lands and the Tabals were with the insurgents when they occupied the city after the fall of the Spanish government. After the Tabals' falling away with the insurgents at the start of the war against the Americans, the Tabals led a wandering life. Having suffered "certain persecutions" after the insurgent surrenders in 1901, the Tabals began to engage in rebel activities once more.

In his meeting with Osmeña, Quintin said he wanted pardon for himself and his men. In his account of this meeting, Osmeña wrote that he told Tabal he could not grant pardon as only the governor-general had this power. He, however, gave assurances that the Tabals would get their pardon. These assurances satisfied Quintin. (Apparently, there was some misunderstanding of the terms of the surrender as, in later years, Osmeña came under criticism for having made promises of pardon and leniency that he was unable to fulfill.)

After the meeting with Osmeña, Tabal returned to the hills with the promise that he would bring in his men. At 10:00 A.M., 25 June, the day after the meeting, Quintin Tabal sent to Osmeña, through an emissary, four rifles (three Krags and one Springfield) and ammunition as a token of the Tabals' good faith. (These rifles were the best in the Tabals' very small arsenal. All they had besides were two Remingtons, only one of which was in good condition, and a Spanish Mauser.)

The formal surrender itself—designed to showcase Osmeña as "peace-and-order" governor—took place in the morning of 22 July 1906 in the plaza of the barrio *capilla* of Guadalupe, Cebu City.[8] On the day of the surrender, *tartanillas* and carriages converged in Guadalupe and a crowd of around a thousand gathered in the sweltering morning to witness the ceremony. Among the notables present were Judge Mariano Cui, Judge Casiano Causin, San Nicolas Mayor Luciano Bacayo, and American civil and military officials. Provincial Secretary Leoncio Alburo announced the names of the surrenderees in the formal presentation. There were some 50 surrenderees led by Quintin and Adoy who appeared dressed in gray suits, wearing shoes and hats.

After Governor Osmeña administered the oath of allegiance, the crowd broke into cheers of "Viva Osmeña!" In a well-applauded speech delivered from the window of a house fronting the plaza, Osmeña spoke of his efforts to effect the surrenders and bring about a reconciliation of the people in Cebu.

A festive mood prevailed. The Tabal brothers were billeted in the Guadalupe convent. In the evening, a dinner was tendered at the house of Filemon Sotto, attended by the Tabals and such personalities as Arcadio Maxilom, Pedro Rodriguez, and Arsenio Climaco. In the conciliatory atmosphere of the surrender, the Tabals were regarded not *as* pulahan or tulisan but as revolutionary leaders who had held out in the hills, according to a newspaper report, "for reasons we cannot now mention."[9]

Thus ended the insurgent career of a family that had waged battle with Spanish, American, and Filipino authorities for close to ten years. After the surrender of the Tabals, "the most complete peace prevailed in this province, for the first time after long years of horrible intranquility."[10] As part of the surrender deal, the Tabals were not jailed in exchange for their active cooperation in tracking down the peasant rebels still in the hills. Many of their followers, however, remained in jail for a long time. With Quintin's help, Naga bandit leader Agustin Pardines was captured and meted a prison term. In 1907, Petronilo Esnardo was captured by the police in Borbon and jailed.[11] Another account says that Esnardo surrendered personally to Sergio Osmeña in a meeting in the sitio of Natin-ao in

Tabogon. In the same year, Roberto Caballero was in prison serving a life term.[12] Eugenio Alcachufas surrendered to Gov. Dionisio Jakosalem on 21 January 1911 and was sentenced by the Cebu court of first instance to a prison term of 20 years.[13]

The pulahan phenomenon, however, did not become entirely a thing of the past. Events in the years that followed indicated how a folk tradition of protest remained close to the surface. In 1908, a "prophet" named Anastacio Quejada was baptizing people in the district of Guadalupe and a man presenting himself as "José Rizal" was organizing a cult in some northern Cebu barrios. At around the same time, there were reports that in Olango (Santa Rosa, Mactan) there was a Tagalog who called himself Santiago Apostol, had a sword whose brightness, when unsheathed, could smite nonbelievers, and who traveled in the company of "Mary Magdalene" and a preacher named Segundo Tilana.[14]

Prophets and rebels continued to walk the Cebu countryside.

17

Osmeña Begins

T HE SURRENDER of the Tabals gave added luster to the career of one man, Sergio Osmeña (1878–1961).[1] When the Americans came to Cebu in 1899, Osmeña was one of the rising young men in the city, connected to the wealthy landowning and merchant family of the Osmeñas, educated in Manila, with interests in law and journalism, fields that, at the time, were the avenues towards a public life. Osmeña's career is expressive of the changes of the time, the shifts of temper and practice that brought the war to an end and created much of the foundation of contemporary Philippine politics.

Although born to a modest home—he was the illegitimate child of Juana Suico Osmeña, who operated a bakery and sweet shop in Cebu City—he had such relatives and patrons as Tomas Osmeña, one of the wealthiest men in the city at the time. After attending the Seminario-Colegio de San Carlos, Osmeña studied law at the University of Sto. Tomas (1892–1898) and, during breaks in his studies (with the interruptions of the Revolution and the Spanish-American War), he contributed articles to *El Boletin de Cebu* and Manila's *El Comercio* at the same time that, in the period 1896–1898, he worked as an employee in the Cebu audiencia. He served as an "official reporter" and protege of the Spanish governor of Cebu, Don Celestino Fernandez Tejero, and of Arturo Pereiro, who became interim governor after Tejero's departure in 1896. He was—like many of his social class—associated with the pro-Spanish voluntarios leales during the first flush of the revolution. When the revolution broke out in Luzon in 1896, Osmeña wrote articles in *El Comercio* in support of the Spanish government. For this and other services, he was given in 1898, when he was only nineteen, the Medalla de Merito Civil, the highest award given by the colonial government to civilians in the Philippines.

When the revolution broke out in Cebu on 3 April 1898, Osmeña prudently stayed out of harm's way, seeking refuge in Liloan together with his family. The story that he dressed as a woman in order to get past hostile lines was preserved by political cartoonists and enemies in the decades that followed through the standard caricature of Osmeña in *baro't saya* (skirt and blouse).

Osmeña became a republican after the Spanish withdrawal, although he played a very peripheral role in the events of the day. In 1899, he was reportedly sent to Luzon as an emissary by the local leadership to discuss the situation in Cebu with Aguinaldo. He met Aguinaldo briefly in Tarlac at the time when the Malolos Republic was already on the retreat. This gave rise to later glorified accounts that "he secretly performed several missions for the revolutionary junta of Cebu." A very deliberate person even at a young age, Osmeña quickly saw, not long after the start of Filipino-American hostilities, the inevitability of American victory. He saw that both personal and national aspirations had to be pursued within the realities of American rule. Towards this end, he assiduously applied himself to the understanding of American law, politics, and government. (This included his taking English lessons in early 1900 from Rizal's widow, Josephine Bracken.)

In the provincial election of 16 April 1899, Osmeña was one of those who received some votes (but did not win) for the position of "provincial representative to Manila."[2] Then, in early 1900, Osmeña invited writers Jaime C. de Veyra and Rafael Palma to come to Cebu and work with him in putting out *El Nuevo Dia*, to be financed by the wealthy Chinese business-man who would soon become his father-in-law, Nicasio Chiong-Veloso. *El Nuevo Dia* was launched on 16 April 1900.

As publisher of *El Nuevo Dia*, Cebu's first daily newspaper, Osmeña became a figure of public consequence in Cebu. The newspaper, with its "independent and critical" stance gave him a reputation as one of the "na-tionalists" of the day. The paper's run-in with American censors helped build up this reputation. *El Nuevo Dia* was suspended just a month-and-a-half after it came out (and stayed suspended for two months) due to its issue of 19 May 1900, which carried a report on a Filipino-American en-counter in Leyte. The American censor reduced the American losses to seven dead and 11 wounded, three or four times less than the figures in the report the paper received from a source in Ormoc, Leyte. (At this time, newspaper proofs had to be sent to the American censor prior to publication.) De Veyra and Palma printed the original report but introduced in parentheses the American censor's figures.[3]

El Nuevo Dia was suspended twice, its offices searched by American soldiers, and management threatened with banishment of its personnel or throwing of its printing equipment into the sea. Yet, it was far from being a revolutionary paper and the editorial decisions that upset the U.S. censors may have been as much (or more) the making of De Veyra or Palma as of Osmeña himself.

El Nuevo Dia showed Osmeña's skills at survival. Its maiden-issue editorial statement (16 April 1900) is characteristic of Osmeña: reasonable, conservative, and pragmatic. It stays within "the limits of the possible," balancing the interests of conflicting parties, adopting that tone of conciliation that Americans themselves, including Governor-General Taft, were beginning to sound:

> We shall not stir up hatreds; we shall not plant distrust;
> seeking the national good, we shall urge harmony upon the
> two nations that continue to fight in our land, appeasing the
> fire of war and muffling the roar of artillery with words of
> peace and phrases of love. . . so that all wounds may heal and
> all rancor may disappear.[4]

The editorial acknowledges American strength ("an inflexible circle of steel") but invokes the "liberal tradition" of the United States and sees in it hope that Filipino aspirations can be served.

Osmeña was developing his skills in the art of the possible. He took his oath of allegiance to the U.S. on 23 March 1901. In the first election for the governorship of Cebu in 1902, he was one of the important men who worked for the election of Juan Climaco. A symbiotic relationship was to develop between the ambitious Osmeña and the retired revolutionary who was almost 20 years his senior. Osmeña was Climaco's precocious political lieutenant while Climaco, in turn, promoted the young Osmeña's career. That the two were drawn together seems odd only on the surface. The Climacos and Osmeñas were bound together by multiple marital and social ties. For one, Juan Climaco's nephew, Arsenio Climaco, was married to a cousin of Osmeña. Arsenio stood as best man at Osmeña's wedding to Estefania Chiong-Veloso on 10 April 1901. The Climacos and Osmeñas were both of the Filipino-Chinese merchant elite of the city. Llorente, the Hispanic aristocrat who was Climaco's opponent for governor in 1902 was, at least ethnically, an outsider to the larger, more powerful circle of Chinese mestizos.

In 1903, Osmeña placed second in the bar examinations and set up his *bufete* at the Osmeña residence on corner Felipe II (now Juan Luna) and Lapulapu Streets in the inner city. He went on to have a short stint as an elected member of the municipal council of Cebu (1903–1904). He had begun to catch the admiring eye of American officials and businessmen in Cebu—men like Judge Carlock, Cebu collector of customs James J. Rafferty, lawyer Martin M. Levering, and businessman John M. Switzer. On 10 January 1903, Carlock wrote to Taft recommending Osmeña for appointment as registrar of deeds for Cebu. Of the young Osmeña, Carlock wrote: "He is a popular, progressive and honorable young man."[5] (It is not clear what came out of the recommendation but Osmeña at this time was clearly setting his sights on higher things.)

In 1904, after Climaco's reelection as Cebu governor, Osmeña was appointed provincial fiscal of Cebu in place of Mariano Cui who was promoted to a judgeship. In 1905, he was made concurrent provincial fiscal for Negros Oriental. As a fiscal, Osmeña impressed Americans with his progressive ideas, particularly when he was tasked in March 1905 to take charge of replanning the burned central business district of Cebu City.[6]

When Climaco left for the United States in April 1904 as one of the commissioners to the St. Louis Exposition of 1904, Climaco designated Osmeña as acting governor with Governor-General Luke Wright's approval. Though he served for only two months, the appointment gave notice of Osmeña's growing prominence in Cebu.

His political skills were made evident in the visit of Secretary of War William Howard Taft on 22 August 1905. In what was considered "the grandest welcoming ceremony in the city since 1898," Cebu laid out the royal welcome mat for the 24-hour visit of a distinguished party that included Taft, U.S. senators and congressmen, and Governor-General Luke Wright.[7]

Organized by provincial officials and the city's leading residents, the welcome was intended to dramatize "popular acceptance" of American tutelage. "The people of Cebu endeavored specially to demonstrate by that splendid reception that they wished to be courteous and hospitable to the representatives of the great people." At the same time, Cebuanos took the occasion to demonstrate their aspirations within American rule. Days before the arrival of Taft, in a convention held at Teatro Junquera on 6 August 1905, Cebuano leaders, including municipal presidents, gathered to lay down preparations for the visit and ratify resolutions to be presented to the Congress of the United States and the Philippine Commission. Framed as a memorial, these resolutions were to be "the expression of the will" of the people. The memorial, which was formally presented to Taft during the visit, had 53 signatories, among them such leading citizens as Celestino Rodriguez, Vicente Sotto, Arsenio Climaco, Luciano Bacayo, Clodoaldo Rocamora, and Dionisio Jakosalem.

Running for some 38 pages, the carefully crafted memorial began thus:

> Honorable Gentlemen: Designs, superior to the will of men,
> have placed the fate of the Filipinos in the hands of the
> people of the United States. Fortunately, the people of the
> United States have assumed this responsibility before all
> Nations, through motives of liberality and altruism.[8]

The memorial invoked "the principle that the people of the United States cherish no other purpose towards us than that of making us a free and happy people" and liberally quotes from various American presidents and from Taft himself. It presented 24 "propositions" for the proper governance of the Philippines. Its core propositions asked that the U.S. Congress "declare its intention with regard to the future and definite status of the Philippines"; that such decision be based solely on "the happiness of the inhabitants of these islands and the demonstration that the Filipinos may have made of their capacity for self-government"; and that this "capacity for self-government" be assessed "from the viewpoint of Philippine interests" and not on criteria exclusively American. The rest of the propositions covered a wide range of topics, ranging from municipal rule and the establishment of a Philippine Assembly to matters of tariff and taxation. (During the visit, articles of sugar and hemp adorned the parade route to demonstrate before the visitors the Cebuanos' support for tariff reductions in the U.S. for Philippine agricultural products.) Underlying the various propositions was the desire for expanding and strengthening Filipino participation in government, particularly on provincial and municipal levels.

Sergio Osmeña played a leading role in these events. He had gained the reputation of being the "brains" behind Governor Climaco and was instrumental in crafting the memorial to Taft and thus shaping "the sentiments and ideas of the people."

Taft was impressed. In his speech at the banquet and ball held in honor of his party in the evening of 22 August, he commended the Cebuanos, saying—in the ill-disguised tones of imperium—"there is in this community a feeling among thinking men that it is better that their thinking men should take part in this great work (of the U.S.) and deal with facts and not waste their energies and their strength in theories that are impossible."[9] Taft took notice of the young Osmeña. During his speech, he digressed to laud the young Cebuano: "If it shall be that (Osmeña) is to be called to higher honors, we may be confident that the people of Cebu will lose nothing in his administration of any office to which he may be called." Taft was undoubtedly privy to political goings-on in Cebu. A member of his staff, James LeRoy, recorded in his diary: "(Osmeña) has evidently been groomed by the American officials here as a candidate for provincial governor."[10]

Prior to the gubernatorial elections of 5 February 1906, Climaco decided not to seek a third term for reasons of poor health. (Climaco, whose relations with the U.S. military had not been completely harmonious, died at the age of 47 in 1907.) Sponsored by Climaco, Osmeña ran unopposed, garnering 378 votes out of the 404 votes cast. (Climaco still received 21 votes and three other nominal candidates had four votes.)

No effort was spared to make Osmeña's inauguration as governor on 5 March 1906 a truly grand affair.[11] It was to be not just the inauguration of a man but of an era. The two-day festivities (5 and 6 March) opened with fireworks, band music through the city streets, and the sounding of boat whistles and horns. The celebration included a grand feria at Plaza Rizal, a musical concert, a horse race at Hipodromo sponsored by the Cebu Jockey Club, parades through streets lined with gaily decorated houses, and a public dance. Osmeña took his oath of office before Judge Adolph Wislizenus at noon of 5 March. The oath taking was followed by a public reception in the plaza fronting the provincial capitol building on Martires Street. In the afternoon, a civic parade took place with U.S. troops, business and civic groups, and departments of the government participating.

As governor of Cebu, Osmeña had the stage to demonstrate his political leadership. Osmeña's first annual report to the governor-general communicates that "getting-things-done" ethic that must have impressed American authorities. In an assured, self-congratulatory account of plans and accomplishments, Osmeña enumerates initiatives in bringing the government close to the municipalities, streamlining local administration, improving peace and order and social services, improving tax collection and fiscal management, and promoting public works. He goes on to suggest electoral and administrative reforms, increased power for local governments, expanded judicial and educational systems, and measures for improving business conditions. The upbeat report ends by saying that, with the economic crisis having passed, with the "wealthy man feeling secure in his home, his property and tranquillity, and the tiller of the soil being free to devote his energies to the art of husbandry; with universal confidence in the officials of government keeping wide open the doors of law and justice, the political situation does not offer evidence other than that of general satisfaction."[12]

Osmeña quickly won the patronage of high American officials. He also actively courted this patronage. He worked in close consultation with Governor-General Henry C. Ide in his antipulahan campaign of 1906. Taft and William Cameron Forbes were impressed by the young governor's reasonable, efficient, and pragmatic approach to governance, which conformed to conservative American ideas of "good government." He was a political leader after their own heart and one with whom, they knew, they could work.

In the task of balancing Filipino aspirations with American goals, the Americans saw the value of Osmeña as a leader. Governor-General Forbes said Osmeña "has shown such marked executive ability and. . . has really played ball with us in everything we have undertaken to do."[13] American leaders were impressed by Osmeña's political skills, his ability to fuse and ride out contradictory interests. Leonard Wood remarked: "He is cunning and persistent and secret."[14] Elsewhere, Forbes also assessed Osmeña thus: "Osmeña is clever enough politician to put himself in the forefront of the popular movement in order to hold his power. He is not a fighter; he is always a maneuverer and conciliator and trader."[15]

In the space of less than a decade, Sergio Osmeña steadily rose as a partaker of the power of the evolving political order. His career was a signal illustration of the triumph of the ethos of collaboration. Osmeña would become not only the leading political figure of Cebu but of the country as well. As early as 1905, on his own and as surrogate for Governor Climaco, he already had contacts with Manila-based Filipino leaders. Teodoro M. Kalaw writes that Osmeña took several trips to Manila to participate in meetings of Nacionalista leaders at the home of Don Pablo Ocampo on Calle Palma. These meetings drafted the Nacionalista Party memorials presented to Taft in 1905. Apparently, the young man from Cebu quickly established his presence. Kalaw credits Osmeña with having coined the slogan of "Immediate Independence" which, he says, "caused a great deal of talk because of its radicalism." (In its use, of course, the phrase proved quite elastic.) Perhaps no other person exerted as much an influence in shaping and articulating the elite, post-revolutionary position on "independence" as did Osmeña. Osmeña, Kalaw says, was the one who recast the old appeals for independence and placed them on "a more practical basis." Instead of arguing that independence should be granted because liberty is "the natural right of all peoples" or that Filipinos have a "high degree of culture," Osmeña—in a speech at a banquet in honor of Commissioner W. Morgan Shuster in 1906—laid "the case of the Filipino people" by saying that independence would be "the logical result of the develop-

ment of the American policy in the Islands, as enunciated by those responsible for the occupation." Kalaw remarks: "To present for the first time the
issue of independence, not as a thesis wholly and separately that of the
Filipinos, but as the logical result and final flowering of the American occupation of the Philippines, is doubtless an indication of an exceptional
insight."[16]

While what Kalaw meant to be praise is exaggerated (and, in an important sense, misguided in the manner that it cancels the meaning of the
anti-American resistance), it illustrates how skillfully Osmeña placed himself at the head of the parliamentary movement for independence.

In October 1906, Osmeña was elected presiding officer of the convention of provincial governors in Manila. In the 30 July 1907 elections for
the First Philippine Assembly, he ran as a candidate of the Partido
Nacionalista and was elected one of the delegates from Cebu province. In
seeking the speakership of the assembly, he did his homework and left
nothing to chance. He impressed his fellow delegates with his knowledge
of the various parliamentary systems of the world and arrived in Manila
ready with policies and a code of procedure to propose for the assembly.
On 16 October 1907, he was elected by acclamation to the post of Speaker.
He thus became the highest Filipino official in the American government
of the Philippines.

The rise of Sergio Osmeña marks the beginning of a new story. The
time of war gave way to the time of politics. During the first decade of the
century, groundwork was laid for an electoral process, a new civil service,
an extensive judicial system, a new system of municipal, provincial, and
national governments, a Filipino legislature, and a political party system.

The Americans provided Filipino leaders with an expanding arena
for political participation. In the Spanish regime, Filipinos could aspire for
no higher offices than junior posts in the provincial government. The provincial governor was appointed by the Spanish government. The four members of the provincial council (junta) were elected by the municipal captains (mayors), who were in turn elected by 12 delegates of the town
principalia, which is made up of all persons who have held certain offices
and persons who had paid $50 land tax. American policies, therefore, of-
fered the Filipino elite a frontier for political expansion. By 1906, the Filipino elite was at the head of municipal and provincial governments. With
the elections for the Philippine Assembly in 1907, the elite moved into an
even wider, supralocal field of power.

Politics remained an elite preserve. In municipal elections, suffrage
requirements barred those who did not fulfill any of the following qualifications: legal residents 26 years old or over who were (1) previous office

holders, (2) paid at least 300 pesos in taxes or had property valued at 500 pesos or more, or (3) could speak, read, and write in English or Spanish. In 1903, less than 3 percent of the population of the archipelago was qualified to vote. In the 1907 Philippine Assembly elections, there were only 4,416 qualified electors in Cebu province in a total population of around 700,000. In the municipal elections of this time, qualified electors in the province numbered only 8,681.

The elite composition of officeholders can be seen in the profile of the First Philippine Assembly (1907–1909). There was, countrywide, a total of 80 delegates with an average age of 37. Of the delegates, 47 were lawyers, 57 had university education, and 75 were educated in Manila or Spain. Continuities in elite dominance can be seen in the fact that of the 80 delegates, 21 had served in the Spanish government, 54 held a civil or military office or both in the republican interregnum, and 54 had served in the American government in the islands.[17]

"Filipinization" focused Filipino attention on the quarrying of power and sinecures. By 1910, provincial governments were virtually controlled by Filipinos. Out of a total of 1,069 regular officials and employees at the province level, only 36 were American (or barely one per province). By 1924, less than 2 percent of positions in the Philippine government, outside of schoolteachers, were held by Americans.[18]

With the advent of the Philippine Assembly elections in 1906, factions of the elite girded for power. The Federalistas, hounded by their "collaborationist" image, regrouped and rejuvenated their party under a new name, Partido Nacional Progresista. The Nacionalistas were riven by internal dissension among three factions—Inmediatistas, Urgentistas, Unionistas—all of whom professed commitment to "immediate independence," but were divided in their leaders and working relations with American officials. These factions were to merge into a single Nacionalista Party on 12 March 1907 under the leadership of Sergio Osmeña and Manuel Quezon.

In Cebu, all seven of the elected assemblymen were Nacionalistas: Osmeña, lawyer Celestino Rodriguez, planter Pedro Rodriguez, lawyer Filemon Sotto, planter Alejandro Ruiz, lawyer Casiano Causin, and lawyer and former revolutionary Troadio Galicano. The Nacionalistas received 3,088 out of the 3,692 votes cast in the elections. The total number of qualified electors in Cebu province was 4,416.[19]

There was much interest in striking up alliances and consolidating local power bases. The theme of "immediate independence" was on everybody's lips but definitions of national purpose were less important in themselves as they were a way of staking out space in the power system

which one, or one's class, could occupy. Governor-General Forbes remarked
that the politicians were exploiting the "independence issue" because it
was "a great vote-getter and makes a fine series of phrases in the campaign
oratory."[20] On the eve of the assembly elections, Forbes privately sounded
out the Nacionalista leaders on how strongly they would push for independence if elected. Forbes wrote in his journal:

> They practically admitted to me that it was really a catch way
> of getting votes; that what they wanted was office, not
> independence; that they understood very clearly that the
> present existing condition of affairs would not change and
> that we need have very little anxiety about what they would
> do when they got in; that they would be friendly to the
> government and not attempt to start any waves.[21]

In Cebu, the municipal elections of 1905 were hotly contested. In
the 41 towns where elections were held, the results in 25 were protested.
Sixteen of the protested elections were approved and nine were annulled.
Of the nine, three were again annulled after a second election. Osmeña
reported: "The interest of political factions in the pueblos which are the
source of agitation during elections is rapidly increasing."[22]

Cebu had quieted down and conditions were ready for men like
Osmeña. In 1906, the junta of Cebu City declared that "never before during American occupation has there existed in this city a greater general
spirit of welcome to the Military than prevails here today."[23] The local
elite had been won over almost entirely to the American side. This is seen,
for instance, in the public meeting jointly held in Cebu on 27 February
1908 by the provincial board, Cebu municipal council, and the Cebu chamber of commerce, at which a resolution was passed urging the American
government to establish a U.S. military reservation in Cebu. At this time
there were plans for a 3,000-acre reservation for U.S. troops to be established in the city suburb of Mabolo. (Plans were afoot for a reservation
either in Mabolo or in Mactan as early as 1905.) Addressed to Secretary of
War Taft in Washington, the resolution said that the stationing of American troops would encourage business investment in Cebu. "The citizens
of Cebu are now and always have been anxious to encourage the stationing of large bodies of troops near the City," the resolution declared. A committee was formed to urge adoption of the measure, composed of such
men as Speaker Sergio Osmeña, Gov. Dionisio Jakosalem, Assemblymen
Celestino Rodriguez, Filemon Sotto, Pedro Rodriguez, Troadio Galicano,
Alejandro Ruiz, Casiano Causin, and Jaime de Veyra, Cebu municipal presi-

dent Martin Llorente, Cebu Chamber of Commerce president Bernard Cogan, and such wealthy businessmen as Lucio Herrera, Florentino Rallos, Martin M. Levering, and Mariano Veloso.[24]

There were occasional strains in Filipino-American relations in Cebu and, from time to time, there were cases of "banditry" reported from the hinterlands—from the activities of brigand leader Eugenio Alcachufas in 1907–1909, running into the *colorum* activities of Laureano Solar after 1914. The political strife, however, had shifted to the periodic electoral contests held under U.S. auspices. There was practically only one political party in the province—the Nacionalista Party—and dissensions, given liberal coverage in the local press, were personal and factional in nature.

The old leaders of the revolution and the war against the Americans faded into the background or into the crevices of the emerging political order. A few years after their surrender, Nicolas Godines was municipal president of Opon, Saturnino Echavez municipal president of Aloguinsan, and Angel Libre municipal president of Toledo. Pantaleon del Rosario served as deputy to Governor Climaco in 1902, became a Cebu City councilor in 1904, and then moved on to higher positions in government. Troadio Galicano was a Cebu City councilor in 1904 and became a member of the Philippine Assembly in 1907. Arsenio Climaco was also a Cebu City councilor in 1904 and later went on to become provincial governor of Cebu. Gervasio Padilla went on to serve as chief of police of Cebu City, deputy to the provincial treasurer and, in 1912, member of the Philippine Assembly. Tomas Alonso also went on to become a member of the Philippine Assembly.

Mateo Luga joined the Philippine Constabulary and became a zealous and valiant soldier for the Americans, then resigned to work for the American-owned Philippine Refining Company. Luga later retired to Negros island. Melquiades Lasala also joined the Philippine Constabulary, rising to the rank of "sub-inspector" in 1903. He was accidentally killed in Asturias in 1904.[25]

Other leaders receded into the shadows. The Pacañas returned to Labangon and lived out their years in relative obscurity. Enrique Lorega played a peripheral role in local politics in the years after his surrender. In 1941, at the age of 86, he died in his shack on Lopez Jaena Street, blind and virtually forgotten. He was so poor, the state assumed the expenses for his funeral. After his surrender in 1902, Marcial Velez became active in civic and political affairs in Cebu City, but he died early.

After the war, Alejo Miñoza was employed by Governor Climaco as a deputy (*mensajero especial*) of the provincial government. He took up residence in a barrio of Opon where he died a poor man in 1925. After his surrender, Potenciano Aliño was harassed by church authorities for his advocacy of Aglipayanism. He worked as a journalist and, in 1907, died in poverty at the age of 42.

Hilario Aliño escaped to Negros after the surrenders and was never heard from since then. Since systematic records for the Cebuano side of the war have not been kept, history is silent on the many who fell in battle and the others who survived the war.

Julio Llorente, after serving as governor, served as a court of first instance judge in Samar and then in Luzon. He sold his properties and left Cebu to live in Manila, feeling his fellow Cebuanos had not given him sufficient recognition. He died a poor and largely forgotten man sometime in the 1950s. Much earlier, Luis Flores, somewhat unjustly maligned for having delivered the revolution to its enemies, bore the illness he contracted in the hills and died a poor and obscure man in 1904. Juan Climaco, too, died relatively early, at the age of 47, on 16 July 1907, the year after he left the governorship.

The Maxiloms suffered a tragic fate. The brothers Samuel and Nemesio met violent deaths after their surrender. Arcadio Maxilom, after his imprisonment, returned to his hometown in Tuburan where he was unsuccessful in local politics against old enemies. He was paralyzed and died on 10 August 1924 after a long and painful illness. The Tabals were more fortunate. On 4 October 1907, after their surrender, Quintin and Anatalio were sentenced to life imprisonment for bandolerismo. A few days after their conviction, they were pardoned by the governor-general, after they took the oath of allegiance, in recognition of their help to the authorities in bringing in "over 100 outlaws."[26] Many ordinary peasants, however, branded bandits and rebels, were forgotten and continued to languish in jails. Their names had not been recorded.

The war had ended.

Epilogue

A WAR NEVER really ends. When the causes for resistance remain, then a war never really ends. It assumes other forms, becomes an illusion of itself, a subversion of what it intends; it is submerged and yet can rise again, find itself once more in the tenacious imagining of a better order of things.

War casts a stark light on society: It brings into sharp relief a political field in which people have to define themselves in relation to each other and the Other. Who and what are threatened by what or whom? On the other hand, war raises not only the threat of loss and destruction but, by unhinging a world, it opens up (as it also closes) possibilities. How and what possibilities are discerned?

In studies of the war against Spain and the United States there has been a tendency to lean towards a simple dichotomy that distinguishes between the response of the elite and that of the masses, ascribing to either one or the other the primary role for the resistance.[1] What is inadequately appreciated is the complex social formation of Philippine society at the turn of the century. A "two-class" model makes for a net too widely spaced it allows a lot of significant data to fall through the sieve. For sure, the model is too cumbersome for the case of Cebu.

On the eve of the war, Cebu province was a socially irregular, unstable and inchoate landscape. Nineteenth-century economic changes created new social groups, revised old social relations, and primed the appearance of new social formations. This was most evident in the increasingly differentiated economy and ethnically complex port society of Cebu City. The city was the headquarters of an export-oriented economy, the point for the collecting, processing, and transshipping of goods from a hinterland that included not only the island of Cebu but provinces in the Eastern Visayas and Northern Mindanao.

Who were the primary beneficiaries of this order? To begin with, there were the Spaniards who stood at the helm of the colonial government (and, in Cebu, the central figures were the governor and the bishop): They extracted wealth from such assets as land and people as well as from taxes and duties on services, industries, and trade. Yet, Spanish power was more parasitic than dynamic. Outside the Augustinian estates in the Mandaue and Talisay areas, Spaniards were not directly engaged in agricultural production. Spaniards constituted a minuscule portion of the provincial population and they did not own land in the Cebu countryside.[2] Their prominence largely resided in their control of the civil and ecclesiastical bureaucracy.

The most dynamic sector in local society was the foreign merchant houses that presided over the export and import of goods. In the early nineteenth century, these houses had provincial agents that supplied them with the products needed in the markets of Great Britain, United States, Australia, and Spain. After the opening of the port of Cebu to world trade in 1860, they established permanent offices in Cebu. The American firm of Russell and Sturgis and the English houses of Loney, Kerr and Company and Smith Bell and Company established control of the trade. They bought agricultural products, supplied credit, accepted funds at interest, had direct access to trade information, operated ships or acted as consignees for shipping lines, and performed insurance and brokerage functions.

On the eve of the war, the Cebuano elite was no longer a homogeneous group.[3] Principalia status came from a mix of factors: wealth, public office, lineage, and education. The principalia was made up of merchants, landowners, shopkeepers, doctors, lawyers, pharmacists, as well as artisans, tanners, carpenters, bakers, and seamstresses. Titles of don and doña were used by people of divergent statuses. A carriage-maker or clerk, who comes from a family that had at one time served in the Spanish administration, may carry such a title. As a social category, then, principalia does not quite define the position of persons in the existing power system.

Within the principalia, the important distinction was between those who stood close to the center of the port economy (foreign merchant houses, the highest Spanish officials, and a few Filipino families based in the city) and those who were at its peripheries. The most powerful Cebu families were almost wholly of mestizo stock (Spanish or Chinese), or foreigners, who resided in the city (or headquartered in it), controlled sizeable landholdings, capital, and a network of clients in the hinterland. They had direct links with the foreign merchant houses for which they usually served as agents or compradores. In the 1890s, these included the Velosos, Llorentes, Climacos, Osmeñas, and Mejias. These families built up their wealth throughout the nineteenth-century, profiting from a symbiotic relationship with both the Spanish administration and the foreign merchant houses. They were almost wholly mestizo in ethnic character—Spanish and Chinese—easily straddling local and global worlds.

At the periphery of the "elite" were a large number of property owners whose holdings were on a much lesser scale than the families earlier mentioned, and were less aggressive or less favorably positioned to fully exploit the opportunities of the port-oriented economy. Growing educational opportunities (there were 662 students enrolled in the Colegio-Seminario de San Carlos in 1895) and expanding communications raised social expectations.[4] There were cracks and fault lines in the social system: dividing the municipal gentry in the countryside from the aggressive, port-based entrepreneurs; the emerging proletariat and petty bourgeoisie from the Spanish bureaucrats and their allies; and the marginal indios from the economically dominant mestizos.

The city population was internally divided by the pressures of a rising cash economy. An occupational census of the city in 1900 shows that 6,014 were employed in trade and transportation and 5,170 in domestic and personal services as opposed to only 814 city residents involved in agriculture.[5] The city was increasingly populated by people who lived off industry, trade, and the service sectors: wage laborers, skilled craftsmen, market gardeners, domestic servants, hawkers, employees and professionals. Moreover, the increased circulation of population within the colony in the nineteenth century made for a more diverse, volatile society.

The larger mass of the provincial population, as far as the written records go, was a largely anonymous entity. By the 1890s, however, the shift to commercial agriculture and the export trade had brought large sections of Cebu island into the orbit of the port of Cebu. The rural population was increasingly peasantized and enmeshed in widening networks of social and economic dependency.

Due to the different positions of persons and groups in the social field, they perceived and participated in events differently. Among the elite, the war against Spain was animated by libertarian ideas as well as by the awareness, sharpened by nineteenth-century changes, of the irrelevance of the Spanish presence. The Spanish colonial administration had become excess baggage to a local elite grown confident in their ability to take matters of governance in their own hands.

The war against the United States was fueled by the same sentiments. Nevertheless, it was also a different war. The elite knew that, in
the course of the nineteenth century, the Philippines had come within the
orbit of a world economy, locked into a dependent relationship with the
developed nations of the West (particularly the rising nation of the United
States). The elite must have perceived the imbalance in the relationship.
Yet, they profited from it, enjoying a prosperity they never experienced
before. Collaboration was a stance taken not simply out of self-interested
calculations of profit but by the politically demobilizing sense of what, to
many, must have seemed the inexorability of historical process. Spain was
a country receding into the past, the United States loomed in the future.

On the other hand, there were elements of the elite, more particularly of the lower orders, who participated only peripherally or indirectly in
the new prosperity, transcended class-bound interests, and were moved
by racial pride and ideas of liberte. The most active leaders of the resistance came from this group: socially displaced political agents (Pantaleon
del Rosario, Mateo Luga), young students (Andres Jayme, Tomas Alonso),
municipal landowners (Jacinto Pacaña, Arcadio Maxilom), and urban bourgeoisie (Alejo Miñoza, Enrique Lorega). They fought a war that, in a sense,
was doomed from the very beginning—not only because of the superior
martial powers of the United States but because, given the society, Filipinos could not have acted as one.

And what of the now largely anonymous mass of resisters? To say
that they simply followed patrons and kinsmen is to deny them political
knowledge of the social and economic positions they occupied. The growing intensification in the movement of men and ideas through the countryside in the nineteenth century must have equipped rural dwellers with
a sense of membership in an evolving national brotherhood. To this extent, they knowingly participated in what was a national war, first, against
the Spaniards, and then, against the Americans. Yet, their expectations of
what the goals of this war were must have been shaped by the economic
and cultural positions they occupied in a native society where exploitation
wore not only the face of the foreigner but that of fellow Filipinos. Hence,
what many of them fought was also a social war, one heavy with the idiom
of millenarianism and peasant egalitarianism. This became most visible
after the surrender of the republican generals in 1901 when the complexion of
the war changed with the spread of the so-called pulahan movement.

All these made for a highly asymmetrical war in which who was fighting whom, and for what reasons, was not always clear. Indeed, a war is
never simple. In Cebu, complex social tensions played themselves out in a

complex war in which Cebuanos fought not only against the Americans but also against each other.

How was the war of resistance structured? A national army waged war against the United States. Provincial troops, as in Cebu, maintained communications with central organs in Luzon, acknowledged the leadership of Aguinaldo, followed orders from higher authorities, adhered to standard commissions and procedures and, in other respects, operated as units of a larger army. In other ways, this national army was a fiction (as much recent scholarship tends to argue). There were groups that operated apart from, as well as against, the Aguinaldo army; the army was often "national" more in form than in substance; the bulk of the population did not actively join in the fighting; and the ideology and motives of the ordinary soldiers who fought within this army may have been different from those of their leaders. Nevertheless, the fact remains that it was a "national" army—albeit inchoate, plagued by contradictions—that embodied the main resistance against the Americans from 1899 to 1901. That it lost the war is to be explained, in large measure, by its failure to become what it claimed to be. This failure was less a matter of strategy and tactics as it was, in the final instance, an outcome of the conditions of social and national formation at the time the war was fought. The resistance was stymied by crosscutting and opposing interests. However, given the society as it was constituted at the time, as well as the shortness of time into which events were collapsed, it could not have been otherwise.[6]

What did it all amount to? The meaning of the Filipino-American War is both diverse and dense. Writ large, America tried to remake Philippine society by implanting "democracy" through a process of guided self-government, popular education, and economic development. It was an enterprise undermined by political cross-purposes, imperial conceit, and parochial naivete. Contemporary scholarship suggests that the impact of U.S. rule has been less beneficent and more limited than claimed in the past. America embarked on a fresh "adventure" but also worked within the limited (and, often, conservative) parameters of her own culture, which predisposed her to a partnership with the local elite and a simple faith in "popular education" and economic "developmentalism."[7]

On the other hand, the resilience and integrity of Philippine society were underestimated. Filipino response to U.S. rule was mediated by tenacious facts of social structure and historical experience. In the accommodation of American and Filipino conservatisms, much was preserved. The basic problems of poverty and dependency remained and were heightened, the basic social configuration was preserved, and the character of the economy sustained. The U.S. built on earlier economic accomplishments. The major changes in the economy took place in the nineteenth century, before the U.S. occupation, in the shift from subsistence cultivation to cash cropping. In 1855, the value of goods exported by the Philippines amounted to 5.9 million pesos; 18.9 million pesos in 1875; 36.6 million pesos in 1895. This increased to 69.8 million pesos in 1909, then to 95.9 million pesos in 1913. In 1913 as in 1900, the four principal exports of the archipelago were abaca, copra, tobacco, and sugar. The United States "captured" and presided over a society that, in the nineteenth century, was already increasingly locked into larger worlds.

All these have fostered a tendency in recent scholarship to mitigate the responsibility of the Americans by focusing on the active complicity of local elites and arguing that U.S. occupation had little effect. This tendency must not erase the fact of massive destruction wrought by the American invasion. It must not, at the same time, obscure the fact that the U.S. occupation cleared the ground for the institutionalization of a neo-colonial Philippines.

Nothing changed, much was changed. An American military officer, who was stationed in Cebu in 1902, revisited the city in 1911. In 1911, American soldiers were still very much in evidence in Cebu City. Six companies of the Ninth Infantry, under Col. Charles J. Crane, were stationed in Warwick Barracks. The Americans also occupied 12.5 hectares of private land for military reservation and target range purposes, in addition to 19 houses and rooms in 8 other houses in the city as "officers' quarters." Most of these were located on Colon, Magallanes, and other streets close to the Recollect Plaza (which the Americans renamed Plaza Washington).[8]

The officer saw a changed city.[9] What used to be just two wooden piers in 1902 had become a million-and-a-quarter-peso wharf that could accommodate at the same time five ocean-going vessels as well as a number of small coasters. At the port could now be seen a brand-new customs house and a row of concrete warehouses with foreign names (Castle Bros., McLeod, Stevenson and Company, Ltd.). In the inner city itself were new concrete buildings and thriving British, Chinese, and American commercial establishments. There used to be just three foreign export-import houses in Cebu. Now there were thirteen, in addition to two commercial banks, all foreign-owned.

A new waterworks system was in the process of being built and there was talk of building an electric railway within the city. Philippine Railway Company operated a line that extended from Cebu to Danao in the north and Argao in the south, with four trains dispatched daily in either direction from the Cebu station. The city electric plant (Visayan Electric Company) was in the process of being expanded to generate not just night but also day service. The city had a telephone service, an English-language newspaper (Alfred G. Andersen's *The Cebu Chronicle*), two 10-ton ice plants, and several hotels. At the waterfront was a new public market with nearly 300 stalls. A public high school and trade school had just opened; the government had 43,003 students in the whole province. Foreign residents found modern amenities at such social clubs as Club Ingles and United Service Club. Movies were shown with increasing regularity at several cinematografos in the city. At Plaza Washington (now Freedom Park), Cebuanos were taking enthusiastically to the game of baseball.

The visiting American marveled at the changes. The honking of cars had become part of the sounds of the city for, by 1911, livery stable operators had Overlands, Buicks, and Fords for rent. In 1902, it was unsafe for foreigners to walk beyond the inner city, say to Sambag, as insurgents and bandits lurked in the city outskirts. Now, peace-and-order and sanitation conditions had markedly improved. He learned that one could now run up to Danao in an automobile, over a fine road, in 40 minutes. It used to be a two-day hike.

The American visitor called on an old friend, Florentino Rallos, the former Cebu presidente. At his house on Colon Street, smaller than the one he occupied in 1901, Rallos reminisced about the past, bitter about how the new politics had left him behind. He had lost a great part of his wealth and, half-paralyzed, he now rarely ventured outside his home. (He died the year after.) He lamented how things had not changed entirely for the better, the young men were leaving the fields, crowding into the towns, seeking work. Asked by the visitor what he thought about what the American occupation had wrought, the old man said: The poor are still poor.

The American wandered back to old Plaza Independencia, looking over the scorched grass towards the fort, and was visited by melancholy over the war he and his friends had fought. Looking landwards, he saw once more the barren mountain range of the island and recalled interminable hikes over those burning hills, and the apparent fruitlessness of it all.

It is a different city but the hills are still there.

Sources

The principal sources for this narrative are (1) the original U.S. military records classified as Record Group 395 at the U.S. National Archives in Washington D.C., USA, and (2) the "Philippine Insurgent Records," in particular those pertaining to the Visayan islands, referred to as the "Noble Papers" (microfilm rolls 637–43 from the U.S. National Archives, at the Cebuano Studies Center in Cebu City), and the assorted files classified as Selected Documents (SD) (microfilm rolls 4, 13, 59, 62, and 68 from the U.S. National Archives, at the National Library in Manila).

In the United States, I also availed of related record groups at the U.S. National Archives as well as other materials—personal papers, manuscripts, and books—at such institutions as the Library of Congress (Washington, D.C.), U.S. Military History Institute (Carlisle, Pennsylvania), Harvard University (Boston, Massachusetts), Duke University (Durham, North Carolina), University of North Carolina (Chapel Hill, North Carolina), University of Michigan (Ann Arbor, Michigan), and the New York Public Library (New York).

In the Philippines, I worked with resources at the National Library, Manila, and the Cebuano Studies Center, University of San Carlos, Cebu City. These included manuscripts, Cebu newspapers, and other publications.

The popular histories of the war are by James H. Blount, *The American Occupation of the Philippines, 1898–1912* (New York: G. P. Putnam's Sons, 1912); and Leon Wolff, *Little Brown Brother* (London: Longmans, 1961). For studies of the American side of the war, see Daniel B. Schirmer, *Republic or Empire: The American Resistance to the Philippine War* (Cambridge: Schenkman Publishing Co., 1972); Richard E. Welch, Jr., *Response to Imperialism: The United States and the Philippine-American War, 1899–1902* (Chapel Hill: University of North Carolina Press, 1980); and Stuart C. Miller, *Benevolent Assimilation: The American Conquest of the Philippines, 1899–1903* (New Haven: Yale University Press, 1982).

For the Filipino response to the war, see Teodoro Agoncillo, *Malolos: The Crisis of the Republic* (Quezon City: University of the Philippines, 1960); and Bonifacio S. Salamanca, *The Filipino Response to American Rule, 1901–1913* (Quezon City: New Day Publishers, 1984).

Fresh perspectives on the war are offered in two important scholarly works: Reynaldo C. Ileto, *Pasyon and Revolution: Popular Movements in the Philippines, 1840–1910* (Quezon City: Ateneo de Manila University Press, 1979); and Milagros C. Guerrero, "Luzon at War: Contradictions in Philippine Society, 1899–1902" (Ph.D. diss., University of Michigan, 1977). For a recent reassessment, see Peter W. Stanley, ed., *Reappraising an Empire: New Perspectives on Philippine-American History* (Cambridge: Harvard University Press, 1984).

Notes

Abbreviations

ARWD	Annual Report of the War Department
BIA	Bureau of Insular Affairs
CSC	Cebuano Studies Center (University of San Carlos, Cebu City)
HDP	Historical Data Papers (National Library, Manila)
HU	Harvard University (Boston, Massachusetts)
LC	Library of Congress (Washington, D.C.)
PIR	Philippine Insurgent Records
PNA	Philippine National Archives (Manila)
RG	Record Group
RPC	Report of the Philippine Commission
TNL	The National Library (Manila)
UM	University of Michigan (Ann Arbor, Michigan)
USMHI	U.S. Military History Institute (Carlisle, Pennsylvania)
USNA	U.S. National Archives (Washington, D.C.)

Chapter 1: A Time Between Times

1. For a profile of Cebu in 1900 see USNA, RG 395, entry 5701, box 3, item 1520, "Information on Philippine Islands: Cebu, 1900."

2. No full and satisfactory history of the anti-Spanish revolution in Cebu exists. Useful references are articles in *Bag-ong Kusog* and other early twentieth-century Cebu newspapers; Fe Susan Go, "*Ang Sugbu sa Karaang Panahon*: An Annotated Translation of the 1935 History of Cebu (by Felix Sales)" (1976 M. A. thesis, at the University of San Carlos, the main part of which is soon to be published by the Ateneo de Manila University Press); Manuel Enriquez de la Calzada, *Ang Kagubut sa Sugbu, 1898* (Sugbu: Rotary Press, 1951); and Jovito S. Abellana, "Bisaya Patronymesis Sri Visjaya" (Ms., Cebuano Studies Center, ca. 1960). A short eyewitness account is Elisa Krapfenbauer, "Outbreak of the Revolution in Cebu in '98," *Special Boost Edition of the Cebu Chronicle*, ed. A. G. Andersen (Cebu: Cebu Chronicle, 1910), 41–44. (Krapfenbauer's husband owned the Botica Antigua, a pharmacy established in Cebu in the 1850s.) Also see John Foreman, *The Philippine Islands* (London: Sampson Low and Co., 1899), 551–54.

There are also primary documents on the anti-Spanish revolution in TNL, PIR, Selected Documents (SD), such as roll 13, SD 144, E. Verdeflor, "Diario de las operaciones," 30 November 1898; V. Garcia, "Diario de las operaciones," 6 December 1898; and M. Angulo, "Diario de las operaciones," 10 January 1899.

3. John R. M. Taylor, *The Philippine Insurrection Against the United States, 1898–1902*, 5 vols. (Pasay: Eugenio Lopez Foundation, 1971), 2:417–18; 3:113–16. For a discussion of the decree of 18 June 1898, see Agoncillo, *Malolos*, 228–32.

4. Teodoro M. Kalaw, *The Philippine Revolution* (Mandaluyong: Jorge B. Vargas Filipiniana Foundation, 1969), 82.

5. Go, "*Sugbu*," 253, 368.

6. Go, "*Sugbu*," 473–74, et passim.

7. Quoted in Wolff, *Little Brown Brother*, 75.

8. On moves to organize a Visayan government, see Kalaw, *Philippine Revolution*, 129–34; CSC, Noble Papers, roll 638, n982; Agoncillo, *Malolos*, 420–29. The sending of Mejia and Logarta to Iloilo is referred to in *Reseña Historica del Seminario Colegio de San Carlos de Cebu, 1867–1917* (Manila: E.C. McCullough and Co., 1917), 192; and Go, "*Sugbu*."

9. This meeting is discussed in "Kinsa ang Unang Gobernador Pilipinhon sa Sugbu," *Bag-ong Kusog* (25 December 1930), 12, 40; and "'Big Three' sa Sugbu sa Panahon sa Kagubut," *Bag-ong Kusog* (9 January 1931), 1, 16, 17.

10. Go, "*Sugbu*," 342–43.

11. *Reseña Historica*, 84–85, 135.

12. Taylor, *Philippine Insurrection*, Exhibit 1387.

13. The text of the proclamation is in Blount, *American Occupation*, 147–50.

14. Go, "*Sugbu*," 349–50.

15. Go, "*Sugbu*," 357–58.

16. Taylor, *Philippine Insurrection*, 418; *Go*, "*Sugbu*," 314.

17. USNA, RG 395, entry 2601, T. Hamer to A. A. General, 4 May 1899. References to the Llorente family are to be found in Bruce L. Fenner, *Cebu Under the Spanish Flag, 1521–1896* (Cebu: San Carlos Publications, 1985).

18. "Kinsa ba si Luis Flores sa Kagubut sa Sugbu," *Bag-ong Kusog* (23 December 1938), 27, 51, 64–65; "Heneral Luis Flores: Bayani ug Makilungsod," *Bag-ong Kusog* (6 April 1928), 8, 16; Go, "*Sugbu*," 385, 446.

19. *Reseña Historica*, 86–87, 135–36; Go, "*Sugbu*," 387–88; and John N. Schumacher, *Revolutionary Clergy: The Filipino Clergy and the Nationalist Movement, 1850–1903* (Quezon City: Ateneo de Manila University Press, 1981), 138.

20. Felix Sales says that Cebu was divided into 18 zones at the beginning of 1899 (Go, "*Sugbu*," 356–60). Discrepancies are partly explained by changes in military plans with shifts in the political or military situation.

21. Go, "*Sugbu*," 371–72.

22. For the extensive Climaco estate and the Climacos' relations to other families, see PNA, Protocolos, Cebu, bundle 1348, no. 339 (Inventory of the estate of D. Juan Climaco), 11 October 1875; bundle 1351, unnumbered (other Climaco documents), 1877. For biographical data on Juan Climaco, see "Kinsay Unang Gobernador sa Sugbu nga Pinili sa Lungsod," *Bag-ong Kusog* (31 July 1931), 4, 9, 32–33; Andres Jayme, "Hon. Juan Climaco," *Homenaje al Seminario-Colegio de Sebu*

en el Cincuentenario de la Toma-Posesion del Mismo por los Padres Paules (Sebu: Falek's Printing House, 1917), 96–99. Also scattered data in Go, "*Sugbu*," 486–87, and Fenner, *Cebu Under the Spanish Flag*, 155, et passim.

23. TNL, PIR, roll 59, SD 979.1, "Hojas de servicio" (of A. Maxilom), ca. February 1899. Additional biographical data on Maxilom are from an interview with Felisa Maxilom Timog, Jose T. Timog, and Daniel Timog, Tuburan, 2 December 1973, done by Resil B. Mojares and Michael Cullinane.

24. Go, "*Sugbu*," 372–73.

25. For the text of the decree, see Taylor, *Philippine Insurrection*, Exhibit 35.

26. This is based on Climaco's account in Taylor, *Philippine Insurrection*, Exhibit 1389.

27. For an account of the occupation of Iloilo, see *Annual Report of the Major-General Commanding the Army, 1899* (Washington D.C.: Government Printing Office, 1899), pt. 3.

28. Go, "*Sugbu*," 374.

Chapter 2: The Coming of the Americans

1. Certain details vary in the accounts of the first days of the Americans in Cebu. These are, however, minor details, e.g., one account says that Cornwell's letter to the Cebuano leaders was delivered by Sidebottom while another says it was carried by the Tagalog pilot of the *Metralladora*. Accounts include: Taylor, *Philippine Insurrection*, Exhibit 1386; "The Taking of Cebu, Described by an Officer of the United States Navy," *Harper's History of the War in the Philippines*, ed. Marion Wilcox (New York: Harper and Brothers, 1900), 142–44; an account of the German consul in Cebu at the time as cited in Irving Faust and Peter MacQueen, *Campaigning in the Philippines* (San Francisco: Hicks-Judd Company, 1899), 245; and Vernon Williams, "The U.S. Navy in the Philippine Insurrection and Subsequent Native Unrest, 1898–1906" (Ph.D. diss., Texas A and M University, 1985), 145–48.

For Cebuano accounts of these events, see Go, "*Sugbu*," 375–83; "Unang Pagkayab sa Bandilang Amerikanhon sa Sugbu," *Bag-ong Kusog* (12 August 1932), 1, 10, 27, 31; and "'Big Three' sa Sugbu sa Panahon sa Kagubut," *Bag-ong Kusog* (9 January 1931), 1, 16, 17.

2. Go, "*Sugbu*," 376–77.

3. It is to be noted that at the time of Dewey's arrival in Manila, British, German, Japanese, and French war vessels were also on the prowl in Manila Bay (Agoncillo, *Malolos*, 158–68). References to foreign vessels in Cebu at this time are to be found in Go, *Sugbu*, and other sources.

At this meeting, Cornwell also notified the Cebuanos that the following day, 22 February, the *Petrel* would be firing a naval gun salute to mark the birthday of George Washington, and that the residents should not be alarmed over the firing of the guns (Go, "*Sugbu*," 377).

4. An important document on the deliberations of Cebuano leaders is CSC, Noel Papers (Minutes of proceedings, Cebu, 21 and 23 February 1899). This is an official copy found in the papers of Vicente Noel, a town official of Carcar, Cebu.

5. The plan to burn the city was probably modeled after what was done in Iloilo. Wilcox (*Harper's History*, 144) says that to prevent the burning of Cebu, "two Filipino priests secured all the coal-oil in town, and have had it under lock and key ever since."

6. Hagaw-haw (pseud.), "Si General Luis Flores," *Tingog sa Lungsod* (21 and 24 May 1904).

7. The text of this document is reprinted in *Harper's History*, 144; and, in a slightly different translation, in *Facts About the Filipinos: Taking the Southern Islands* (Boston: Philippine Information Society, 1901), 8–9.

8. The German consul's account (Faust and MacQueen, *Campaigning in the Philippines*, 245) says that a force of 40 Americans was landed at 9:30 A.M. and the American flag was hoisted at 9:40 A.M. Historian Felix Sales (Go, *Sugbu*, 377–78) says the flag was raised at 8:00 A.M. Another account says that the flag-raising ceremony took place in the afternoon: ("Unang Pagkayab sa Bandilang Amerikanhon sa Sugbu," *Bag-ong Kusog* [12 August 1932], 1, 10, 27, 31). *Harper's History* (144) records that the flag was raised at 9:56 A.M.

9. *Harper's History*, 144.

10. For a biographical sketch of Hamer, see Hiram T. French, *History of Idaho* (Chicago: Lewis Publishing Co., 1914), 3: 1176–77. I owe this source to Sally Allen Ness.

11. The use of the church as horse stables is cited in Go, *"Sugbu,"* 381.

12. *Annual Report of the Major-General Commanding the Army, 1899* (Washington, D.C.: Government Printing Office, 1899), pt. 3:350.

13. Ibid., 350.

14. USNA, RG 395, entry 2601, T. Hamer to Adj. General, First Separate Brigade, Visayan Military District, 8 June 1899.

15. Ibid.

16. USNA, RG 395, entry 2601, T. Hamer to A. A. A. General, First Independent Brigade, 6 April 1899.

17. USNA, RG 395, entry 2601, T. Hamer to Adj. General, Visayan Military District, 1 May 1899.

18. Quoted in *Harper's History*, 237; *Facts about the Filipinos*, 11.

19. Kalaw, *Philippine Revolution*, 261.

20. USNA, RG 395, entry 2601, T. Hamer to Adj. General, First Separate Brigade, Visayan Military District, 8 June 1899.

Chapter 3: A Society Comes Apart

1. On the assassination: USNA, RG 395, entry 2601, box 1, T. Hamer to A. A. General, 28 July 1899; "'Big Three' sa Sugbu sa Panahon sa Kagubut," *Bag-ong Kusog* (9 January 1931), 1, 16, 17.

2. "Kinsa ba si Luis Flores sa Kagubut sa Sugbu," *Bag-ong Kusog* (23 December 1938), 27, 51, 64–65. See also Hagaw-haw, "Si General Luis Flores."

3. Agoncillo, *Malolos*, 294–308; Salamanca, *Filipino Response*, 15–16.

4. Go, "*Sugbu*," 350–52, 361.

5. See text of edict in *La Justicia* (16 April 1899), 2.

6. Taylor, *Philippine Insurrection*, 2:418.

7. CSC, Noel Papers (Minutes of proceedings, Cebu, 21 and 23 February 1899).

8. Taylor, *Philippine Insurrection*, Exhibit 1389.

9. Taylor, *Philippine Insurrection*, 2:423.

10. Taylor, *Philippine Insurrection*, Exhibit 1390.

11. Ibid.

12. An American source (*Harper's History*, 144) claimed that the public coffers were bankrupt since the Cebuanos inherited only $14 from the Spaniards, which money they had spent by the time the Americans came. An official source, however, acknowledges that $2,383.96 in public funds in Cebu was turned over to the Americans at the start of the occupation (ARWD 1901, X:621).

13. Taylor, *Philippine Insurrection*, Exhibit 1390.

14. Taylor, *Philippine Insurrection*, Exhibit 1391.

15. CSC, Noel Papers, Acta de eleccion, Cebu, 24 April 1899.

16. Faust and MacQueen, *Campaigning in the Philippines*, 246.

17. Hagaw-haw, "Si General Luis Flores."

18. USNA, RG 395, entry 2601, T. Hamer to A. A. General, 4 May 1899. See also Faust and MacQueen, *Campaigning in the Philippines*, 246.

19. USNA, RG 395, entry 2601, T. Hamer to A. A. General, 28 July 1899; *Annual Report of the Major-General Commanding the Army, 1899* (Washington, D.C.: Government Printing Office, 1899), pt. 3:350.

20. Taylor, *Philippine Insurrection*, 422.

21. Taylor, *Philippine Insurrection*, Exhibit 1393.

22. CSC, Noble Papers, roll 642, no. 3793–98, Minutes of meeting, San Nicolas, 17 May 1899; Taylor, *Philippine Insurrection*, 423.

23. TNL, PIR, roll 13, SD 144.2, A. Maxilom to A. Mabini, 30 May 1899; Taylor, *Philippine Insurrection*, Exhibit 1394.

24. Taylor, *Philippine Insurrection*, Exhibit 1395.

25. Taylor, *Philippine Insurrection*, 423.

26. Taylor, *Philippine Insurrection*, Exhibit 1399.

27. Taylor, *Philippine Insurrection*, Exhibit 1321.

28. USNA, RG 395, entry 2601, T. Hamer to A. General, 1 May 1899.

29. USNA, RG 395, entry 2601, T. Hamer to A. A. General, 13 May 1899.

30. USNA, RG 395, entry 2604, box 1, T. Barry to T. Hamer, 21 May 1899.

Chapter 4: Widening the Orbit

1. USNA, RG 395, entry 2604, box 3, W. Mann to T. Hamer, 14 June 1899.

2. USNA, RG 395, entry 2601, T. Hamer to R. P. Hughes, 27 June 1899; entry 2604, W. H. Allaire to A. A. A. General, 28 June 1899.

3. USNA, RG 395, entry 5701, box 3, item 1520; information on Philippine Islands: Pardo, 1900.

4. On the occupation of Talisay and Minglanilla see USNA, RG 395, entry 2604, W. H. Allaire to A. A. A. General, 2 July 1899.

5. For the text of the San Nicolas protest, see USNA, RG 395, entry 2604, box 1, Junta Popular, San Nicolas, Cebu, 16 June 1899.

6. USNA, RG 395, entry 2601, T. Hamer to A. A. General, 28 July 1899; entry 2604, box 1, J. Ferraris to T. Hamer, 27 June 1899.

7. Taylor, *Philippine Insurrection*, Exhibit 1396.

8. *Annual Report of the Major-General Commanding the Army, 1899* (Washington, D.C.: Government Printing Office, 1899), pt. 3:352. See also *Facts About the Filipinos*, 11–12.

9. Ibid., 351; *Facts About the Filipinos*, 11. See also USNA, RG 395, entry 2601, F. G. York, 2nd endorsement, 13 July 1899.

10. CSC, Noble Papers, roll 642, no. 3901, "Cuadro demostrativo para la reforma de las zonas militares," Pardo, Cebu, 21 April 1899; Taylor, *Philippine Insurrection*, Exhibit 1392.

11. TNL, PIR, roll 13, SD 144.5, A. Maxilom to A. Mabini, 15 May 1899.

12. Taylor, *Philippine Insurrection*, 422.

13. This assassination is alluded to in a 1900 short story by Vicente Sotto, "Ang Gugma sa Yutang Natawhan," in *Mga Sugilanong Pilipinhon* (Barili: Barili Press, 1929), 91–95.

14. For some reports see USNA, RG 395, entry 2601, T. Hamer to A. A. General, 26 July 1899; entry 2604, box 1, W.H. Allaire to A. A. A. General, 28 June 1899; entry 2604, box 3, W.H. Allaire to A. A. A. General, 27 July 1899. See also item in *El Nacional* (9 September 1899), 3.

15. USNA, RG 395, entry 2601, F. G. York to E. P. Pendleton, 12 July 1899; RG 395, entry 2604, box 2, F. McIntyre to A. General, U.S. Troops, Cebu, 11 November 1899.

16. USNA, RG 395, entry 2604, W. T. Merry to T. Hamer, 12 July 1899; W. T. Merry to T. Hamer, 8 July 1899. On the occupation of Dumanjug see USNA, RG 395, entry 2604, W. T. Merry to A. A. A. General, 5 August 1899.

17. USNA, RG 395, entry 2604, W. H. Allaire to A. A. A. General, 28 June 1899; entry 2604, W. H. Allaire to T. Hamer, 27 August 1899.

18. Taylor, *Philippine Insurrection*, Exhibit 1402.

19. USNA, RG 395, entry 2607, box 4, Endorsement of A. S. Rowan to F. McIntyre, to Commanding Officer, 25 March 1901.

20. USNA, RG 395, entry 2607, box 2, J. L. Malley to H. B. McCoy, 5 September 1900.

Chapter 5: The Siege of Sudlon

1. For an account of the battle see USNA, RG 395, entry 2604, box 1, G. D. Moore to A. A. A. General, 29 July 1899.

2. Aliño's circular, dated 24 July 1899, is appended to USNA, RG 395, entry 2604, box 1, W. T. Merry to A. A. A. General, 29 July 1899.

3. Taylor, *Philippine Insurrection*, Exhibit 1397.

4. USNA, RG 395, entry 2601, T. Hamer to A. A. General, Visayan Military District, 26 July 1899.

5. A description of the area, with sketch map, is in USNA, RG 395, entry 2604, box 1, G. D. Moore to A. A. A. General, Cebu, 29 July 1899.

6. Ildefonso P. Miñoza, "Mga Kaagi sa Kinabuhi ni Alejo Miñoza" (Ms., ca. 1926); and Hermenegildo Solon, "Handum sa Kamatayon ni Alejo Miñoza, Han-ay sa Iyang Kaagi" (Ms., 2 December 1925), copies at the Cebuano Studies Center.

7. USNA, RG 395, entry 2604, box 3, W. H. Allaire to A. A. A. General, 23 August 1899; W. H. Allaire to A. A. A. General, 23 August 1899.

8. USNA, RG 395, entry 2604, A. B. Bayless to A. A. A. General, 28 August 1899.

9. USNA, RG 45, entry 464, box 15, P. J. Werlich, "Report of Bombardment of Insurgent Fortifications in the Vicinity of Cebu, P.I., Oct. 5, 1899"; Williams, "U.S. Navy in the Philippine Insurrection," 161–64, 331–32.

10. For an account of this offensive see USNA, RG 395, entry 2602, S. Snyder to A. General, 2 October 1899.

11. USNA, RG 94, entry 294931, box 1973, W. W. Fiscus to A. General, 4 October 1899.

12. *Harper's History*, 237. An account of the Battle of Bocaue is in Elkanah Babcock, *A War History of the Sixth U.S. Infantry* (Kansas City: Hudson-Kimberly Publishing Co., 1903), 66–68.

13. *Harper's History*, 237.

14. CSC, Noble Papers, roll 642, nos. 3842–43, A. Maxilom to J. Cabajar, 23 September, 17 October, 28 October, 14 December, and 20 December 1899.

15. USNA, RG 395, entry 2604, box 2, A. S. Rowan to A. General, 15 October 1899.

16. For a short popular account of the battle see Publio S. Piedad, "Sudlon: A Historical Landmark," *History: Cebu's 4 Cities and 49 Municipalities*, ed. Gervasio L. Lavilles (Cebu: Mely Press, 1965), 149–51.

17. For the siege of Sudlon see USNA, RG 395, entry 2602, S. Snyder to T. Mann, 13 January 1900; and documents filed under RG 395, entry 2607, dispatches of 8–11 January 1900. See also USMHI, Spanish-American War Survey, US Infantry, Nineteenth Regiment, folder "Ray, Elmer F.," item: "The Assault on Insurgent Forts, Sudlon Mountain, January 8th, 1900, Camp Rowan, Cebu, Jan. 15, 1900." *Harper's History* (349) also contains an article, "The Battle of Sudlon," based on McClernand's report.

18. USNA, RG 395, entry 2602, Snyder cablegram, 29 January 1900.

19. See Allan L. MacDonald, *The Historical Record of the First Tennessee Infantry, U.S.V., in the Spanish War and Filipino Insurrection* (N.p., 1900).

Chapter 6: Fire in a Field of Dry Grass

1. RPC 1906, VIII:251–52. See also Gov. Juan Climaco's report in RPC 1903, I:808.

2. For this decree, see Taylor, *Philippine Insurrection*, Exhibits 1404 and 1405. See also USNA, RG 395, entry 5706, vol. 1, Circular no. 6, Post of Cebu, 1 February 1900; entry 5698, box 1, "Translation of Decree of A. Maxilom, Cebu, P.I., Jan. 16, 1900, captured by Lieut. Fiscus, Nineteenth Inf., in Entrenchment in Mountains of Danao, Jan. 27, 1900." Also in CSC, Noble Papers, roll 640, no. 2587, Maxilom's decree, 16 January 1900.

3. CSC, Noble Papers, roll 640, no. 2586, Maxilom's decree, 17 January 1900.

4. CSC, Noble Papers, roll 643, no. 4717, "Ejercito Filipino. Organizacion de guerrillas. Provincia de Cebu," undated. Some names may have been misspelled since this is a U.S. Army copy of the Cebuano original.

5. CSC, Noble Papers, roll 640, nos. 2473–79, diary of Gervasio Padilla, entries 27–29 January 1900. In the version later related by Fr. Cecilio Sanchez, parish priest of Sogod, two American soldiers had entered his convent on January 27 seeking food. After dinner, armed guerrillas barged into the convent and started firing, killing one American and wounding the other. See Noble Papers, roll 640, no. 2480, Father P. Singson to Father C. Sanchez, 7 June 1900, and Father C. Sanchez to Father P. Singson, 10 June 1900.

6. On this and the skirmishes that followed see USNA, RG 395, entry 2602, Snyder cablegrams, 5 February 1900, 6 February 1900, and 9 February 1900; RG 395, entry 2607, J. L. Bond to A. General, 28 February 1900; J. L. Bond to A. General, 27 February 1900; W. W. Fiscus, Jr. to A. General, 4 February 1900; and E. P. Lawton to A. General, 27 February 1900.

7. USNA, RG 395, entry 2607, box 1, W. W. Fiscus, Jr. to A. General, 7 February 1900.

8. USNA, RG 395, entry 5698, box 1, A. S. Crossfield to Adjutant, 6 February 1900.

9. USNA, RG 395, entry 2602, Snyder cablegram, 8 February 1900.

10. CSC, Noble Papers, roll 640, nos. 2473–79, Gervasio Padilla diary, entry 27 February 1900.

11. USNA, RG 395, entry 2607, box 1, E. P. Lawton to A. General, 28 February 1900; entry 2602, Snyder cablegram, 1 March 1900; entry 2607, J. L. Bond to A. General, 28 February 1900; J. L. Bond to A. General, 27 February 1900.

12. USNA, RG 395, entry 5698, box 1, L. L. Roach to Adjutant, 1 April 1900.

13. USNA, RG 395, entry 2602, Snyder cablegram, 23 March 1900.

14. USNA, RG 395, entry 5706, vol. 1, General Order No. 5, Headquarters, U.S. Troops, Cebu, 4 October 1899.

15. USNA, RG 395, entry 2602, E. McClernand to H. McCoy, 20 May 1900.

16. USNA, RG 395, entry 5698, box 1, G. D. Moore to Post Adjutant, 7 April 1900.

17. USNA, RG 395, entry 2602, E. McClernand to H. B. McCoy, 20 May 1900.

18. USNA, RG 395, entry 2602, E. McClernand to H. B. McCoy, 22 May 1900.

19. USNA, RG 395, entry 2607, W. W. Fiscus, Jr. to A. General, 21 June 1900.

20. USNA, RG 395, entry 2607, box 2, F. G. Lawton to A. General, 22 June 1900.

21. CSC, Noble Papers, roll 640, no. 2520, Troadio Galicano's report of operations, entry 27 July 1900.

22. USNA, RG 395, entry 2503, box 1, E. J. McClernand, "Diary of Events 15 days Ending August 15, 1900."

23. I have not found an account of this battle in the U.S. military records. See Benjamin L. Aliño, "A Crumbling Monument to a Nearly-Forgotten Battle for Freedom" (Ms., Cebuano Studies Center, 1990), with a photograph of a historical marker in Bugas, Badian, erected in 1954 by the Badian Provincial High School.

24. CSC, Noble Papers, roll 640, no. 2520, Troadio Galicano's report of operations, entry 19 October 1900.

25. USNA, RG 395, entry 3191, F. G. Lawton to A. General, 23 October 1900.

26. USNA, RG 395, entry 2607, J. L. Malley to Adjutant, 9 May 1900.

27. USNA, RG 395, entry 2607, box 3, J. L. Malley to H. B. McCoy, 25 December 1900.

28. Another document says he was killed on 31 March 1900 (USNA, RG 395, entry 2607, box 4, Insurgent Papers, Cebu, 20 May 1901). He was also erroneously reported to have died when, betrayed by Cebuano spies, he was surprised and killed by the Americans in his house sometime in April 1900. See CSC, Noble Papers, roll 642, no. 3791, "O. Dormell" to G. Padilla, 5 April 1900.

29. USNA, RG 395, entry 2607, box 5, J. Climaco to T. Galicano, 1 February 1901.

30. *A Hundred Years of Catholicism* (Souvenir program of the First Centenary of San Roque Parish, Asturias, Cebu, 1985), unpaged.

31. These diaries and reports are in CSC, Noble Papers, roll 640, nos. 2520–34 and 2473–79.

32. USNA, RG 395, entry 2607, box 1, A. S. Rowan to A. General, 18 February 1900; CSC, Noble Papers, roll 640, nos. 2620–49, "Diario de un oficial insurrecto," entry 12 February 1900.

33. USNA, RG 395, entry 2607, box 2, A. S. Rowan to A. General, 18 September 1900; box 3, A. S. Rowan to A. General, 12 December 1900.

34. USNA, RG 395, box 3, A. S. Rowan to A. General, 17 January 1901.

35. USNA, RG 395, box 3, A. S. Rowan to E. J. McClernand, 27 January 1901.

36. USNA, BIA, Annual Report of the Governor of Cebu, 1 January 1902.

37. CSC, Noble Papers, roll 642, no. 3847, A. Pepito to Jefe de Operaciones del Norte, 9 February 1900.

38. On this affair: USNA, RG 395, entry 2607, A. S. Rowan to A. General, 24 September 1900; entry 2761, C. Stacey to Commanding Officer, 16 September 1900; C. Stacey to Commanding Officer, 16 September 1900.

39. USNA, RG 395, entry 2761, C. Stacey to Commanding Officer, 16 September 1900.

Chapter 7: Running a War

1. For a sample of a receipt of contributions to the insurgent cause, see USNA, RG 395, entry 2607, box 3, receipt dated 9 July 1900, signed by Anastacio Miranda with the seal of "Guerrillas Filipinas, Cebu. Cuarta Fraccion."

2. CSC, Noble Papers, roll 642, no. 4051, J. Climaco to Presidentes Locales, 30 April 1900, with a list of the quotas for the southern towns. References to the monthly quotas levied on towns are also to be found in CSC, Noble Papers, roll 640, nos. 2555–57: P. del Rosario to T. Galicano, 29 January 1901; P. del Rosario to T. Galicano, 29 January 1901.

3. CSC, Noble Papers, roll 643, no. 4723–25, Minutes of meeting, Opon, 27 January 1901; Taylor, *Philippine Insurrection*, Exhibit 1416.

4. USNA, RG 395, entry 2607, box 1, Li Yung Yeu to E. S. Otis, 13 March 1900.

See also list of voluntary subscriptions to the insurgent cause in CSC, Noble Papers, roll 640, no. 2561, "Relacion de los pudientes de la provincia de Cebu o vecinos caracterizados que han donado por suscriciones voluntarias." This list, which pertains to Troadio Galicano's zone of operations (the Argao-Sibonga area), contains 79 names with contributions ranging from one to 20 pesos. Total amount indicated is 253 pesos.

5. CSC, Noble Papers, roll 640, no. 2582, A. Maxilom and J. Climaco to Presidente Local de Naga, 12 December 1899. For the 26 November 1899 circular of P. del Rosario, see Taylor, *Philippine Insurrection*, Exhibit 1400.

6. On the financial system of the Aguinaldo government, see Taylor, *Philippine Insurrection*, 2:453–85.

7. USNA, RG 395, entry 2602, F. McIntyre to Commanding Officer, 11 October 1899; F. McIntyre to Commanding Officer, 10 November 1899; F. McIntyre to Commanding Officer, 18 December 1899.

8. See "Kinsay Unang Gobernador sa Sugbu nga Pinili sa Lungsod," *Bag-ong Kusog* (31 July 1931), 4, 9, 32–33.

9. Taylor, *Philippine Insurrection*, Exhibit 1398.

10. USNA, RG 395, entry 2607, box 2, J. Climaco to B. Reyes, 16 April 1900.

11. USNA, RG 395, entry 2601, T. Hamer to Senior Naval Officer, 18 September 1899.

12. See Frederick L. Sawyer, *Sons of Gunboats* (Annapolis: United States Naval Institute, 1946), 107–29.

13. Taylor, *Philippine Insurrection*, 419.

14. See Taylor, *Philippine Insurrection*, 2:419, 462–65.

15. USNA, RG 395, entry 5701, box 3, item 1520, Post and Town of Cebu, Preliminary Report of Intelligence Officer, March 1902.

16. CSC, Noble Papers, roll 643, no. 4678, "Ejercito Filipino. Resumen del estado demostrativo de las fuerzas, armamentos, y municiones de las diez fracciones guerrillas que forman las tres columnas denominadas: l.a, 2.a, y 3.a destinadas en el Norte, Centro y Sur," 23 December 1900. See also nos. 4674–77.

17. CSC, Noble Papers, roll 640, no. 2581, Maxilom circular, 15 March 1900.

18. Historian Glenn May (In Stanley, *Reappraising*) focuses on patron-client factors as the "real underside" to mass involvement in the war. I think he overstresses the point. See also Glenn May, "Filipino Resistance to American Occupation: Batangas, 1899–1902," *Pacific Historical Review*, 48 (November 1979): 531–56.

19. CSC, Noble Papers, roll 643, no. 4675, "Relacion de los individuos que prestan sus activos servicios en la Jefatura volante de la partida del Norte," undated; USNA, RG 395, entry 5705, box 1, "Relacion de los insurrectos se presentaron," undated.

20. USNA, RG 395, entry 3494, box 7, E. J. McClernand to A. General, 28 October 1900.

21. See CSC, Noble Papers, roll 640, nos. 2558–59: N. Godines to T. Galicano, 20 November 1900 and 25 November 1900.

22. CSC, Noble Papers, roll 642, no. 3769, P. del Rosario to M. Luga, undated.

Elsewhere in the Philippines, Filipinos were as hard pressed in raising arms. In Samar, church bells were melted down for bullets; copper bands were stripped from shells fired by the U.S. Navy and laboriously beaten out into sheet copper for the manufacture of cartridge shells; melted silver ornaments of churches were used for solder; and substitutes from galvanized iron roofing replaced cartridge shells that were hopelessly worn out. Unexploded navy shells were opened and the powder withdrawn; or powder was made from sulphur, saltpeter obtained from niter beds, and charcoal from native woods. A fulminate for the cartridges was obtained from match heads. So crude was the ammunition that it was effective only when fired on very close range or, in any case, good enough for making noise. See Taylor, *Philippine Insurrection*, II:453–85 and Exhibit 1321.

23. USNA, RG 395, entry 2607, box 3, J. Malley to Adjutant, Forty-fourth Inf., USV, 16 January 1901.

24. CSC, Noble Papers, roll 640, nos. 2555 and 2560: Commissions given by P. del Rosario to M. Lasala to seek assistance from Leyte and Samar, dated 8 November 1899 and 4 December 1899.

25. USNA, RG 395, entry 5698, box 3, A. P. Blockson to A. A. General, 30 October 1901.

26. CSC, Noble Papers, roll 640, nos. 2620–49, "Diario de un oficial insurrecto," 12 November 1899–23 February 1900.

27. For pictures and descriptions of insurgent forts and earthworks, see *Harper's History*, 19, 217–18.

28. See copy of code in RG 94, P.I.R., 1896–1906, documents pertaining to the Visayan group, 1898–1902, vol. 30, page 4824 (M254, roll 634). See also Agoncillo, *Malolos*, 266–67; Enriquez, *Kagubut*, 63.

29. Taylor, *Philippine Insurrection*, Exhibits 1414 and 1420.

30. CSC, Noble Papers, roll 643, no. 4818. "Ejercito R. Filipino. Cebu" (Declaration from P. E. del Rosario, "Jefatura de operaciones de la primera columna del norte"), 2 September 1900.

31. CSC, Noble Papers, roll 642, no. 3819, J. Climaco to T. Galicano, 24 January 1901; no. 3820, P. del Rosario to T. Galicano, 29 January 1901; no. 3836, A. Maxilom to F. Rodriguez, 12 May 1901; no. 3854, A. Maxilom to A. Tabal, 20 March 1899.

32. Taylor, *Philippine Insurrection*, Exhibit 1417; CSC, Noble Papers, roll 640, no. 2555, instructions from P. del Rosario to T. Galicano on submission of financial reports.

33. See seals of Cebu guerrilla groups in CSC, Noble Papers, roll 640, no. 2432.

34. USNA, RG 395, entry 2604, box 2, A. Maxilom to F. Sotto, 28 October 1899.

35. USNA, RG 395, entry 2607, box 3, G. D. Freeman, Jr., to Commanding Officer, 12 December 1900; E. P. Lawton to A. General, 18 December 1900.

36. See, for instance, CSC, Noel Papers, "Proclama," San Isidro, 16 April 1899.

37. Agoncillo, *Malolos*, 788; Taylor, *Philippine Insurrection*, Exhibits 673–74.

38. Gen. Henry W. Lawton died in the battle of San Mateo on 19 December 1899. *Weler* must be a reference to Gen. Joseph ("Fighting Joe") Wheeler. I have found no reference to Wheeler having been captured by the insurgents.

39. USNA, RG 395, entry 2607, box 2, Comite Central Filipino, Hong Kong, General Order, 15 May 1900. Also see Maxilom's letter, dated 28 June 1901, to Galicano Apacible, president of the Central Filipino Committee (Taylor, *Philippine Insurrection*, Exhibit 1424).

40. Taylor, *Philippine Insurrection*, Exhibit 1403; CSC, Noble Papers, roll 642, no. 3789, "Telegrama," undated, with annotation by F. R. Fabie. See also CSC, Noble Papers, roll 643, no. 4816, "Carta de Cebu" (by Sergio Osmeña), 20 January 1900.

41. CSC, Noble Papers, roll 642, nos. 3787–90, miscellaneous items, with annotations by F. R. Fabie, 1899–1901.

42. Taylor, *Philippine Insurrection*, Exhibit 1373.

43. Taylor, *Philippine Insurrection*, Exhibit 1409.

44. CSC, Noble Papers, roll 643, no. 4711, "Instrucciones para el cuerpo de 'Magdudukut' o 'Agocoy' (vengadores secretos)," A. Maxilom, 22 June 1900. See also Taylor, *Philippine Insurrection*, Exhibit 1409.

45. Taylor, *Philippine Insurrection*, Exhibit 1410; CSC, Noble Papers, roll 643, no. 4733, Felix Aliño to Comandante Superior Militar, 17 October 1900.

46. Taylor, *Philippine Insurrection*, Exhibit 1418.

47. USNA, RG 395, entry 2607, J. L. Bond to A. General, 7 September 1900.

48. USNA, RG 395, entry 2607, box 3, N. Godines, "Warning to Tax Collectors for Americans," Bulac, Cebu, 14 October 1900.

49. USNA, RG 395, entry 2607, box 5, A. Ruiz to J. Llorente, 13 July 1901.

50. See the memo of "Liberato Cui," dated 5 May 1901, addressed to insurgent generals in the country on deliberations on the Spooner Amendment (CSC, Noble Papers, roll 640, no. 2351).

51. CSC, Noble Papers, roll 640, nos. 2620–49, "Diario de un oficial insurrecto," 12 November 1899–23 February 1900, entries for 13–14 November 1899 and 19–20 February 1900. The problem of raising funds is also cited by Juan Climaco. See CSC, Noble Papers, roll 642, "Ydioc" (J. Climaco) to "Querido Primo," 5 February and 4 September 1900.

52. CSC, Noble Papers, roll 642, nos. 3876–77, J. Cabajar to A. Maxilom, 17 October 1899; A. Maxilom to J. Cabajar, undated.

53. Circular No. 17, Headquarters, Department of the Visayas, Iloilo, P.I., 10 December 1900. See U.S. Army, Philippines Division, Department of the Visayas, General Orders and Circulars (Bound compilation of orders and circulars at the Library of Congress, Washington, D.C.) 19 vols., 1900–1909.

Chapter 8: Cracks in the Resistance

1. Data on the biographies of personalities have been pieced together from various sources. On Pacaña see "Ang Banay Pacaña sa Labangon sa Panahon sa Kagubut sa Sugbu," *Bag-ong Kusog* (3 May 1929), 9, 21, 25; Felipe Pacaña, "Kinsay mga Matuod nga Manggugubot, ang mga Alangalang ug ang 'Ultima Hora'," *Bag-ong Kusog* (7 November 1930), 12, 16. On Miñoza: Miñoza, "Kaagi sa Kinabuhi"; Solon, "Handum sa Kamatayon"; "Los heroes de nuestro ayer," *Nueva Fuerza* (22 October 1921), 14. On P. Aliño see "Mahinuklugong Kaagi sa Kinabuhi ni Aliño," *Bag-ong Kusog* (10 August 1934), 11, 19, 22. On Lorega see "Kalandrakas," *Bag-ong Kusog* (27 June and 4 July 1941), 31. On Padilla see *Reseña Historica*, 187. On Galicano see Anthony R. Tuohy, *Album Historico de la Primera Asamblea Filipina* (Manila: n.p., 1908), 43–44.

Scattered data on these and other personalities are to be found in Go, *Sugbu*, and Elisea Alvarez-Rizada, "A Historical-Biographical Study of the Lives of Persons After Whom the Streets of Cebu City are Named" (M.A. thesis, University of the Visayas, 1956).

2. USNA, RG 395, entry 2607, box 4, descriptive card of inhabitants: Nicolas Godines (22 April 1901).

3. USNA, RG 395, entry 2602, F. McIntyre to F. G. Lawton, 5 May 1900. On Verdeflor see Taylor, *Philippine Insurrection*, 2:416–17.

4. USNA, RG 395, entry 5701, box 8, A. S. Rowan to A. General, 17 June 1900.

5. TNL, PIR, roll 59, SD 979, "Acta," Pardo, Cebu, 22 December 1898.

6. TNL, PIR, roll 59, SD 979.1, "Hojas de servicio" (of A. Maxilom), ca. February 1899.

7. Taylor, *Philippine Insurrection*, Exhibit 1385.

8. USNA, RG 395, entry 5697, J. F. Huston to A. General, 5 April 1902.

9. TNL, PIR, roll 62, SD 1030.9, "Relacion nominal y plantilla," 10 November 1899.

Early rosters of leaders of the revolution vary in names and ranks or titles ascribed to persons. For rosters, see also Go, "*Sugbu*," 297, 359–60; Enriquez, *Kagubut*; "Ang Kaagi sa Katipunan ug Kagubut sa Pilipinas," *Bag-ong Kusog* (31 October 1930).

10. Miñoza, "Kaagi sa Kinabuhi"; Solon, "Handum sa Kamatayon."

11. On Leoncio Alfon see *El Precursor* (6 and 30 July, 13 and 20 August 1901).

12. USNA, RG 395, entry 5695, vol. 1, G. D. Moore to Post Commander, Cebu, 21 November 1899. See *Ang Suga* (3 October 1906); *El Precursor* (3 and 22 August 1901). A report in *El Precursor* (18 April 1901) says Llamas surrendered to the Americans in Talisay on 18 April 1901.

13. USNA, RG 395, entry 5712, "Oaths of Allegiance, Island of Cebu," 1899–1901.

14. TNL, PIR, roll 62, SD 1030.6, P. del Rosario to Chief of the Sixth Fraccion, "Centro," Cebu, 10 January 1901.

15. CSC, Noble Papers, roll 642, nos. 3815–16, "A. Sandobal" to T. Galicano, undated; Galicano's decree, 7 January 1901; roll 642, no. 3820, P. del Rosario to T. Galicano, 29 January 1901; Taylor, *Philippine Insurrection*, Exhibit 1420.

16. In this tentative analysis, we have either identified or associated these names with the following places: San Nicolas (Abadia, Abarca, Abellana, Cabajar, Enriquez, Ferraris, Labrador, Llamas, Lopez, Pacaña, Padilla, Rama, and Ylaya); Talisay (Abarquez, Abatayo, Aliño, Campo, Cañeda, Dabasol, Fernandez); and Tuburan-Asturias (Alburo, Allego, Alonso, Estrella, Maxilom, Novicio).

17. See Glenn May's criticism of Aguinaldo in "Why the United States Won the Philippine-American War, 1899–1902," *Pacific Historical Review*, 52 (November 1983); 353–77.

Chapter 9: Fire Above, Fire Beneath

1. LC, Carlock Papers, M. A. Cuenco to L. J. Carlock, 31 March 1903.

2. Faust and MacQueen, *Campaigning in the Philippines*, 246.

3. Ibid.

4. May, "Why the United States Won," 366.

5. See Ileto, *Pasyon*.

6. USNA, RG 395, entry 2607, box 3, F. Rallos to Governor, 10 December 1900.

7. USNA, RG 395, entry 2601, T. Hamer to Senior U.S. Naval Officer, 14 November 1899. For other restrictions, see the following: USNA, RG 395, entry 2604, box 2, W. H. Allaire to A. General, 18 October 1899; entry 5698, box 1, F. Rallos to Post Commander, 20 March 1900; entry 5698, box 2, L. L. Roach to Post Adjutant, 27 October 1900; entry 2604, box 2, F. G. Stritzinger, Jr., to Adjutant, 23 October 1899.

8. USNA, RG 395, entry 2604, box 1, P. E. Heermann to W.H.W. James, 12 September 1899.

9. USNA, RG 395, entry 2601, T. Hamer to Commanding Officer, 6 December 1899. Also, *El Nacional* (2 September 1899) for text of F. Rallos circular, 2 September 1899.

10. For sample, see USNA, RG 395, entry 2607, box 4, Descriptive Card of Inhabitants, 1901.

11. USNA, RG 395, entry 5701, box 3, item 1520, "Information on Philippine Islands," 1900. These are printed forms, accomplished for each town.

12. USNA, RG 395, entry 2601, A. J. MacNab, Jr., to Manager of Printing Press, San Carlos Seminary, 20 September 1899.

13. USNA, RG 395, entry 2601, F. G. York to Manager of Printing Press, San Carlos Seminary, 27 May 1899.

14. USNA, RG 395, entry 5701, box 3, item 1520, "Post and Town of Cebu. Preliminary Report of Intelligence Officer, March 1902."

15. USNA, RG 395, entry 2601, permission issued by A. J. MacNab, Jr., 1 November 1899.

16. Norman G. Owen, "Winding Down the War in Albay, 1900–1903," *Pacific Historical Review*, 48 (November 1979), 562.

17. See Jorge I. Dominguez, "Responses to Occupations by the United States: Caliban's Dilemma," *Pacific Historical Review*, 48 (November 1979), 557–89.

18. *Reseña Historica*, 84–85; Taylor, *Philippine Insurrection*, 418.

19. CSC, Noble Papers, roll 642, no. 3853, Singson's circular to parish priests, 24 July 1899.

20. Quoted in Schumacher, *Revolutionary Clergy*, 139. The examination of Father Sanchez is in CSC, Noble Papers, roll 640, no. 2480, Father P. Singson to Father C. Sanchez, 7 June 1900.

21. See Schumacher, *Revolutionary Clergy*. For Fr. Pablo Singson, see *Reseña Historica*, 103–13.

22. Schumacher, *Revolutionary Clergy; Reseña Historica*, 137–39. See also, CSC, Noble Papers, roll 642, no. 3888–91, "Daniel" to P. del Rosario, 26 January 1900; no. 3911, "Daniel" to P. del Rosario, 6 February 1900; TNL, PIR, roll 68, SD 1120, "Daniel" to P. del Rosario, 2 and 6 February 1900; F. Blanco to Quintin Tabal, 14 June 1899; and other items. "Daniel" is obviously Father Blanco. The letters show his active support for the revolutionary cause. See also Taylor, *Philippine Insurrection*, Exhibit 1406.

23. USNA, RG 395, entry 2503, box 1, E. J. McClernand, "Diary of Events 15 Days Ending August 15, 1900."

24. USNA, RG 395, entry 2604, box 2, M. de Arrieta to Military Governor, 20 October 1899.

25. CSC, Noble Papers, roll 642, no. 4447, M. de Arrieta to F. McIntyre, 1 April 1901.

26. USNA, RG 395, entry 2604, box 2, M. de Arrieta to Military Governor, 20 October 1899.

27. USNA, RG 395, entry 5701, box 3, item 1520, Post and Town of Cebu, Preliminary Report of Intelligence Officer, March 1902.

28. USNA, RG 395, entry 5698, box 1, F. Rallos to Governor of Cebu, 8 March 1900.

29. Taylor, *Philippine Insurrection*, Exhibit 1413.

30. USNA, RG 395, entry 2601, T. Hamer to A. A. General, 7 August 1899; entry 2604, box 1, W. T. Merry to A. A. A. General, 29 July 1899.

31. USNA, RG 395, entry 2604, box 1, G. O'Brien to A. A. A. General, 12 September 1899; T. Mejia to "Paco," 25 September 1899; G. O'Brien to A. A. A. General, 24 August 1899; entry 2604, box 2, C. R. Tyler to A. General, 16 October 1899 and 6 November 1899.

32. USNA, RG 395, entry 2607, box 5, A. Ruiz to Military Governor, Argao, 1 August 1901. On Alejandro Ruiz see *Reseña Historica*, 187–88; Tuohy, *Album Historico*, 91.

33. USNA, RG 395, entry 2601, T. Hamer to Commanding Officer, 27 September 1899.

34. USNA, RG 395, entry 2604, box 1, T. Mejia to "Paco," 25 September 1899.

35. CSC, Noble Papers, roll 642, no. 3821, P. del Rosario to T. Galicano, 6 February 1901; Taylor, *Philippine Insurrection*, Exhibit 1419.

36. USNA, RG 395, entry 2607, box 2, S. Ferraris to Military Governor, 17 July 1900.

37. USNA, RG 395, entry 2607, box 2, H. Alquizola to Gobernador Militar, 30 June 1900.

38. USNA, RG 395, entry 2602, Capt., Nineteenth Infantry, to Commanding Officer, 21 January 1900; entry 2607, box 3, E. Espina to Military Governor, 3 October 1900.

39. USNA, RG 395, entry 2607, box 3, F. Rallos to Military Governor, 3 October 1900.

40. USNA, RG 395, entry 2604, box 1, G. O'Brien to A. A. A. General, 12 September 1899.

41. "Bantugang Makilungsodnon Nanaug sa Lubnganan," *Bag-ong Kusog* (28 October 1932), 12, 20, 22, 25, 26.

42. CSC, Noble Papers, roll 642, no. 3787, "Ecos de Cebu," 2 September 1899; no. 3788, "Cronica de la campaña," undated.

43. USNA, RG 395, entry 2604, box 1, V. Sotto to Military Governor, 14 September and 20 September 1899.

44. CSC, Noble Papers, roll 642, no. 3786, V. Sotto to Gobernador Militar, undated.

45. USNA, RG 395, entry 2601, T. Hamer to Commanding Officer, 4 November 1899.

46. See Vicente Sotto, "Nuestros derechos," *La Justicia* (25 June 1899), 2.

47. USNA, RG 94, entry 455906, encl. 3, F. A. Smith to A. General, 7 August 1902.

48. USNA, RG 395, entry 5705, box 2, C. J. Crane to Officer-in-Charge, Military Information Division, 12 September 1910.

49. *Facts About the Filipinos*, 8.

50. CSC, Noble Papers, roll 642, no. 3774, "Sentimiento Manifestado en el Mundo Filipino," undated.

51. USNA, RG 395, entry 2607, box 5, N. Veloso to Commanding Officer, 27 July 1901.

52. USNA, RG 395, entry 2604, box 1, Petition of Cebu merchants, 29 June 1899.

53. USNA, RG 395, entry 2607, box 3, "Memoranda from the Public Archives," 15 August 1900.

54. ARWD 1901, IV:53.

55. LC, Carlock Papers, "The Experiences of an American Judge in the Philippines" (Ms., 1902), 3.

Chapter 10: Infrastructure of Consent

1. An example is an election called in Dumanjug on 1–2 August 1900 by the ranking American military officer in the area, Major H. B. McCoy of the Forty-fourth Infantry. Appointed "secretaries" to administer the oath of electors were Dionisio Jakosalem, Antonio de la Cerna, and Miguel Gandiongco. Named judges were Juan Losada, Juan Noel, and Bonifacio Garcia. Tellers were Fabio Beltran and Juan Llenos. See USNA, RG 395, entry 2607, box 2, "Election Proclamation Issued at Dumanjug, July 1900."

2. The best short study of the American reorganization of local governments in this period is Michael Cullinane, "Implementing the 'New Order': The Structure and Supervision of Local Government during the Taft Era," *Compadre Colonialism*, ed. N. G. Owen (Ann Arbor: University of Michigan, Center for South and Southeast Asian Studies, 1971), 13–75.

3. USNA, RG 395, entry 2602. McClernand cablegram, 5 April 1900.

4. ARWD 1901, X:733–35.

5. CSC, Noble Papers, roll 642, no. 3780, A. Maxilom, "Ynstrucciones," undated. On the Schurman Commission, see RPC 1900, 1.

6. Taylor, *Philippine Insurrection*, Exhibit 1411.

7. CSC, Noble Papers, roll 642, no. 3809–12, "El Comisionado" to "Señor Presidente" of Carcar, 11 May 1900.

8. See *Protests against American Civil Government in the Island of Cebu, Philippine Islands* (U.S. Senate, 56th Congress, 2nd Session, Doc. no. 234, 27 February 1901).

9. For the case of Danao, see *Facts About the Filipinos*, 14–16.

10. For the text of this petition, see Andres Jayme, "Breve Reseña Historica de Sebu," *Homenaje al Seminario-Colegio de Sebu*, 70–78.

11. USNA, RG 395, entry 2607, box 2, A. S. Rowan to E. J. McClernand, 7 July 1900.

12. USNA, RG 395, entry 5698, box 4, J. Climaco to J. F. Huston, 9 June 1902.

13. RPC 1900, I:90.

14. ARWD 1901, X:736.

15. UM, Department of Rare Books and Special Collections, Worcester Philippine Collection, Notes and Documents 337–44. "Journal dictated by Dean C. Worcester Jan. 1 to June 30, 1901." For an account of the visit, see Edith Moses, *Unofficial Letters of An Official's Wife* (New York: D. Appleton, 1908); Daniel R. Williams, *The Odyssey of the Philippine Commission* (Chicago: A.C. McClurg, 1913), 219–25.

16. USNA, BIA, United States Philippine Commission, Minutes of proceedings, 17–18 April 1901; Williams, *Odyssey*, 219–25.

17. For the text of Act No. 116, see ARWD 1901, X:246–48. Case was an engineer in the Eighth Army Corps and had been in the Philippines since 1899 while Young was a lieutenant in the Forty-fourth U.S. Infantry.

18. On the organization of the towns, see USNA, BIA, Annual Report of the Governor of Cebu, 1 January 1902.

19. USNA, RG 395, entry 2607, box 4, J. Llorente to Comandante Militar, 22 June 1901.

20. In Salamanca, *Filipino Reaction*, 25.

21. CSC, Noble Papers, roll 642, no. 3823, "Al Pueblo Cebuano," 24 March 1901.

22. CSC, Noble Papers, roll 642, no. 3832, J. Climaco to Presidentes Locales, 16 April 1901.

23. USNA, RG 395, entry 2607, box 4, F. G. Lawton to A. General, 4 March 1901.

24. USNA, RG 395, entry 2607, box 5, J. Llorente to Military Commander, 14 July 1901.

25. ARWD 1902, IX: 136–78.

26. Ibid.

27. LC, Carlock Papers, diary, entry 25 July 1901.

28. Quoted in Salamanca, *Filipino Reaction*, 37–38.

Chapter 11: Decade of Death

1. For estimates of war losses, See Wolff, *Little Brown Brother*, 360; Blount, *American Occupation*, 595–99; William T. Sexton, *Soldiers in the Sun* (Harrisburg, Pa.: Military Service Publishing, 1939), 19–20.

The measurement of war losses is a matter of controversy because of the lack of reliable census figures, deficiencies in battle records (particularly for the Filipino side), and the problem of determining what deaths can be considered "war-related." Estimates of Filipino deaths in the Filipino-American War range from 200,000 to 700,000 (around 10 percent of the estimated population of the Philippines in 1898). Reviewing available data, John M. Gates estimates that for the period 1898 to 1903 (which includes part of the anti-Spanish revolution) Filipino soldiers killed in action and war-related civilian deaths must be around 220,000, with the cholera epidemic of 1902 accounting for close to 200,000 of these deaths. See John M. Gates, "War-related deaths in the Philippines, 1898–1902," *Pacific Historical Review* (1984): 367–78. For a close analysis of mortality in a specific province see Glenn A. May, "150,000 Missing Filipinos: A Demographic Crisis in Batangas, 1887–1903," *Annales de Demographie Historique* (1985): 215–43.

2. See USNA, RG 395, entry 2607, box 2, E. McClernand to A. General, Cebu, 23 April 1900; RG 395, entry 2503, box 1, F. McIntyre to A. General, Cebu, 3 November 1900; RG 395, entry 2607, box 3, J. G. Leefe, "Weekly Report of Strength, Cebu," 30 November 1900; RG 395, entry 2607, box 3, "Consolidated Report. Stations. Troops," 13 December 1900.

3. Canute Vandermeer, "Corn on the Island of Cebu" (Ph.D. diss., University of Michigan, 1962), 17.

4. See Peter C. Smith, "Demographic History: An Approach to the Study of the Filipino Past," in *Perspectives on Philippine Historiography*, ed. J. A. Larkin (New Haven: Yale University Southeast Asia Studies, 1979), 27–46. For a general study see Dean C. Worcester, *A History of Asiatic Cholera in the Philippine Islands* (Manila: Bureau of Printing, 1909). See also, Norman G. Owen, "Measuring Mortality in the Nineteenth-century Philippines," in *Death and Disease in Southeast Asia*, ed. N. G. Owen (Singapore: Oxford University Press, 1987), 91–114.

5. *Reseña Historica*, 83–84.

6. For the health situation, see RPC 1903, I:808–9, II:123, 174, 231, 246–47; RPC 1904, I:480, II:131, 236. See also the annual reports of the Cebu Governor in USNA BIA files and the news reports in *Ang Suga* of these years.

7. *Census of the Philippine Islands: 1903* (Washington, D.C.: United States Bureau of the Census, 1905), 81, 139.

8. RPC 1903, II:233.

9. RPC 1905, IV:490.

10. RPC 1904, II: 236.

11. Vic Hurley, *Jungle Patrol: The Story of the Philippine Constabulary* (New York: E. P. Dutton, 1938), 119.

12. RPC 1903, III:242.

13. RPC 1904, I:480–81.

14. USNA, RG 395, entry 2604, box 2, Marron to Bratton, 4 November 1899; Marron to T. Hamer, 7 November 1899; Tyler to A. General, 6 November 1899.

15. USNA, RG 395, entry 2604, box 2, A. Ruiz to W. T. Merry, Argao, 17 November 1899.

16. USNA, RG 395, entry 2607, box 5, A. Ruiz to Military Governor, Argao, 1 August 1901.

17. USNA, RG 395, entry 5698, box 1, petition, Junta Popular de Dalaguete, 28 June 1900.

18. USNA, BIA, Annual Report of the Governor of Cebu, Cebu, 1 January 1902.

19. RPC 1903, I:715, 805–6.

20. RPC 1903, I:805–6

21. ARWD 1905, XIV:164–65.

22. *Ang Suga* (1 August 1902).

Chapter 12: Surrender of the Generals

1. CSC, Noble Papers, roll 640, no. 2580; roll 642, no. 3831. The same circular was issued on 6 April 1901 by Maxilom (Taylor, *Philippine Insurrection*, Exhibit 1421).

2. CSC, Noble Papers, roll 642, nos. 3912–13, "Al Pueblo Sebuano," 24 June 1901; "Carta del General Maxilom," 28 June 1901; Taylor, *Philippine Insurrection*, Exhibit 1423.

3. USNA, RG 395, entry 2607, box 2, M. Logarta, G. Sepulveda, and P. Rodriguez to Governor, 28 July 1900.

4. Taylor, *Philippine Insurrection*, Exhibit 1401; Noble Papers, roll 642, no. 3771, "Ydioc" (J. Climaco) to "Querido Primo," undated.

5. Taylor, *Philippine Insurrection*, Exhibit 1424. See reference to Malvar's instructions.

6. CSC, Noble Papers, roll 643, no. 4715, A. Maxilom to Gobernador Militar Americano, 15 April 1901.

7. For the text of Act No. 173 see ARWD 1901, X:368.

8. ARWD 1902, IX:136–78, 614.

9. LC, Carlock Papers, diary, entry 21 September 1901.

10. USNA, RG 395, entry 2607, J. L. Bond to A. General, 8 September 1900.

11. USNA, RG 395, entry 5697, W. S. Scott to Adjutant, 11 April 1904.

12. The mayors are not named in U.S. military reports and available Cebu newspaper accounts of the day. Identification of the mayors is also rendered difficult by the lack of local data and the frequent changes of officials during this period. In supplying the names, I have pieced together fragmentary and inferential data from various accounts (e.g., *Reseña Historica*, 135, 137).

13. USNA, RG 94, entry 455906, encl. 4–13, F. McIntyre to A. General, 20 November 1901. See other related items in this file.

14. On Llorente's pacification campaign, see USNA, BIA, Annual Report of the Governor of Cebu, 1 January 1902.

15. USNA, BIA, Annual Report of the Governor of Cebu, 1 January 1902.

16. Texts of circulars in USNA, RG 350, file 3019/10, HQ, Department of the Visayas, Circulars, 25 September and 4 October 1901. Also, USNA, RG 350, Entry

3019/10, Circulars nos. 5 and 6, HQ, Department of the Visayas, 25 September and 4 October 1901.

17. USNA, RG 395, entry 2607, box 3, J. Climaco to A. Medalle, 22 December 1900; CSC, Noble Papers, roll 642, no. 3771, "Ydioc" (J. Climaco) to "Querido Primo," undated. See also Taylor, *Philippine Insurrection*, Exhibit 1401.

18. *El Precursor* (12 February 1901).

19. USNA, RG 395, entry 2607, box 4, J. Climaco to Military Governor, 27 April 1901.

20. USNA, BIA, Annual Report of the Governor of Cebu, 1 January 1902.

21. ARWD 1902, IX:136–78.

22. USNA, BIA, Annual Report of the Governor of Cebu, 1 January 1902; Jayme, "Breve Reseña Historica," 79–86.

23. LC, Carlock Papers, diary, entries for October 1901. For Cebuano accounts and the text of the *Acta de la Paz*, see Jayme, "Breve Reseña Historica," 61–86; Juan F. Alcazaren, *Tinipsing sa Kasaysayan sa Filipinas* (Sugbo: Imprenta Falek, 1925), 79–81.

24. LC, Carlock Papers, diary, entries 9 and 29 October 1901.

25. TNL, PIR, roll 62, SD 1030.3, (Manifestation), Barili, Cebu, 18 October 1901.

26. ARWD 1902, IX:136–78; USNA, RG 395, entry 5697, J. Climaco to F. McIntyre, 2 April 1902. Another source cites that Lasala surrendered on 30 October 1901.

27. Our data are based largely on ARWD 1902, IX:136–78. See also USNA, RG 395, entry 5697, J. Climaco to F. McIntyre, 2 April 1902.

28. On Maxilom's surrender, see USNA, RG 395, entry 2989, Balamban: Post Letters Received (August 1901–May 1902).

29. LC, Carlock Papers, diary, entry 29 October 1901.

30. CSC, Noble Papers, roll 642, nos. 4135–136, A. Maxilom to F. McIntyre, 19 January 1902; A. Maxilom to D. Papa, 17 January 1902.

31. USNA, RG 395, entry 5698, box 3, P. Rodriguez to Military Commander, Bogo, 12 November 1901. Other surrenders may be inferred from USNA, RG 395, entry 5712, "Oaths of Allegiance, Island of Cebu," 1899–1901. This list contains 1,824 names, with the earliest entry dated 28 October 1899 and the latest 11 November 1902.

32. *Reseña Historica*, 187.

33. USNA, RG 395, entry 5705, box 1, J. K. Wiggins to A. General, 28 April 1901. See also, *El Pueblo* (4 July 1900), 3.

34. *Reseña Historica*, 194–5; *El Precursor* (6 July 1902); Alcazaren, *Tinipsing*, 82.

35. *El Precursor* (22 October and 7 November 1901, 4 January, 15 February and 2 August 1903, 12 February 1905); *Nueva Era* (12 February 1904); interview with Benjamin L. Aliño, Cebu City, 11 August 1989. Also see the safe-conduct passes issued to Potenciano and Fermin Aliño by the U.S. authorities: USNA, RG 395, entry 5695, vol. 2, "To Whom It May Concern" (by F. McIntyre, 4 November 1901, and S. Snyder, 6 November 1901).

36. USNA, RG 395, entry 5695, vol. 2, J. F. Huston to A. General, 29 January 1902.

37. For a narration of the process, see USNA, RG 350, File 3019/15, F. S. Young and J. G. Holcombe to Executive Secretary, 11 February 1902.

38. USNA, RG 395, entry 5701, box 3, item 1520, "Post and Town of Cebu. Preliminary Report of Intelligence Officer, March 1902."

39. USNA, BIA, Annual Report of the Governor of the Province of Cebu from 1 Jan. 1903 to 30 June 1904, Cebu, 13 September 1904.

40. USNA, RG 395, entry 5701, box 8, item 5209, V. Teves to C. J. Crane, 22 August 1910, with "Resumen de Ordenanzas de Cebu" appended.

41. USNA, BIA, Annual Report of the Provincial Governor of Cebu, from 1 Jan. to 31 Dec. 1902. On other administrative actions, see USNA, BIA, Annual Report of the Governor of the Province of Cebu, 1 July 1905.

42. USNA, BIA, Annual Report of the Provincial Governor of Cebu, 1 Jan. to 31 Dec. 1902; USNA, RG 350, entry 812, J. Riano to Secretary, Washington, D.C., 10 March 1902, and related items in this file.

43. Additional data in *Ang Suga* (16 October 1903), 1.

44. Michael Cullinane, "Playing the Game: the Rise of Sergio Osmeña, 1898–1907," *Philippine Colonial Democracy*, ed. R. R. Paredes (New Haven: Yale University, Southeast Asia Studies, 1988; Quezon City: Ateneo de Manila University Press, 1989), 92–93.

45. "Elecciones Municipales," *Ang Suga* (16 November 1903), 1.

46. USNA, RG 395, entry 5698, box 6, "Relacion de los oficiales municipales de la ciudad de Cebu, Cebu, I.F.," undated.

47. LC, Allen Papers, container 7, folder 10, H. T. Allen to J. F. Bell, 26 March 1902; H. T. Allen to R. P. Hughes, 4 April 1902.

48. LC, Carlock Papers, "Judge Carlock's Statement of Conditions in Cebu" (draft of a report), 30 October 1902.

Chapter 13: Face to Face

1. James C. Scott, *Weapons of the Weak: Everyday Forms of Peasant Resistance* (New Haven: Yale University Press, 1985).

2. Letters written by American soldiers stationed in the Philippines are to be found in various archives and libraries in the United States. I have examined letters at LC, USMHI, and special collections in Duke University (Durham, NC), University of North Carolina (Chapel Hill, NC), and Wisconsin Historical Society (Madison, WI).

3. USNA, RG 395, entry 5695, vol. 3, J. E. Woodward to Presidente de Cebu, Cebu, 28 March 1903; RG 395, entry 5701, box 3, item 1520, C. R. Street, "Report on the Station at Camp Warwick, 31 May 1904."

4. For references to such pastimes, see USNA, RG 395, entry 2604, box 3, J. E. Bennett et al., to Commanding Officer, 15 December 1899; F. Rallos to Gobernador, 15 January 1901.

5. USNA, RG 395, entry 5698, box 5, H. H. Baily to Post Adjutant, Cebu, 7 February 1903; entry 5701, box 10, no. 6354, H. F. Rethers to Adjutant, 26 January 1911.

6. Data on Argao: USNA, RG 395, entry 2877, "Argao: Post Letters Sent" (1902–1903), Post Commander to A. General, Argao, 1 October 1902.

7. See, for illustration, USNA, RG 395, entry 2601, T. Hamer to President, Consejo Provincial, 26 October 1899; entry 2604, box 1, V. Z. Funnel to A. B. Bayless, 12 August 1899; entry 2604, box 2, M. Logarta to Military Governor, 7 November 1899; M. Logarta to Military Governor, 14 November 1899; entry 5695, vol. 3, G. Penney to Governor, 27 November 1902.

8. USNA, RG 395, entry 2612, General Orders No. 4, HQ, U.S. Troops, Sub-District of Cebu, 2 October 1899.

9. USNA, RG 395, entry 5698, box 2, L. L. Roach to Post Adjutant, Cebu, 17 January 1901.

10. USNA, RG 395, entry 2607, box 5, A. E. Williams to Colonel Miller, 26 June 1901.

11. Al General Chaffee, *El Pueblo* (29 June 1902), 3; see also issue of 2 November 1902.

12. On these atrocities, see USNA, RG 94, entry 455906, item 455906, "Statement of Diego Cabrera," 7 August 1902, with other testimonies; and file of documents in RG 94, entry 482616.

13. On this case, see USNA, RG 94, entry 455906, item 455906, W. P. Baker to Inspector General, 24 July 1902, with enclosures 3 to 13; RG 395, entry 5705, box 1, A. S. Rowan to A. General, 16 March 1901, with attachments.

14. Miller, *Benevolent Assimilation*, 206.

15. Schumacher, *Revolutionary Clergy*, 145.

16. Charles J. Crane, *The Experiences of a Colonel of Infantry* (New York: Knickerbocker Press, 1923), 506.

17. LC, H. T. Allen Papers, H. T. Allen to R. P. Hughes, 12 September 1901.

18. USNA, RG 395, entry 5701, box 13, no. 8742, C. J. Crane to A. Borromeo, 10 May 1912.

19. Miller, *Benevolent Assimilation*, 54–55, 215–16.

20. USNA, RG 395, entry 5695, vol. 1, J. Leefe to A. General, 28 November 1900.

21. See "Fred M. Baker" and "Ropas y cartas," *El Pueblo* (28 April 1900), 3. There are also references to Baker in "Bantugang Makilungsodnon Nanaug sa Lubnganan," *Bag-ong Kusog* (28 October 1932).

22. USNA, RG 395, entry 5697, "Statement of F. M. Baker," 5 May 1900; entry 2607, box 2, E. J. McClernand to A. General, 5 May 1900.

23. Faust and MacQueen, *Campaigning in the Philippines*, 246.

24. See *Ang Suga* (1 August 1902) and other issues of this newspaper in 1902.

25. CSC, Noble Papers, roll 642, no. 3950, E. Duterte to "Mis queridos hermanos," 30 September 1901. See also TNL, PIR, roll 62, SD 1030.4, E. Duterte, 30 September 1901.

26. USNA, RG 395, entry 5701, box 3, item 1520, "Post and Town of Cebu. Preliminary Report of Intelligence Officer," March 1902.

27. *Ang Suga* (23 October 1903), 1; USNA, RG 395, entry 2607, box 4, H. M. Cohen to Chief Surgeon, Cebu, 22 June 1901. We do not have full records on the total number of Filipino prisoners of war in Cebu or on prison mortality in the province.

28. *Ang Suga* (16 May 1902 and 19 May 1902). See Resil B. Mojares, "Vicente Sotto and the Rise of Realism in Cebuano Literature," *Philippine Quarterly of Culture and Society*, 4 (1976), 101–9. For the plays see Vicente Sotto, *Ang Paghigugma sa Yutang Nataohan* (Cebu: "Imp. Filipina," 1902); Idem., *Elena* (Cebu: Imprenta Filipina, 1903).

29.*El Nacional* (9 September 1899); *El Pueblo* (11 April 1900); and other issues of these years.

Chapter 14: The Underside of the War

1. See Ileto, *Pasyon*, for problematics in the ideology of resistance.

2. While documentation is sparse, all accounts agree on the role of Domingo and Plata in the organization of the Katipunan in Cebu. See Go, *"Sugbu"*; Enriquez, *Kagubut*; Abellana, "Bisaya Patronymesis."

3. Go, *"Sugbu"*; Enriquez, *Kagubut*.

4. Go, *"Sugbu"*; Enriquez, *Kagubut*; Abellana, "Bisaya Patronymesis."

5. See Ileto, *Pasyon*, for a discussion of Katipunan initiation ceremonies.

6. Enriquez, *Kagubut*, provides illustrations and texts of these amulets.

7. No full biography of Leon Kilat has been written, but many short accounts exist, particularly Enriquez, *Kagubut*.

8. Enriquez, *Kagubut*. The connection between Leon Kilat and Buhawi is mentioned in Donn V. Hart, "Buhawi of the Bisayas: The Revitalization Process and Legend-making in the Philippines," *Studies in Philippine Anthropology*, ed. M. D. Zamora (Quezon City: Alemar-Phoenix, 1967), 380.

9. Abellana, "Bisaya Patronymesis."

10. Foreman, *Philippine Islands*. Foreman mistakenly identifies the estate owners as the Wilsons.

11. Go, *"Sugbu."*

12. RPC 1903, I:215.

13. *Ang Suga* (22 March 1902). For Aglipayanism in Cebu, see Geoffrey G. Salgado, "The Dynamics of Aglipayan-Catholic Confrontation in a Cebuano Community: Santa Fe, Cebu (1903–1953)" (M. A. thesis, University of San Carlos, 1978).

14. *Harper's History*, 142.

15. Taylor, *Philippine Insurrection*, Exhibit 1388.

16. *La Justicia* (24 June 1899).

17. Taylor, *Philippine Insurrection*, Exhibit 35.

18. CSC, Noble Papers, roll 642, nos. 3815–16, "A. Sandobal" to T. Galicano, undated; Galicano's decree, 7 January 1901; roll 642, no. 3820, P. del Rosario to T. Galicano, 29 January 1901.

19. Taylor, *Philippine Insurrection*, Exhibit 1420.

20. CSC, Noble Papers, roll 642, no. 3836, P. del Rosario to 1st and 2nd Chiefs, Fourth Fraccion, 27 May 1901.

Chapter 15: Rise of the Pulahanes

1. USNA, BIA, Annual Report of the Provincial Governor of Cebu, from Jan. 1 to Dec. 31, 1902.

2. Sturtevant, *Popular Uprisings*, 119.

3. RPC 1903, III:133.

4. RPC 1904, I:476.

5. RPC 1905, III:96.

6. USNA, BIA, Annual Report of the Provincial Governor of Cebu, from 1 Jan. to 31 Dec. 1902. See issues of *Ang Suga* in 1902 for reports on Philippine Constabulary abuses.

A short story by Vicente Sotto (pseud., Taga-Kotta) in *Ang Suga* (16 June 1909) tells a sympathetic story of the pulahanes. It describes the case of an upland farmer driven to become a pulahan because PC soldiers raped the women in his family and killed his two sons. It also describes other abuses of the PC and says that the pulahanes are not fighting the U.S. and are not insurgents or bandits, but ordinary mountain folk fighting in defense of their rights (Taga-Kotta, "Ang pulahan," *Ang Suga* [16 June 1909], 3).

Another sympathetic account of the pulahanes in Cebuano fiction is Nicolas Rafols, *Ang Pulahan* (Cebu: Cebu Press, 1918).

7. USNA, BIA, Annual Report of the Provincial Governor of Cebu, from 1 Jan. to 31 Dec. 1902.

8. *Ang Suga* (25 June 1902).

9. On the Godines case see *Ang Suga* (16 April and 14 September 1902).

10. On the Maxilom case see *Ang Suga* (22, 25 and 29 March; 10 and 18 April; 16 and 23 June; 7, 9, 14 and 16 July; and 27 August 1902); *El Precursor* (2 November 1902).

11. USNA, RG 395, entry 5697, Commanding Officer, 21 March 1902; J. F. McCarthy to A. General, 27 March 1902.

12. USNA, BIA, Annual Report of the Provincial Governor of Cebu, from 1 Jan. to 31 Dec. 1902.

13. LC, Carlock Papers, "Draft of a Report," 30 October 1902.

14. *Ang Suga* (13 February and 9 July 1902).

15. "Mga balita," *Ang Suga* (12 May 1902).

16. *Ang Suga* (30 June and 23 July 1902); Charles Edward Russell, *The Outlook for the Philippines* (New York: Century Co., 1922), 229–31.

17. USNA, BIA, Annual Report of the Provincial Governor of Cebu, from 1 Jan. to 31 Dec. 1902.

18. The distinction between capioanes and pulahanes is made by a local historian in TNL, HDP, Cebu, Aloguinsan, Cawasan.

19. USNA, BIA, Annual Report of the Provincial Governor of Cebu, from 1 Jan.to 31 Dec. 1902.

20. Ibid.

21. Additional data on Caballero from an interview with Demetrio Macapaz, Colonia, Tuburan, 3 December 1973, done by Resil B. Mojares and Michael Cullinane.

22. USNA, RG 395, entry 2607, box 2, A. S. Rowan to A. General, 18 December 1900.

23. See "Mga Tulisan sa Tuburan," *Ang Suga* (18 June 1902).

24. On the Tabals, see Go, "*Sugbu*," 265–67, 307–12.

25. Go, "*Sugbu*," 310–12. On the battle, see Enriquez, *Kagubut*, 131–32.

26. Francisco Rodriguez (pseud., FER), "Ang mga Pulahan Lain sa mga Rebolusyonaryo," *Bag-ong Kusog* (14 October 1932), 2–4. Rodriguez was an officer in the Maxilom army.

27. CSC, Noble Papers, roll 642, nos. 3799–3800 and 3904, A. Maxilom to A. Tabal, 26 August to 30 August 1899. These are communications about the movement of weapons and the manufacture of bamboo traps. See also TNL, PIR, roll 68, SD 1120, F. Blanco to Q. Tabal, 14 June 1899.

28. Noble Papers, roll 642, nos. 3883–84, L. Flores to A. Tabal, 13 April 1899; A. Maxilom to A. Tabal, 15 August 1899.

29. The source of this account is Rodriguez, "Ang mga Pulahan." Other articles on the case of the Tabals skirt the reason for their quarrel with the Maxilom-Climaco government.

30. CSC, Noble Papers, roll 642, no. 3846, A. Maxilom to Presidente Local de Mandawe and A. Maxilom to Los Jefes de Guerrillas, 23 January 1900.

31. Piedad, "Sudlon," 150.

32. "Mga Salin sa Kagubut," *Bag-ong Kusog* (15 April 1927), 4–5, 22. Reprinted in *Bag-ong Kusog* (29 August 1941), 11, 26. This is an interview with Anatalio Tabal in 1906.

33. Rodriguez, "Ang mga Pulahan."

34. *Ang Suga* (13 February and 9 July 1902).

35. *Ang Camatuoran* (14 January 1903).

36. USNA, BIA, Annual Report of the Provincial Governor of Cebu, from 1 Jan. to 31 Dec. 1902.

37. USNA, BIA, Annual Report of the Governor of the Province of Cebu, from 1 Jan 1903 to 30 June 1904.

38. USNA, BIA, Annual Report of the Provincial Governor of Cebu, 5 August 1908.

39. "Mga Salin sa Kagubut," *Bag-ong Kusog* (15 April 1927), 4–5, 22.

40. USNA, RG 395, entry 5695, vol. 5, W. Paulding to A. General, 24 July 1904.

41. "Mga Salin sa Kagubut," *Bag-ong Kusog* (15 April 1927), 4–5, 22.

42. Taylor, *Philippine Insurrection*, Exhibit 1407; USNA, RG 395, entry 2607, W. W. Fiscus to A. General, 10 March 1900.

43. USNA, RG 395, entry 2607, box 3, I.L. Hunt to A. General, 15 December 1900.

44. Celestino T. Alfafara, "Ang Ika-kawhaan ug Lima nga Sumad sa Republica Filipina: 'Interview' kang General Luga," *Bag-ong Kusog* (28 February 1924), 2, 11; (14 March 1924), 2, 3, 11.

45. Hurley, *Jungle Patrol*, 296–97.

46. For data on pulahan activities, see USNA, BIA, Annual Report of the Governor of the Province of Cebu, 1 July 1905.

47. USNA, RG 395, entry 5695, vol. 5, W. Paulding to A. General, 24 July 1904.

48. "Ang mga Pulahan," *Ang Suga* (12 June 1903), 1.

49. USNA, RG 395, entry 5695, vol. 5, W. Paulding to A. General, 24 July 1904.

50. RPC 1903, III:119–20. See also TNL, HDP, Cebu, Aloguinsan, Cawasan; Hurley, *Jungle Patrol*, 152–54. Hurley calls this battle "an epic of jungle warfare."

51. USNA, BIA, Annual Report of the Governor of the Province of Cebu, from 1 Jan. 1903 to 30 June 1904. Also, TNL, HDP, Cebu, Aloguinsan, Cawasan.

52. In the aftermath of this raid, the provincial government had to loan the municipality of Asturias money for "relieving distress in said municipality caused by fire and by the marauds of bandits." See ARWD 1905, XIV:42.

53. USNA, RG 395, entry 5695, vol. 5, O. Bundy to Military Secretary, 18 July 1905; USNA, BIA, Annual Report of the Governor of the Province of Cebu, 31 July 1906.

54. USNA, BIA, Annual Report of the Governor of the Province of Cebu, from 1 Jan. 1903 to 30 June 1904; Annual Report of the Governor of the Province of Cebu, 1 July 1905.

55. Rodriguez, "Ang mga Pulahan."

56. RPC 1906, VIII:251–52. An interesting encounter with a band of armed men, who must have been pulahanes, is recorded by A. Henry Savage Landor who encountered the pulahanes while hiking from Naga to Toledo in 1903. Landor conversed with the men in Spanish and was gifted with mangoes. He later wrote: "More polite ladrones it would be difficult to imagine" (A. Henry Savage Landor, *The Gems of the East* [New York: Harper and Brothers, 1904], 422).

Chapter 16: The Leveling of the Mountains

1. *Census of the Philippine Islands* (Manila: Bureau of Printing, 1920).

2. On the reconcentration program, see USNA, BIA, Annual Report of the Governor of the Province of Cebu, 1 July 1905.

3. Hurley, *Jungle Patrol*, 151–57. Also cited in RPC 1905, III:86–93.

4. RPC 1905, III:93.

5. USNA, RG 395, entry 5497, Toledo: Post Letters Sent, Commanding Officer to D. MacDonald, 9 March 1906.

6. On Osmeña's anti-insurgency plan, see USNA, BIA, Annual Report of the Governor of the Province of Cebu, 31 July 1906, particularly Exhibit B, dated 30 June 1906, appended to this report.

7. On negotiations for the Tabal surrender, see USNA, RG 395, entry 5695, vol. 7, E. Chandler to Military Secretary, 28 June 1906. The fullest account is by Osmeña himself, USNA, BIA, Annual Report of the Governor of the Province of Cebu, 31 July 1906, Exhibit B, dated 30 June 1906, which is a letter from Osmeña to Governor-General Ide.

8. USNA, RG 395, entry 5698, box 6, Governor of Cebu, Executive Order No. 7–B, 21 July 1906.

9. For accounts of the surrender, see "Mga Salin sa Kagubut," *Ang Suga* (23 July 1906), as well as items in *Ang Camatuoran* (27 June, 21 July, and 24 July 1906).

10. USNA, BIA, Report of the Provincial Governor of Cebu, 5 August 1908.

11. *Ang Suga* (19 June 1907).

12. *Ang Suga* (17 July 1907); *Ang Kauswagan* (21 July 1907).

13. USNA, BIA, Report of the Governor of Cebu, 14 September 1911.

14. *Ang Suga* (17 September and 5 October 1906); *Ang Camatuoran* (17 October 1908); RPC 1908, II:5.

Chapter 17: Osmeña Begins

1. The standard (if somewhat uncritical) biography of Osmeña is Vicente Albano Pacis, *President Sergio Osmeña* (Manila: Philippine Constitution Association, 1971), 2 vols. An excellent study of Osmeña's rise to power is Cullinane, "Playing the Game." For a guide to sources, Resil B. Mojares and Celia B. SyPiecco, *Sergio Osmeña Bibliography* (Cebu: University of San Carlos, Cebuano Studies Center, 1978).

2. CSC, Noble Papers, Acta de eleccion, Cebu, 24 April 1899.

3. Jaime C. de Veyra, "'El Nuevo Dia'—Story of a Youthful Adventure," *The Philippine Republic*, 1 (March 1924), 7, 10. See also Rafael Palma, *My Autobiography* (Manila: Capitol Publishing House, 1953), 13, 37–38.

4. *El Nuevo Dia* (16 April 1900).

5. LC, Carlock Papers, L. J. Carlock to W. H. Taft, 10 January 1903.

6. See ARWD 1905, XIV: 161–63.

7. On this visit, see USNA, BIA, Annual Report of the Governor of the Province of Cebu, 31 July 1906.

8. The text of the memorial is in USNA, BIA, Annual Report of the Governor of the Province of Cebu, 31 July 1906, Exhibit D. See also, USNA, RG 350, entry 1239–50, "Translation: Memorial to the Congress of the United States and to the Philippine Commission. Cebu, Aug. 15, 1905."

9. UM, James LeRoy Papers, "Remarks of Secretary Taft... at Cebu on Aug. 22, 1905," and "Manuscript of Travelogue Account of Trip to the Philippine Islands, 1905."

10. UM, James LeRoy Papers, "Manuscript of Travelogue Account," entry for 22 August 1905.

11. USNA, RG 395, entry 5698, box 6, H. P. Neville to Commanding Officer, 2 March 1906.

12. USNA, BIA, Annual Report of the Governor of the Province of Cebu, 31 July 1906.

13. HU, W. C. Forbes Papers, confidential letter, book no. 1, W. C. Forbes to F. W. Carpenter, 2 March 1910. See also W. Cameron Forbes, *The Philippine Islands* (Boston: Houghton Mifflin Company, 1928), 1: 135–36, 163.

14. UM, J. R. Hayden Papers, box 1, Folder "Correspondence, July–Dec. 1926," 10 July 1926.

15. HU, W. C. Forbes Papers, confidential letter, book no. 1, W. C. Forbes to Secretary of War, 29 November 1910.

16. Teodoro M. Kalaw, "Senator Osmeña," *Philippine Magazine*, 26 (8 January 1930), 494–96, 526, 528, 530.

17. For a profile, see Glenn A. May, *Social Engineering in the Philippines: The Aims, Execution, and Impact of American Colonial Policy, 1900–1913* (Westport, CT: Greenwood Press, 1980), 187–88; Frank Jenista, Jr., "Conflict in the Philippine Legislature: The Commission and the Assembly from 1907 to 1913," *Compadre Colonialism*, 77–101. Jenista presents a slightly different breakdown of the background of the Assembly members.

18. Cullinane, "Implementing the New Order," 31.

19. RPC 1907, I:50–51, 202–3. For biographical data on the Cebu assemblymen see Tuohy, *Album Historico*, 9, 30, 43–44, 87–88, 91, 95.

20. USNA, RG 350, entry 3427, W. C. Forbes to J. M. Dickinson, 26 October 1909.

21. HU, W. C. Forbes Papers, W. C. Forbes to R. Forbes, 14 August 1907, FMS Am 1366, vol. 6.

22. USNA, BIA, Annual Report of the Governor of the Province of Cebu, 31 July 1906.

23. USNA, RG 395, entry 5698, box 6, R. Enriquez and C. Alcantara to J. Buchanan, 28 February 1906.

24. USNA, RG 350, entry 12993/4, M.M. Levering to W. H. Taft, 7 March 1908.

25. *El Precursor* (13 December 1903 and 6 March 1904).

26. *Ang Suga* (7 October 1907); *Manila Times* (8 October 1907); *Cebu Courier* (12 October 1907).

Epilogue

1. Glenn May, for instance, faults Teodoro Agoncillo and Renato Constantino for the "rigid dichotomy" between masses/resisters and elite/collaborators. In his work on the war in Batangas, however, May commits the same mistake by simply reversing the equation, ascribing to an ill-defined "elite" the primary impetus for the resistance.

2. We have no precise data on the number of Spaniards residing in Cebu in the late nineteenth century. There must have been around 30 Spanish merchants and property owners in Cebu in the 1890s. See Fenner, *Cebu Under the Spanish Flag.*

3. Important work on elite formation in Cebu has been done by Michael Cullinane, "The Changing Nature of the Cebu Urban Elite in the 19th Century," in *Philippine Social History*, ed. A.W. McCoy and Ed. C. de Jesus (Quezon City: Ateneo de Manila University Press, 1982), 251–96.

4. For student enrolment, see Fenner, *Cebu Under the Spanish Flag*, 163.

5. *El Pueblo* (9 and 23 May 1900).

6. In what is an otherwise comprehensive analysis of the reasons for the failure of the resistance, Glenn May ("Why the United States Won," 353–77) errs in inadequately defining the social position of his "elites," overstressing clientilism as principle of recruitment and motive for participation, reductively characterizing peasant response to the war as one of "indifference," and in tending towards presentist valuations by not fully taking into account the specificity of nation-formation at the time the war was fought.

7. May (*Social Engineering*, xix) says: "The colony was not a 'laboratory of democracy'; it was, rather, a laboratory for the testing of essentially conservative formulas."

8. USNA, RG 395, entry 2503, box 1, *Roster of Troops Serving in the Department of the Visayas* (Iloilo, August 1911), no. 4, 9–10; RG 395, entry 2503, box 1, "Warwick Barracks, Cebu. Leases. Fiscal Year 1912."

9. The data in the paragraphs that follow are drawn from USNA, RG 350, entry 2055/18, H. M. Cohen to F. McIntyre, 23 October 1911. Additional details on Cebu in 1910 are from James J. Rafferty, "The Story of Cebu's Progress," *The Philippines Monthly*, 2 (October 1911), 16–19; Alfred G. Andersen, "Cebu, the Second City in the Philippines," *Philippine Resources*, 1 (June 1910), 9–13; Alfred G. Andersen, ed., *Special Boost Edition of the Cebu Chronicle* (Cebu: Cebu Chronicle, 1910).

Index of Personal Names

A

B